T0271132

The External Dimension of the Euro Area

Although still relatively closed, the euro area economy is nevertheless subject to a broad range of economic impacts originating from outside its borders. This book aims to improve our understanding of how, and to what extent, such external developments affect the euro area. Using a broad range of methodologies and techniques, chapters analyse the various channels that connect the euro area to its external environment; most notably trade, capital flows and other international macroeconomic linkages. The result is that the interaction between the euro area and its 'external dimension' is shown to be complex and wide-ranging. With contributions from both academics and professionals, this volume will be an invaluable source of information for researchers and policy makers concerned with the interaction between regional European integration and globalisation.

FILIPPO DI MAURO is Head of the External Developments Division at the European Central Bank in Frankfurt.

ROBERT ANDERTON is Adviser in the External Developments Division at the European Central Bank in Frankfurt, and Professor of Economics at the University of Nottingham.

The External Dimension of the Euro Area

Assessing the Linkages

Edited by

Filippo di Mauro and Robert Anderton

CAMBRIDGE
UNIVERSITY PRESS

CAMBRIDGE
UNIVERSITY PRESS

University Printing House, Cambridge CB2 8BS, United Kingdom

Cambridge University Press is part of the University of Cambridge.

It furthers the University's mission by disseminating knowledge in the pursuit of education, learning and research at the highest international levels of excellence.

www.cambridge.org
Information on this title: www.cambridge.org/9780521867009

© Cambridge University Press 2007

First published 2007
First paperback edition 2012

A catalogue record for this publication is available from the British Library

ISBN 978-0-521-86700-9 Hardback
ISBN 978-1-107-41059-6 Paperback

Cambridge University Press has no responsibility for the persistence or accuracy of URLs for external or third-party internet websites referred to in this publication, and does not guarantee that any content on such websites is, or will remain, accurate or appropriate.

Contents

Illustrations

Contributors

FILIPPO DI MAURO is Head of External Developments Division, European Central Bank.

ROBERT ANDERTON is Adviser in the External Developments Division, European Central Bank, and Professor, School of Economics, University of Nottingham, UK.

JOSEPH GAGNON is Assistant Director, Division of International Finance, Board of Governors of the Federal Reserve System.

JOSÉ MANUEL CAMPA is Professor of Finance and Director of Research at IESE Business School and Research Fellow of the CEPR.

LINDA S. GOLDBERG is Vice President of the Federal Reserve Bank of New York and Head of the International Research Function.

JOSÉ M. GONZÁLEZ-MÍNGUEZ is Economist at the Monetary and Financial Studies Department of Banco de España.

PHILIP R. LANE is Director, Institute for International Integration Studies (IIIS), Professor of International Macroeconomics (Trinity College Dublin) and a Research Fellow of the CEPR.

GIAN MARIA MILESI-FERRETTI is Chief of the Economic Modelling Division, Research Dept, International Monetary Fund, and Research Fellow of the CEPR.

W. JOS JANSEN was, at the time of writing a senior economist in the Monetary and Economic Policy Department, De Nederlandsche Bank. He is now a senior policy advisor in the Economic Policy Department of the Dutch Ministry of Social Affairs and Employment.

AD C. J. STOKMAN is a senior researcher in the Economics and Research Division, De Nederlandsche Bank.

RAY BARRELL is Senior Research Fellow, National Institute of Economic and Social Research (NIESR), London, UK

E. PHILIP DAVIS is Professor of Economics and Finance, Brunel University and Visiting Fellow, National Institute of Economic and Social Research (NIESR), London, UK.

ALESSANDRO CALZA is Senior Economist, External Developments Division, European Central Bank.

STEPHANE DEES is Principal Economist, External Developments Division, European Central Bank.

Preface

Although relatively closed in comparison with the individual constituent countries, the euro area economy is subject to a broad range of economic impacts originating from outside its borders, by an extent which remains significant. At the ECB we are well aware of the international linkages of the euro area and in 2004, we hosted a workshop on 'The Importance of the External Dimension for the Euro Area: Trade, Capital Flows and International Macroeconomic Linkages'. Drawing partly from that workshop and using the most recent research, the book edited by di Mauro and Anderton aims at providing an overall understanding of how and to what extent external developments affect the euro area. Using a broad range of methodologies and techniques, the chapters bring together the latest information and results regarding the various channels connecting the euro area to its external environment, most notably the trade, capital flows and other international macroeconomic linkages.

The work is ambitious as it attempts to tackle a number of complex, overarching issues: how good are standard openness measures to ascertain the impact of trade developments on the euro area economy; what are the most relevant economic linkages between the euro area and the rest of the world; what are the channels and mechanisms by which the euro area is influenced by external developments and how are they changing through time; and what can we say regarding claims that there has been an increase in the international synchronisation of economic cycles?

While most of the replies remain work in progress, still a number of results are in my opinion worth mentioning. First, there are significant indicators of an increase in the synchronisation of economic cycles across the major countries of the world since the mid-1990s which seems to be associated with the growth in international economic linkages resulting from globalisation. However, these linkages and mechanisms are not straightforward and the impact on the euro area of external shocks can differ quite considerably depending on the specific nature of the shock. For example, the apparent recent rise in the international synchronisation of cycles may be partly due to the global nature of the ICT shock which led to the downturn in early 2000, but the nature of future external disturbances may be more idiosyncratic or country-specific and, therefore, may not have such a significant impact on the euro area. Second, the explosive growth of FDI since the mid-1990s represents a key mechanism by which globalisation seems to have increased economic spillovers across borders and continents by creating additional channels for the international transmission of shocks. Third, given the greater openness of the euro area compared to the USA and Japan, international trade still remains one of the most important sources of external shocks for the euro area. Finally, financial shocks such as equity price movements play an important role as a channel for external shocks, while the speed with which financial shocks are transmitted across the globe is much faster than shocks to output.

All in all, the comprehensive information contained in this book regarding the euro area's response to external shocks is important to the ECB for the conduct of monetary policy. In particular, external shocks affect the broad set of economic and financial indicators which are analysed under the *economic analysis* pillar of the ECB's monetary policy strategy. As shown in the various chapters, policy makers should be aware that real and financial market linkages between the euro area and the rest of the world may be changing over time both in number and magnitude, with globalisation being likely to be one important driving force behind such changes. Overall, the conclusion is that the 'external dimension' of the euro area has a complex impact on its economic developments. Moreover, increasingly important factors that are common to other economies, such as globalisation, are compounded by the fact that the euro area is a new and still rapidly transforming entity – by virtue of its own economic and financial integration in progress – and therefore many European and global structural changes are at play contemporaneously.

Against the background of larger and deeper global interconnections, the call for increasing the flexibility of the euro area economy becomes even more urgent. In rapidly changing markets and with new world players entering the scene, only timely and flexible responses can ensure a smooth absorption of external shocks. In this context, the continuation of structural reforms in the labour and product markets in the euro area countries is essential. This in turn will also encourage a better and more sustainable utilisation of human and capital resources, while enhancing the euro area's growth potential in an increasingly integrated world economy where the process of globalisation shows no signs of abating.

Jean-Claude Trichet
President of the European Central Bank

1   Introduction

Robert Anderton and Filippo di Mauro[1]

Being a relatively-closed economy in comparison with the individual constituent countries has not exempted the euro area economy from a broad range of economic impacts originating from outside its borders. If anything, the impact of external factors has actually been stronger than previously thought. Against this backdrop, the objective of this book is to study the complex interactions between the euro area economy and the growing set of factors representing its external environment.

A number of reasons are identified in this book as having possibly heightened the importance of a better understanding of the external linkages of the euro area. First, while the process of growing world-wide links among economies related to the process of globalisation of trade in goods and financial services has been universal, it may have impacted on the euro area somewhat differently than elsewhere. For example, though being in aggregate a relatively closed economy, the euro area is in fact composed of some rather open economies which are subject to indirect impacts of external shocks via the strong intra-euro area links between the euro area countries. Second, shifts in trade within the euro area have been taking place, led by an acceleration of the ongoing processes of delocalisation of production towards low cost countries, particularly in Eastern Europe. Against this backdrop, the external environment appears to have interacted with the euro area in a different manner than before. Third, there is evidence that globalisation may have increased the number of channels of international linkages in addition to the most-traditional channels, such as trade and capital flows. In this context, the book identifies some additional factors – such as confidence – which may have increased in importance.

The identification of the main channels of transmission and the evidence available to practitioners is the overall objective of chapter 2 ('The external dimension of the euro area: stylised facts and initial findings' –

---

1 European Central Bank: respectively Adviser and Head of Division, External Developments Division. All views expressed in this chapter are those of the authors and do not necessarily reflect those held by the European Central Bank.

Robert Anderton and Filippo di Mauro). The chapter begins by 'setting the scene' for chapters 3 and 4 which contain a more detailed analysis of individual topics. The structure of the chapter mimics the structure of the book. The first part handles the trade channel, the second the capital flows channel, the third covers the issue of other macroeconomic linkages – such as confidence – as well as measuring the degree of international synchronisation to gauge the overall outcome of the increasing integration of the global economy. Based also on work of numerous ECB colleagues, the chapter provides stylised facts and first findings regarding the external dimension of the euro area alongside comparisons with major competitors. A number of overarching questions are examined and tentative replies are provided. Among them is the issue of how good are standard openness measures to ascertain the impact of trade developments on the euro area economy: and, as mentioned before, how globalisation may have changed the main channels and mechanisms by which the euro area is influenced by external developments and how they may be changing through time. The role of common shocks, such as an increase in oil prices, is examined along with an empirical analysis of the international synchronisation of economic cycles. Overall, the chapter finds that the magnitude of the trade links may have increased over time, while also becoming more complex with the impacts depending on the nature of shocks and how they relate to the product and geographical specialisation of euro area trade. Meanwhile, the global surge in cross-border capital flows has increased the potential magnitude of the impact of capital flows as a channel for the transmission of external shocks to the euro area, particularly the FDI channel. As regards the overall co-movement of output across countries, some empirical measures of synchronisation of international activity reveal that the degree of synchronisation has shown a trend decline over the past three decades in the major economies, although there has also been an increase in synchronisation since the mid-1990s. Despite the fact that the recent increase in synchronisation might be due to a possible increase in the number and magnitude of external linkages due to globalisation, common shocks, such as the oil price shock from 1999–2006, as well as the global ICT shock associated with the downturn in 2000, may also provide part of the explanation.

The trade channel in goods and services is the traditional channel through which economies may affect each other, and experience shows that trade still represents one of the most important building blocks of the euro area external dimension. Following the analysis in chapter 2, key issues relating to the trade channel are addressed in chapters 3 and 4: a) the role of product variety for explaining export performance; and b) the exchange rate pass-through to import prices in the euro area.

Chapter 3 ('Product variety and macro trade models: implications for the new EU Member States' by Joseph E. Gagnon) concerns the trade implications of the new EU Member States. The author argues that standard macroeconomic models may embody a misspecification of the trade sector, as they omit an important effect of a country's potential output on its exports, namely the product-variety impact on exports. According to these macro-models, countries that are expected to grow faster than their trading partners for an extended period of time – as is the case with the new EU Member States (NEUMS), should experience a secular decline in their terms of trade. However, long-term trends in trade can be better explained if alternative trade specifications which incorporate the role of product variety are used. In this alternative specification, which proves to be relevant for the NEUMS, fast-growing countries are able to achieve strong export growth without declining terms of trade once the 'varieties model' of trade is incorporated into standard models. Accordingly, taking variety models into account may help us to better understand the evolution of euro area trade, as well as terms of trade developments, *vis-à-vis* the new EU Member States.

The trade channel is also the topic of chapter 4 'Exchange-rate pass-through to import prices in the euro area' by José Manuel Campa, Linda Goldberg and José M. Gonzalez-Minguez. The impact of exchange rate movements on domestic prices and economic activity has long been a matter of interest in international macroeconomics. More recently, this issue has gained special interest due to the rather strong fluctuations of the exchange rate between the euro and the dollar. The empirical work focuses on the pass-through of exchange rate changes into the prices of extra-euro area imports of individual euro area countries, analysing the differences across industries and countries. A number of factors can affect the pass-through, for example: different degrees of openness of the member countries' economies to extra-euro area imports; heterogeneity in the product composition of imports for given industry-specific rates of pass-through; or, different product and country-specific rates of pass-through to import prices for any given composition. The analysis shows that exchange rate changes continue to lead to significant changes in import prices across euro area countries: on average, the authors find that the exchange rate pass-through to import prices across the euro area countries is around 80 per cent in the long term. Overall, the transmission in the short term proves to be high, although incomplete, and differs across industries and countries; in the long term, the exchange rate pass-through is higher and closer to one. The authors do not find strong statistical evidence that the introduction of the euro has caused a structural change in this transmission process, although some empirical results show that industries producing differentiated goods seem to have been more likely to experience reduced rates of exchange rate pass-through to import prices since the start of EMU.

Cross-border capital and financial flows represent an increasingly-important link of the euro area with its external environment. Two specific aspects are dealt with in chapters 5 and 6. First, the determinants of the euro area's foreign direct and portfolio investment, particularly equity holdings, are analysed in detail. Second, the ways in which FDI may transmit shocks to the euro area are evaluated.

Cross-border capital flows are the subject of chapter 5 ('The international equity holdings of euro area investors' Philip R. Lane and Gian Maria Milesi-Ferretti) which analyses the pattern of the investment of equity holdings for the euro area, providing an analysis of bilateral, source and host factors driving portfolio equity investment. The authors present statistics on stock market size and foreign ownership, and relate the actual geographical pattern of portfolio investment with that predicted by the relative importance of countries' stock markets in the world portfolio. The analysis shows that the euro area is a major portfolio equity investor, second only to the United States, and is even larger if intra euro holdings are taken into account. The results from this study show that the pattern of investment of equity holdings for the euro area is strongly related to the size of host country characteristics such as stock market capitalization, bilateral trade ties and its status as a financial centre. Finally, in a sample of OECD investor countries, the authors find evidence that intra-euro area equity investment is larger than that predicted on the basis of 'fundamentals' such as trade ties, distance, and co-movements in key macroeconomic variables.

Chapter 6 ('Global linkages through foreign direct investment' by Jos Jansen and Ad C. J. Stockman) investigates the relationship between FDI and economic linkages across countries. The increasing globalisation and integration of the world economy in the fifteen years up to the early 2000s has motivated an explosive growth of FDI, possibly associated with a higher degree of synchronicity of economic trends across the world. In particular, the chapter reviews the downturn in the United States in the early 2000s which seems to have exerted a bigger impact on other countries than expected from 'traditional' linkages. The authors begin with a description of some stylised facts on FDI patterns and its significance for the host countries. Looking at both the supply- and demand-side effects, they then turn to the possible international spillover effects of FDI, including labour market channels, given the importance of multinational companies in employing labour across the globe. The empirical results support the evidence that FDI, apart from the foreign trade channel, now constitutes a separate channel through which economies may affect each other in an economically-significant way. In addition, foreign disturbances transmitted through the FDI channel may have a more durable effect on the domestic economy than those transmitted through the trade channel. This research has two policy implications relevant in the analysis of the external dimension of the euro area. The first is that the trend towards greater economic interdependence through FDI implies an underlying tendency for business cycles to display a more-synchronised behaviour than in the past, which amounts to a higher effective openness of the euro area with respect to its external environment. The second is that FDI appears to have become an important channel for the international transmission of disturbances, which therefore needs to be embedded into global macroeconomic models. This latter issue is implicitly dealt with in chapter 8, where a global Vector Auto Regression Model (VAR) is presented as a way to treat the transmission mechanisms beyond the trade channel.

The impact of the external dimension as measured by **global models** is the focus of chapters 7 and 8. Against the background of a quite extensive literature, two rather different approaches are presented, which may illustrate the main issues involved in an overall quantitative assessment of the impact of the external dimension on the euro area. The main conclusion of the section is that one cannot identify one single, overwhelmingly-superior approach. In particular, the choice of the most-adequate modelling technique depends on the issue at hand, most notably whether tractability is more critical than structural detail. For example, structural models may have advantages in terms of capturing impacts of quite specific policy responses, while VAR-based models may be somewhat better at capturing the impacts of external shocks due to their more-transparent modelling of international linkages through various channels.

On the one hand, there is the work carried out by R. Barrell and P. Davis which partly uses the National Institute Global Econometric Model (NIGEM) to calibrate the macroeconomic effects of changes in share prices. On the other hand, A. Calza and S. Dees provide an assessment of the strength of international linkages building on the model used by Dees, di Mauro, Pesaran and Smith (2005) based on the Global Vector Auto-Regressive (GVAR) approach proposed by Pesaran, Schuermann and Weiner (2004). The GVAR approach consists of a modelling framework which covers the macroeconomic responses to various types of global and national shocks through a number of transmission channels, which include both trade and several financial linkages.

Chapter 7 ('Shocks and shock absorbers: The international propagation of equity market shocks and the design of appropriate policy responses', R. Barrell and P. Davis) provides an assessment of the macroe-conomic implications of equity price falls for the US and the major euro area countries using Vector Error Correction Mechanism (VECM) models and those produced using the National Institute Global Econometric Model (NIGEM). The authors assess the implications of equity price falls comparable to those seen in 2000–2002 against the background of the high degree of correlation between equity price changes in recent years. An indication of the effect of different policy responses is also provided. Based on estimated relationships, falls in equity prices of the scale observed over 2000–2002 can have significant recessionary effects on the world economy. According to the VECM results, composition of wealth, openness and trade patterns are among the key factors which influence the scope of output responses internationally. For the US in particular, the dependence of firms on market-based finance helps explain why equity prices have a larger impact on output than they do in Europe (the contribution of equity prices to a variance decomposition of output is around three times greater in the US, at 50 per cent, than in the larger euro area economies). Finally, the authors also show that active policy responses to equity price falls is a wise strategy and that structural models are a useful part of the policy analysis toolkit. Overall, the authors argue that VECM studies can only evaluate the 'average' policy response over the sample period for which they are estimated, while structural models are necessary to explain how policy may mitigate the effect of shocks.

In chapter 8, 'The euro area in the global economy: its sensitivity to the international environment and its influence on global economic developments' A. Calza and S. Dees makes use of the Global Vector Auto-Regressive (GVAR) model to assess the importance of changes in global economic conditions for developments in the euro area and, more generally, evaluate the dependence of the euro area economy on external factors. As a complement to this analysis, they also analyse the impact of shocks originating from the euro area on its main trading partners, which should help in evaluating the relative importance of the euro area in the global economy. By providing a framework capable of accounting for both trade and financial transmission channels, the GVAR model is particularly suitable to analyse the transmission of real and financial shocks across countries and regions, especially taking into account the strengthening in cross-border financial integration. The simulations confirm that trade remains the predominant source of linkages between the euro area and the rest of the world while also highlighting the importance of second- and third-market effects of shocks (particularly those relating to financial variables). The authors underline that financial shocks tend to be transmitted much faster than shocks to output, as they are often amplified as they travel from the originating country to the rest of the world. Finally, the simulations also show that there is a greater degree of synchronicity between financial variables across countries in comparison to inflation and output.

Overall, the book underlines the difficulties in understanding the transmission and the final effects of external shocks on the euro area, and highlights the complexity of the various direct and indirect mechanisms. The conclusion is that the 'external dimension' of the euro area has a complex impact on economic developments in the euro area. Policy makers should be aware that real and financial market linkages between the euro area and the rest of the world may be changing over time both in number and magnitude, with globalisation being one possible driving force behind such changes. Moreover, increasingly important factors that are common to other economies, such as globalisation, are compounded by the fact that the euro area is a new and still somewhat unfamiliar entity, so many structural and possibly, some global changes, are at play contemporaneously.

2　The external dimension of the euro area: stylised facts and initial findings

Robert Anderton and Filippo di Mauro[1]

Although relatively closed in comparison with the individual constituent countries, the euro area economy is still rather open – particularly when compared with the two other largest world economies, the US and Japan. The experience of the first few years of EMU has shown that the euro area continues to be subject to a broad range of economic impacts originating from outside its borders, and that the extent of some external impacts are possibly higher than what might have been expected given the relatively-more internationally-insulated aggregate economy of the euro area. For example, the euro area was affected rather strongly by the ICT-related global downturn in early 2000, despite its relatively-low dependence on the ICT sector.

A full explanation of the above developments is a daunting task, particularly because aspects related to the effects of the creation of the monetary union are occurring at the same time as other impacts which are connected with global trends, such as rapid growth in world trade in goods and services, increased mobility of international capital, rising financial integration across the world, and rapid growth in the internationalisation and relocation of production. These difficulties notwithstanding, in several years of analysis of the external environment of the euro area we have learned quite a lot in terms of identification of the transmission channels of external shocks and their impacts. It is the aim of this chapter to report on such facts and findings, fully aware, however, that the development of a comprehensive framework to gauge the external dimension of the euro area is still not entirely complete.

Based also on the work of numerous colleagues[2] as well as the authors, a number of overarching questions are examined in this chapter, including:

[1] European Central Bank: Respectively Adviser and Head of Division, External Developments Division. All views expressed in this chapter are the authors' and do not necessarily reflect those held by the European Central Bank.

[2] First and foremost, we would like to acknowledge the extremely valuable assistance of Natàlia Mas Guix who put the various elements of this chapter together, particularly the Charts and Tables. The chapter draws heavily on substantial works and advice on the subjects by economist colleagues in the European Central Bank's External

how good are standard openness measures to ascertain the impact of trade developments on the euro area economy? what are the most relevant economic linkages between the euro area and the rest of the world? what are the channels and mechanisms by which the euro area is influenced by external developments? What is the role of common shocks, such as an increase in oil prices, what have we learnt about a possible increase in the international synchronisation of economic cycles and what are the implications? To provide some preliminary answers we look at three sets of channels: trade, financial flows and other linkages.

2.1 The external trade of the euro area

International trade in goods and services is the traditional channel through which shocks are transmitted from one economy to another and seem to be one of the most important channels of the euro area's external linkages. This section aims to analyse how, and to what extent, the trade channel matters for the euro area economy. The objectives are twofold: (1) first, to investigate how the international environment affects the euro area through trade, also in comparison with main competitors; (2) second, to shed light on the mechanisms and magnitudes of the international transmission of shocks via the trade channel.

This assessment is highly relevant in the context of the economic analysis for the monetary policy assessment for at least two reasons. First, as the euro area includes some countries with relatively high degrees of openness, it may be the case that its effective degree of openness towards the rest of the world is higher than standard trade indicators would indicate. Second, the relative competitive position among individual euro area countries since EMU has changed somewhat, partly reflecting the mechanisms through which the external environment affects them and the euro area as a whole. In this context, new structural factors – emerging in parallel to EMU – such as the entrance of new global trade players, most notably China and the new EU Member States, may have also hampered the ability of standard trade equations to be a reliable guide to assess the current impact of the trade channel.

Developments Division, as well as the European System of Central Banks, in particular: Tobias Blattner, Matthieu Bussiere, Alessandro Calza, Matthieu Darracq-Paries, Roberto De Santis, Stephane Dees, Paul Hiebert, Pavlos Karadeloglou, Stelios Makrydakis, Laurent Maurin, Fabio Moneta, Ricardo Pereira, Nuno Queiros, Chiara Osbat, Ruta Rodzko, Rasmus Rueffer and Bernd Schnatz. We would also like to thank the Task Force of the Monetary Policy Committee of the European System of Central Banks who drafted ECB Occasional Paper No. 30 'Competitiveness and the export performance of the euro area' (as this chapter also draws on elements of that paper). We would also like to thank various other colleagues at the ECB who are too numerous to mention.

Table 2.1 *Key real economy characteristics of the euro area in 2004*[1]

	Euro area	United States	Japan
Population (millions)	311.7	293.9	127.6
GDP (calculated at purchasing power parity, EUR trillions)	7.7	10.2	3.3
Share of world GDP (calculated at purchasing power parity, %)	15.3	20.9	6.9
Exports (goods & services, % GDP)	19.3	9.8	13.9
Imports (goods & services, % GDP)	17.6	15.1	11.8
Share of world exports[2]	28.5	15.8	4.6

Source: ECB, Eurostat and World Economic Outlook (WEO, IMF).

[1] All tables and charts referring to euro area trade refer to extra-euro area trade unless otherwise indicated.

[2] The world export share of the euro area includes intra-area trade, which represents roughly 50% of the euro area's total exports.

This section is divided into three parts. The first part provides some stylised facts regarding the measurement of the trade openness of the euro area and its member states along with some comparisons *vis-à-vis* the United States and Japan. The second looks at the factors driving euro area trade also against the background of what standard elasticities would predict. The final part provides a detailed geographical and sectoral analysis of the euro area's external trade which is useful for considering its prospects going forward.

2.1.1   The openness of the euro area

International comparisons

The euro area is one of the world's major economies, comparable in size to the United States and considerably larger than Japan. Measured in terms of population, the euro area, with more than 300 million people, is the largest developed economy in the world (Table 2.1). In 2004, the euro area contributed around 15 per cent of world GDP, somewhat less than the United States (21%), but more than double that of Japan (7%). In terms of world trade, the euro area contributed the most, accounting for 28 per cent of the value of world exports, compared with approximately 16 per cent and 5 per cent for the United States and Japan, respectively.

With regard to both exports and imports, the euro area is significantly more open than either the United States or Japan. In fact, its openness in terms of the combined value of imports and exports of goods and services

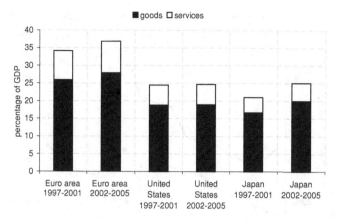

Figure 2.1. Relative openness of the euro area compared with the United States and Japan
(in percentage of GDP; annual data)
Source: ECB and IMF (World Economic Outlook).
Note: The degree of openness is measured as exports plus imports of goods and services as a percentage of GDP, average 1997–2005.

is equivalent (in 2004) to around 37 per cent of its GDP, compared with around 26 and 25 per cent for Japan and the United States, respectively. Particularly as a result of the increasing role of new EU Member States as trade partners, as well as rapidly increasing imports from Asia (especially China), the trade openness of the euro area has actually increased rather markedly through time, especially since the early 1990s (Figures 2.1 and 2.2).

Relative openness within the euro area

An important characteristic of the euro area for understanding the area-wide impact of external shocks is the highly-differentiated degree of openness among individual member states, both with regard to their total trade as well as their internal trade within the euro area.

On the one hand, the largest euro area countries (Germany, France, Italy and Spain) together with Greece tend to be relatively closed, with a total degree of openness (including intra-euro area trade) in the range of 50–60 per cent. On the other hand, smaller countries show a higher degree of openness, with ratios ranging between 70 per cent (Portugal and Finland) to in excess of 100 per cent for the Netherlands, Ireland, Belgium and Luxembourg (Figure 2.3).

With regard to trade within the euro area, while on average it represents about one half of total euro area trade, it varies considerably across

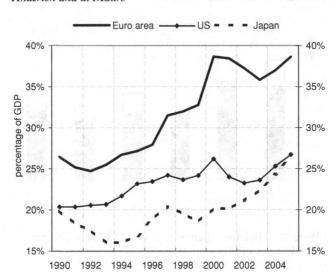

Figure 2.2. Evolution of the trade openness of the euro area, the United States and Japan
(in percentage of GDP; annual data)
Source: ECB and IMF (World Economic Outlook).
Note: Trade openness is measured as exports plus imports of goods and services as a percentage of GDP. Last observation refers to 2005Q4.

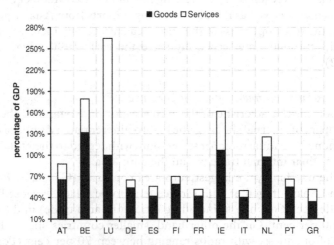

Figure 2.3. Openness of the euro area countries
(in percentage of GDP; annual data)
Source: Eurostat, IMF and ECB calculations.
Note: The degree of openness is measured as exports plus imports as a percentage of GDP, average 1997–2005. Last observation refers to December 2005.

individual countries, both for imports and exports. In particular, while Germany, France and Italy tend to be close to the euro area average (as they lie near to the diagonal of the two panels in Figure 2.4), smaller countries behave rather differently. The countries plotted to the right of the euro area have a higher degree of external openness than the average for the euro area, while those to the left have a relatively lower degree of external openness. Accordingly, Belgium, Luxembourg, Ireland, the Netherlands and Finland are, in relative terms, substantially more 'open' than the other euro area countries. Another interesting observation that can be drawn from Figure 2.4 is related to the rather wide dispersion among euro area countries of their relative magnitudes of intra-and extra-area trade as a proportion of GDP. For example, the large size of extra-relative to intra-euro area trade for Ireland can be partly explained by the strong historical trade links with specific partners such as the United Kingdom.

Imports, exports and the net contribution of trade to GDP
After looking at the traditional measures of openness for the euro area and its member countries, we now turn to the impacts of the external environment through the trade channel. To do so we first look at the interaction between exports, imports, GDP and the net trade contribution to GDP over the last decade (Figure 2.5). Three points seem particularly relevant: first, euro area exports and imports tend to move closely together over the medium term, possibly due to a higher share of the production processes being delocalised abroad in order to benefit from lower labour costs, therefore generating additional trade flows partly via an increase in imported intermediate inputs. Second, as the chart illustrates, on several occasions the net trade contribution to GDP growth has been negative even during periods of strong export growth (e.g. at the end of 1999 and start of 2000). However, when considering the impacts of trade activities one must also take into account the wider impacts of exports on an economy rather than just the basic contribution to growth of net trade.[3] Third, the magnitude of the euro area's net trade contribution has fallen over the past ten years, which again is consistent with exports and imports moving more closely together.

[3] For example, one should remember that the contribution to growth of net trade does not take into account the multiplier effects that result in exports having a greater impact on euro area activity than their initial impact. Accordingly, these export-multiplier effects will also increase imports which will therefore reduce the net trade contribution to growth – as measured by exports minus imports weighted by their share in GDP – and give a misleading impression of the contribution to domestic activity of an increase in exports.

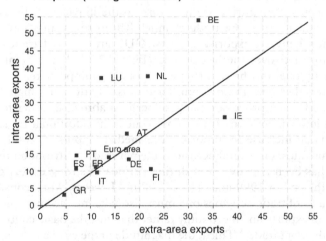

Imports (average 2002-2005)

Exports (average 2002-2005)

Figure 2.4. Extra- and intra-euro area exports and imports of goods for each of the euro area countries
(in percentage of GDP; annual data)
Source: ECB and IMF (*World Economic Outlook*).
Note: Last observation refers to 2005Q4.

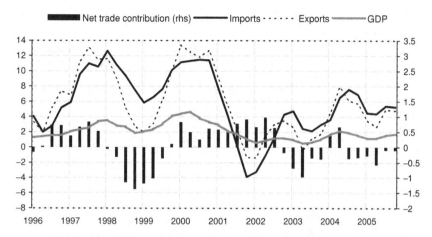

Figure 2.5. The evolution of net trade
(Annual growth in percentages; net trade contribution in percentage points)
Source: ECB computations based on Eurostat national accounts data.
Note: Exports and imports cover goods and services and include intra-euro area trade.

One possible implication of the trend increase in the internationalisation of production is that production off-shoring may have had a negative spillover on economic activity as it could have reduced the value added of export activities by increasing the reliance of euro area exporters on imported intermediate inputs. However, this conclusion is somewhat misleading. Table 2.2 shows indeed that the import content of exports (which is the mirror image of the value added per unit of export) – measured as the long-term elasticity of imports with respect to a one unit increase in exports – has risen for the euro area from 38 per cent in 1995 to around 44 per cent in 2000. Furthermore, this rise in the import-intensity of exports is almost entirely due to trade external to the EU, as the import-intensity of internal EU trade did not change much over this period.[4] However, since the internationalisation of production – which partly explains the rise in imported intermediate inputs – has also boosted exports as well,[5] the first-round net impact of a one per cent increase in exports on GDP growth has roughly remained constant in the euro area.

[4] As the data relate 1995–2000, the EU excludes the new EU Member States who joined the European Union in 2004.
[5] For the euro area, the share of (intra plus extra) exports in GDP rose from 23% in 1995 to 30% in 2000.

Table 2.2 *Import content of exports for the euro area and euro area countries (in percentages)*

	1995			2000		
	Total	Intra-EU	Extra-EU	Total	Intra-EU	Extra-EU
Euro area	37.6	23.3	14.4	44.2	23.9	20.3
Germany	34.7	20.3	14.1	42.8	22.4	20.4
France	34			40.6		
Italy	31.6			35.4		
Netherlands	52.3	34.2	18.1	58.7	30.2	28.4
Austria	46.7	33.9	12.7	51	34.5	16.5
Finland	37.5	22.5	15	42	23	19.1

Source: ECB calculations using Eurostat and OECD input-output tables.
Reproduced from ECB Occasional Paper No. 30 'Competitiveness and the export performance of the euro area.'

2.1.2   *What drives external trade in the euro area?*

Some stylised facts

Figure 2.7 below illustrates the main developments in the euro area's external trade, both in price and volume terms. There are four main drivers of such developments, exchange rate fluctuations and oil price changes as well as developments in domestic and foreign demand.

First, euro area external trade has been strongly influenced by the sizeable fluctuations of the effective exchange rate of the euro – most notably the strong depreciation between early 1999 and the end of 2000, followed by a significant appreciation which started towards the end of 2001 and continued until the second half of 2004. A second relevant factor is the significant increase in oil prices from the end of 1998 until the latter part of 2001, followed by an even sharper and prolonged rise during 2003–2005. The impact of oil prices on the oil trade deficit during this latter period was mitigated somewhat by the appreciation of the euro, particularly the more-marked bilateral appreciation of the euro against the US dollar. Nevertheless, import prices – as proxied by unit value indices – and import values have risen sharply during these two episodes of oil price increases. Finally, developments in foreign and domestic demand also had an important impact on euro area exports and imports of goods (see Figure 2.8). In the second half of 1998 the marginal decline of foreign demand – and the associated fall in extra-euro area export volumes – can be mainly explained by the Asian crisis. In 2001, foreign demand strongly declined, due to the global downturn, before recovering in 2002 and,

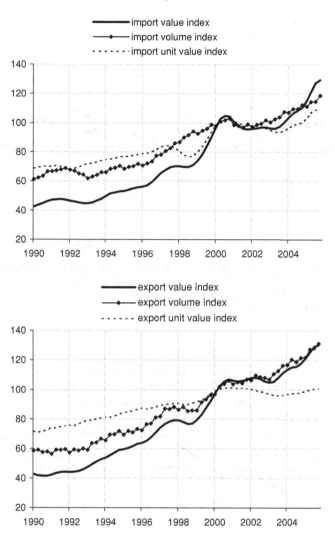

Figure 2.6. Euro area import and export values, volumes and unit values (index 2000 = 100, seasonally adjusted, monthly data, three-month moving average)
Source: Eurostat and ECB calculations.
Note: Last observation refers to December 2005.

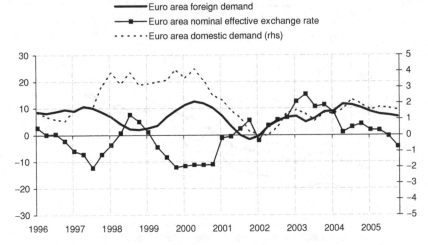

Figure 2.7. Three main determinants of euro area external trade
(index 2000 = 100, annual percentage changes, quarterly data)
Source: Eurostat and ECB calculations.
Note: Last observation refers to December 2005.

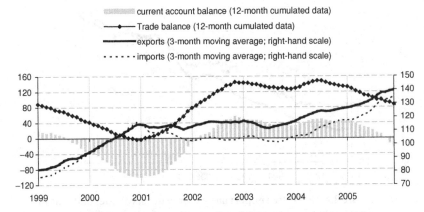

Figure 2.8. Current account and trade balance (goods and services)
(EUR billions, balances are cumulated over 12 months, monthly data)
Source: Eurostat.
Note: Last observation refers to December 2005. Trade balances,
exports and imports are for goods and services.

combined with the impact of the euro appreciation, largely explains the weakness of exports over this period. However, from the second half of 2003 onwards, the growth of foreign demand started to accelerate strongly and was the driving force behind the recovery in export volumes over this period. Nevertheless, at the same time, the euro area still lost export market share as a result of the losses in competitiveness due to the euro appreciation and possibly structural factors (see Box 2.1).

Meanwhile, the growth of import volumes is not only explained by the strength of euro area demand, but also by the composition of expenditure. As described above, exports embody a rising import-content hence the significant degree of co-movement between export and import volumes (Figure 2.5), while investment expenditure is also quite import-intensive.[6] Further information on the evolution and impacts of import and export prices and values on the current account of the euro area are given in Box 2.1 below.

Box 2.1

The euro area current account

The euro area current account is mostly determined by trade in goods given the relative stability of the other components (services, income and current transfers) and their comparatively-smaller magnitudes (see Table 2.3). Therefore, shifts in the current account balance have been largely driven by developments in the euro area goods surplus.

Table 2.3 *Euro area current account (EUR billions, balances)*

	Current Account					Current account as a percentage of GDP[1]
	Goods	Services	Income	Current transfers	Total	
1999	54.9	−9.6	−37.7	−40.2	−32.6	−0.43
2000	8.3	−10.4	−47.5	−49.1	−98.7	−1.23
2001	75.7	−3.9	−39.7	−51.1	−19.0	−0.23
2002	131.2	13.5	−36.8	−49.3	−58.6	0.67
2003	109.1	19.6	−37.0	−57.6	34.1	0.38
2004	105.9	28.6	−34.1	−56.8	43.6	0.47
2005	58.5	31.8	−52.0	−66.4	−28.1	−0.29

Sources: ECB (extracted from ECB Monthly Bulletin, April 2006).
Note: Greece is included from 2001.
[1] GDP data are nominal and seasonally adjusted.

---

[6] For the euro area, the import content of total investment was 29% in 2000, compared to around 20% and 8% for private consumption and government consumption respectively (see ECB Occasional Paper No. 30, p. 65).

Overall, the increase in the goods balance between 1999–2002 in response to the euro depreciation seems somewhat muted. One explanation seems to be that the euro area depreciation resulted in only a limited improvement in the relative price competitiveness of the euro area as exporters passed through only part of the depreciation to export prices, while instead increasing their profit margins. Rather symmetrically, during the euro appreciation in 2001 and 2002, export prices stopped rising – and declined in 2002 – as exporters started to squeeze their profit margins to limit the loss in price competitiveness. Similarly, on the import side, although the import price increased significantly partly as a result of the oil price hike between 1999–2005, the depreciation and subsequent appreciation were not fully passed through to extra-euro area import prices (further details are given below in the section on trade elasticities).

A second explanation relates to the limited response of extra-euro area trade volumes to changes in competitiveness and foreign demand. One reason might be that a loss of export market share by developed economies as emerging economies are catching up is to be expected. Hence the emergence of China and other newcomers as major players in world export markets may, in addition to the euro appreciation, explain some of the more recent losses in export market share. In addition, the large scale net FDI outflows from the euro area since the mid-1990s may have substituted for euro area exports, as outward FDI from the euro area may be used to purchase or set up production plants abroad so that euro area companies can sell goods directly in those foreign markets. As a result, some goods which were previously exported from the euro area may now be manufactured and sold directly in those export markets.

On the import side, it seems that the strong growth of import-intensive categories of euro area expenditure during 1999–2000 – such as investment and exports – partly explains why import volumes grew so robustly over this period, thereby contributing to the weaker than expected response of the goods balance to the euro depreciation. Meanwhile, in the following years, import volumes declined in line with the relatively-slower growth of domestic expenditure in these import-intensive categories.

Contribution analysis

The contribution analysis shown in Figure 2.10 provides information on how individual factors explain export growth in the euro area. One findingfrom this analysis is that the growth of world demand turns out to be the most important determinant of exports over the sample period 1992–2003, with competitiveness indicators playing a much smaller role.

Extra-euro area trade elasticities

This sub-section describes some econometric findings on extra-euro area trade as estimated by ECB staff, which provide information on the possible magnitude of the impact of changes in competitiveness and foreign and domestic demand on extra-euro area export and import volumes, as well as the impact of changes in exchange rates on both exports and import prices. Given that import values are highly sensitive to the development in oil prices, and import volumes of oil seem somewhat price-inelastic, imports of goods are described in terms of their separate non-oil and oil components.

Regarding *import prices*, econometric estimates suggest that around 50–70 per cent of a change in the effective exchange rate of the euro is passed through to manufacturing import prices with most of the long-run exchange rate impact passed through to import prices in about fifteen months, and at least half of the impact occurring in the same quarter as the exchange rate shock (Table 2.4). Meanwhile, in contrast to highly-differentiated manufactured goods, the exchange rate pass-through for more homogeneous and widely-traded goods and commodities such as oil and some non-oil commodities – where the so-called 'law-of-one-price' might hold – is close to 100 per cent. In terms of longer-term trends in import prices, Box 2.3 explains how the rising share of low-cost countries in extra-euro area imports may be putting downward pressure on import prices.

On the *import volume side*, the estimated demand elasticity is quite high, suggesting that a one per cent increase in total final expenditure leads to a 2.8 per cent increase in non-oil import volumes in the long-run, while the long-run relative import price elasticity is approximately 0.8 per cent. However, the estimated equation for non-oil import volumes also includes a negative time trend which partly offsets the ostensibly high impact of a rise in total final expenditure. With respect to oil import volumes, the long-run demand elasticity is about 0.5. This is much lower than the demand elasticity for non-oil import volumes, as it captures the significant decline in the utilisation of oil in production over time. Moreover, the long-run price elasticity of oil is also relatively lower at

Table 2.4 *Estimates of long-run elasticities for extra-euro area import volumes and prices*

Non-oil import volumes[1] (Oil)[2]	
Relative prices	Euro area demand
0.81 (0.18)[2]	2.77[1] (0.51)[2]
Manufacturing import prices[3,4]	
Foreign costs	Domestic prices
0.51–0.71	0.49–0.29

Source: ECB staff estimates.
Notes: Reproduced from ECB Occasional Paper No. 12.
Sample period for estimation varies by equation but the majority of equations used data for the period 1989Q1–2001Q4.
[1] The non-oil import volumes equation also includes a negative time trend which partially offsets the impact of the high demand parameter.
[2] Parameters for oil import volumes are given in parentheses.
[3] Exchange rate pass-through is given by the 'foreign costs' parameter in the import price equation.
[4] A range of estimates is given for manufacturing import prices, as in Anderton (2003).

Table 2.5 *Estimates of long-term elasticities for extra-euro area export volumes and prices*

Export volumes	
Relative prices	Foreign demand
0.50	1.0
Export prices[1]	
Domestic costs	Competitors' prices
0.50	0.48

Source: ECB staff estimates.
Notes: Reproduced from ECB Occasional Paper No. 12.
[1] Exchange rate pass-through is given by the 'competitors' prices' parameter in the export price equation.

around 0.18, reflecting the fact that demand for oil is relatively price elastic.

Regarding *export volumes*, estimates suggest that a one per cent increase in foreign demand will increase extra-euro area export volumes by one per cent in the long-run, while the long-term impact of a one per cent improvement in relative export price competitiveness is estimated to result in a 0.5 per cent increase in export volumes (see long-run parameters reported in Table 2.5). With regard to *export prices*, extra-euro

Box 2.2

The effects of globalisation on import prices

The increasing role of low cost countries global trade seems to have played a significant role in euro area import price developments. As shown in Table 2.6, between 1995–2004 the share of imports from low-cost countries in extra-euro area imports has increased from around one-third (35.4%) to almost half (49.2%). China accounted for 7.2 percentage points and the new EU Member States for another 6 percentage points of the increase. Mechanical simulations indicate that if the share of low-cost countries in euro area imports had stayed at its 1995 level, extra-euro area import prices would have been significantly higher than the actual level of import prices by 2004. This is partly due to the fact that the absolute level of import prices of low-cost countries is significantly lower than for high-cost countries, while the low-cost countries also exhibited slower export price inflation relative to high-cost countries over most of the sample period.

Table 2.6 *Country shares in extra-euro area manufacturing imports* (value terms, per cent)

	High-cost	US	JP	UK	Low-cost	China	NMS
1995	64.6	15.8	10.5	20.0	35.4	4.9	7.8
1998	63.3	17.7	9.4	19.9	36.7	5.6	9.2
2000	60.8	18.2	9.5	18.2	39.2	7.1	10.0
2002	57.0	16.5	7.7	17.7	43.0	8.7	12.4
2004	50.8	13.8	7.2	15.2	49.2	12.1	13.8
Change over 1995–2004	−13.8	−2.0	−3.3	−4.8	13.8	7.2	6.0

Source: Eurostat and ECB calculations.
Notes: NMS is new EU Member States.

However, there are likely to be further impacts on euro area prices that go beyond this direct impact on import prices. For example: the increasing share of low-cost producers in world exports may have put additional downward pressure on the export prices of higher-cost exports via competition effects, hence having a downward impact on world export prices. In addition, the rising share of low-cost suppliers in euro area imports is likely to have put downward pressure on prices in euro area domestic import-competing sectors. Similarly, it may be the case that the threat of relocation of production to low-cost countries by firms may also have had a dampening effect on wage increases in the euro area.

area exporters give virtually equal weight to the pricing-to-market and the costs components. This implies that a one per cent increase in either costs or competitor's prices brings about a 0.5 per cent increase in export prices, with most of the long-run impact coming through in about a year. As competitors' prices include the impact of changes in exchange rates, the results indicate that the pass-through of changes in the effective exchange rate of the euro to extra-euro area export prices of goods is around 50 per cent. This implies that euro area export profit margins are reduced (increased) in response to an appreciation (depreciation), thereby limiting the impact on export price competitiveness of movements in exchange rates. This partly explains why the goods balance showed a somewhat muted response to the significant depreciation of the euro during 1999–2000.

2.1.3   Euro area export performance and its product and geographical composition

We now turn to examine how the euro area's export performance was influenced by its composition in terms of products and destination markets. One objective is to assess possible weaknesses going forward, which may influence the response of the euro area in relation to external shocks.

Putting together the results of a product and market decomposition (the so called 'Constant market share analysis' reported in greater detail in Box 2.3), euro area exports appear to be more concentrated – relative to the world average – in medium-technology products and towards European markets. In the past, the product specialisation of euro area exports has not hampered export performance since medium technology products grew reasonably well, while the growth of European export markets – which has been rather sluggish for most countries – has been sustained by the dynamism of the new EU Member States. Looking forward, however, the low specialisation in high-tech exports and the relatively low penetration in the most dynamic Asian markets could be a source of weakness for euro area exports.

Box 2.3

The product and geographical composition of euro area exports (Constant market share analysis)

The so-called 'constant market share analysis' provides useful policy-related information on whether euro area exporters have, on average, out- or under-performed their competitors in selecting high-growth destination markets and sectors. Without entering into the detail provided elsewhere, the following results indicate the possible risks (or opportunities) for future euro area exports.[7] The overall assessment of the constant market share analysis is that over the past fifteen years or so, the product composition of euro area exports (the *product effect*) had a roughly neutral effect on the euro area's export market share, while the geographical specialisation (the *market effect*) had a negative effect.

The product effect (sectoral specialisation)

Euro area exports are mostly concentrated in the medium-tech sectors (most notably chemicals, agricultural and industrial machinery and transport equipment), which account for almost half of euro area exports compared with one-third for world exports (see Figure 2.9). By contrast, the euro area has a comparatively low export share for high-tech products as they only represent about one-fifth of euro area exports, compared with one-third for world exports. Overall, and somewhat contrary to expectations, the specialisation of the euro area in medium-tech products, helped to support export performance as world demand in medium-tech sectors maintained a robust and stable pace of growth during the period 1985–2001. The under-specialisation of the euro area in the high-tech sectors meant that it was unable to capitalise fully on the relatively-faster growth of these products in world demand. This represents a potential risk for the future as these markets tend to be more dynamic. However, euro area exporters benefited from being less exposed to the volatility of these sectors linked with the technology boom and bust of the second half of the 1990s and early 2000s.

The market effect (geographical specialisation)

Euro area export performance has been hampered by a relatively-low export penetration in the most-rapidly-growing geographical markets. Overall, the geographical structure of euro area exports shows an 'under-specialisation' in fast-growing markets (such as Asian countries, the US and, to a lesser extent, Japan and China) and a 'specialisation' in European markets, with the latter growing relatively slowly with the exception of the new EU Member States (see Figure 2.10). The role of the UK in counterbalancing the negative market effects has rather sharply decreased over time because of the slower growth of the UK market relative to world markets in more recent years.

---

[7] See ECB, Occasional Paper Series No. 30 'Competitiveness and the export performance of the euro area' for full details of the constant market share analysis of euro area exports.

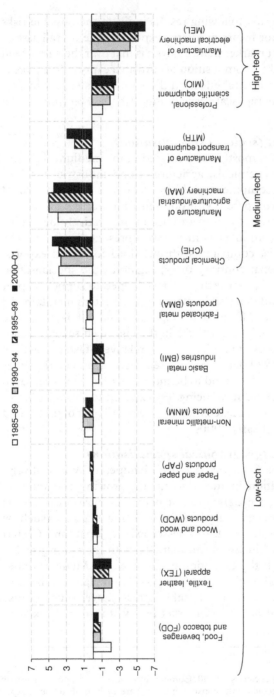

Figure 2.9. Euro area: relative product specialisation (percentages, period average)

Sources: WTA, ECB calculations. Reproduced from ECB Occasional Paper No. 30 'Competitiveness and the export performance of the euro area'.

Note: This indicator is defined as the difference between the share of the sector in euro area exports and the share of the sector in world exports. A value higher (lower) than zero for a sector indicates that the euro area is relatively specialised (despecialised) in the sector.

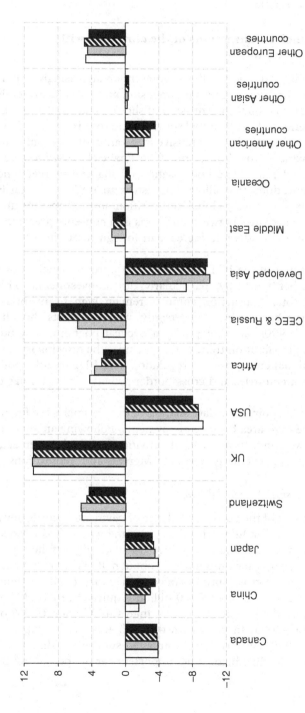

Figure 2.10. Euro area: relative market specialisation
(percentages, period average)

Sources: WTA, ECB calculations. Reproduced from ECB Occasional Paper No. 30 'Competitiveness and the export performance of the euro area'.

Note: This indicator is defined as the difference between the share of the destination market in euro area exports and the share of the destination market in world exports. A value higher (lower) than zero for a destination indicates that the exports of the euro area are relatively specialised (despecialised) in that destination.

2.2 The financial transactions of the euro area with the rest of the world

Cross-border capital and financial flows represent an increasingly important aspect of the euro area's external dimension and provide a notable channel for the international transmission of shocks. During the 1990s, the euro area experienced a substantial surge in cross-border capital flows in parallel with the sustained and extensive integration of financial markets across the world. Cross-border portfolio financial flows increased in magnitude stimulated by the liberalisation of financial markets and technological innovations that allowed investors to trade more easily on global markets. Moreover, global competition spurred merger and acquisition (M&A) activities between euro area and non-euro area companies, leading to a considerable increase in foreign direct investment (FDI).

Following the burst of the ICT bubble in 2000, gross financial flows have declined rather markedly, particularly direct investments. This notwithstanding, total transaction volumes remain high by historical standards and have been increasing recently, which suggests that the boom in the late 1990s was not purely a cyclical phenomenon, but may be related to globalisation trends. This includes the growing importance of multinational enterprises, deregulation, and FDI-friendly policies in a number of countries and cross-border activities in ICT-related sectors.

The classic starting point for a data analysis of this channel is the financial account of the euro area balance of payments. Following an analysis of that account, we concentrate on FDI activities for which other data sources are available, particularly related to Mergers and Acquisitions.

2.2.1 *The overall size of financial flows*

The financial account of the euro area balance of payments records flows of financial assets and liabilities with the rest of the world. It is divided into two sub-components, foreign direct investments, and portfolio transactions (Table 2.7), with each amounting to about half of the gross transactions. Average annual gross outflows in combined direct and portfolio investment declined from almost €700 billion (equivalent to 10.3% of GDP) over the period 1999–2001 to more than €480 billion (6.3% of GDP) during 2002–2005. In net terms, the euro area was an exporter of capital during 1999–2001 (i.e. the combined sum of net direct and portfolio investment), while being a net importer over the period 2002–2005.

Table 2.7 *Euro area financial flows* (EUR billions)

	1999	2000	2001	2002	2003	2004	2005	Average annual values		Average annual values as % of nominal GDP	
								1999–2001	2002–2005	1999–2001	2002–2005
Direct investment											
Abroad	−321.5	−445.6	−311.9	−175.1	−147.2	−141.7	−216.1	−359.7	−170.0	−5.37	−2.24
In the euro area	199.9	429.5	193.8	177.2	134.9	100.5	70.7	274.4	120.8	4.10	1.59
Balance	**−121.6**	**−16.1**	**−118.1**	**2.1**	**−12.3**	**−41.2**	**−145.4**	**−85.3**	**−49.2**	**−1.27**	**−0.65**
Portfolio investment											
Assets	−301.3	−399.2	−283.9	−177.4	−278.5	−343.5	−447.2	−328.1	−311.7	−4.90	−4.10
Equities	−156.9	−286.3	−101.6	−39	−81.2	−106.8	−144.3	−181.6	−92.8	−2.71	−1.22
Debt instruments	−144.4	−112.9	−182.3	−138.4	−197.3	−236.7	−302.9	−146.5	−218.8	−2.19	−2.88
Bonds and notes	−147	−103	−156.5	−89	−175.9	−179.8	−283.8	−135.5	−182.1	−2.02	−2.40
Money market instruments	2.6	−9.9	−25.8	−49.4	−21.4	−56.9	−19.1	−11.0	−36.7	−0.16	−0.48
Liabilities	265.2	299.7	349.9	284.6	351.4	398.7	605.7	304.9	410.0	4.56	5.40
Equities	90.8	52	232.5	85.5	110.3	128.1	280.2	125.1	151.0	1.87	1.99
Debt instruments	174.4	247.7	117.4	199.1	241.1	270.3	325.5	179.8	259.0	2.69	3.41
Bonds and notes	116.9	236.6	113.3	157.2	198.9	254.9	260.3	155.6	217.8	2.32	2.87
Money market instruments	57.5	11.1	4.1	41.9	42.2	15.4	65.2	24.2	41.2	0.36	0.54
Balance	**−36.1**	**−99.5**	**66**	**107.2**	**72.9**	**54.9**	**158.5**	**−23.2**	**98.4**	**−0.35**	**1.29**
Combined net direct and portfolio investment	**−157.7**	**−115.6**	**−52.1**	**109.3**	**60.6**	**13.7**	**13.1**	**−108.5**	**49.2**	**−1.62**	**0.65**

Source: Eurostat and ECB computations (extracted from the ECB Monthly Bulletin, May 2006).
Note: Last observation refers to 2005Q4.

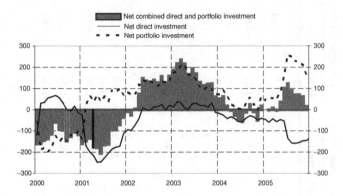

Figure 2.11. Net direct and portfolio investment flows
(EUR billion; 12-month cumulated data)
Source: ECB.
Note: A positive (negative) number indicates a net inflow (outflow) into
(out of) the euro area.

2.2.2   Determinants and recent developments in the euro area's FDI

Given the potentially-important role of FDI in the international transmission of shocks, this section provides a more-detailed analysis on the
determinants and recent developments in the euro area's FDI, focusing
in particular on mergers and acquisitions transactions (M&A), given their
significant magnitude.

In order to understand how FDI by multinational corporations affects
international linkages, it is divided into two broad categories. The first,
'horizontal' FDI occurs among countries which have similar GDP per
capita and where trade costs are relatively high. In particular, trade barriers and transport costs can cause a substitution effect away from trade and
towards foreign direct investment. More recently, FDI among developed
countries has been explained by the competitive advantage of firms in
acquiring new technologies abroad. The technology boom in the United
States and the desire of euro area firms to acquire the new technologies
developed by US companies seem to have been a factor behind the large
euro area FDI outflows to the United States, particularly in the second
half of the 1990s through M&As. The second category is 'vertical' FDI,
such as in the new EU Member States, which is mostly aimed at utilising
their low labour costs through the internationalisation of production.

A large part of the FDI flows relating to 'horizontal' FDI have been
channelled through M&A deals. An approximate calculation suggests that
M&A represented almost 70 per cent of FDI assets and 58 per cent of
FDI liabilities in the period 1998–2001. Until 1997, M&A activity by

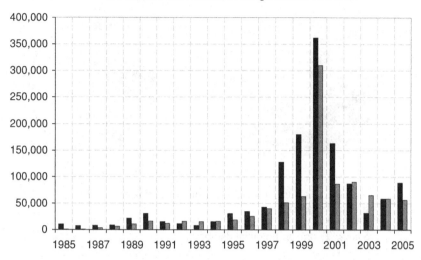

Figure 2.12. Euro area M&A activity (1985–2005)
(EUR millions)
Source: Thomson financial database.
Note: Last observation refers to July 2005.

euro area companies was relatively subdued, but from 1998 onwards, M&A investment by euro area companies increased strongly, especially cross-border investments, reaching a peak in 2000, when the value of euro area M&A flows abroad reached in excess of €350 bn, or around six per cent of GDP (see Figure 2.12). Thereafter, it decreased markedly to around €160 bn in 2001 and declined further to approximately €30 bn by 2003 before gradually recovering to almost €100 bn midway through 2005. Over the past ten years, the value of euro area M&A transactions with companies located outside the euro area has usually been significantly higher relative to the M&A of companies located in the euro area by foreign companies. Therefore, it seems relevant to examine to which countries, and in which sectors, these large M&A outflows have been directed.

As Figure 2.13 shows in greater detail, the USA is, by far, the major destination for euro area M&A investments (in value terms), with the acquisitions of high-tech (or 'new economy') US companies increasing dramatically in the late 1990s.

This is consistent with Figure 2.14 which shows that, in terms of values, a significant part of euro area M&As moved away from manufacturing and

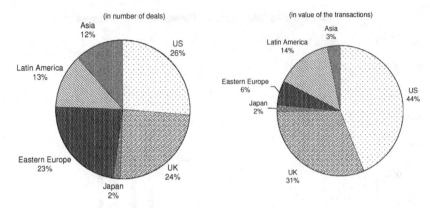

Figure 2.13. Euro area M&A abroad by region (1985–2005)
(in number of deals)
(in value of the transations)
Source: Thomson financial database.

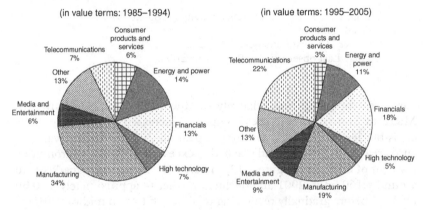

Figure 2.14. Sector of extra-euro area M&As by euro area residents
(1985–2005)
Source: Thomson financial database.

towards telecommunications, indicating that this represents horizontal
FDI as euro area firms seemed to be trying to catch up with their US
counterparts by investing heavily in acquiring US technology companies
associated with the 'new economy', thereby internalising the knowledge
capital of the US economy.[8] However, as shown in Figure 2.13, euro

---

[8] For further analysis of the knowledge-seeking motive behind euro area FDI to the US in
the second half of the 1990s, see De Santis, Anderton and Hijzen (2004). Also see ECB
Occasional Papers Nos 12 and 30.

area M&A activity in Eastern Europe has become as large as that in the USA and the UK in terms of the number of deals, reflecting vertical FDI and the internationalisation of production (described in greater detail later).

In addition to the desire of euro area firms to gain know-how, a factor that may explain the large wave of M&A is the surge in equity prices in the second half of the 1990s. The latter made it easier for firms to raise finance for acquiring domestic or foreign firms, while the rise and expectations of further increases in equity prices made M&As appear more attractive and profitable. Indeed, the peak in euro area M&A activity at home and abroad at the end of 1990s coincided with the stock market boom. This seems to support the notion that M&A transactions were, at least partly, driven by stock market valuations. The bursting of the stock market 'bubble' in 2000 was likewise accompanied by a plunge in M&A.

Most of the euro area's vertical FDI is in the Central and Eastern European economies (CEECs), fuelled in the 1990s by privatisation, economic liberalisation, deregulation and the prospect of EU enlargement. The relatively-low wage costs (along with good education levels) and the establishment of strategic positions in these relatively-new markets are the two main pull factors behind euro area FDI in the CEECs. Euro area FDI in this region is focused on a few countries: around 70–80 per cent of the total FDI inflows into the Czech Republic, Hungary, Poland and Slovakia were from the euro area (mostly from Germany, the Netherlands and Austria).[9] Greenfield foreign investment in manufacturing in the CEECs also plays an important role as 35–40 per cent of FDI activities are in the traditional manufacturing sectors.

2.2.3   Some preliminary assessments of the impact of the FDI channel

Little hard empirical evidence exists as yet regarding the relevance of the FDI channel for spillovers of external shocks to the euro area, although the magnitudes involved seem to be significant and increasing.[10] Against this background, we try to sketch at least some of the mechanisms at work, distinguishing horizontal from vertical FDI.

'Horizontal' FDI channel

Changes in the valuation of M&A investment abroad represent an obvious channel of transmission of shocks to the euro area. First, because such

---

[9] For more details see Table 12 (p. 62) of ECB Occasional Paper No. 30 'Competitiveness and the export performance of the euro area'.
[10] See chapter 6 in this volume.

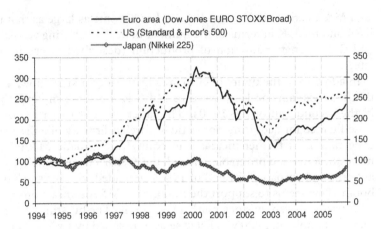

Figure 2.15. Evolution of stock market indices (1994–2005)
index (January 1994 = 100; monthly averages)
Source: ECB.
Note: Last observation refers to 31/12/2005.

changes may influence market expectations of the profits of the company world-wide and therefore affect the euro area parent company. This can have repercussions on the availability of external financial resources (quantity effect) for these firms and on the risk premium embedded in the cost of the financing (price effect). In this way, or simply via the impact on corporate wealth, employment and investment decisions of the acquirer/parent company can also be affected.

Given the amount of outstanding M&As, the impact of such valuation changes on firms' balance sheets can be substantial. Previous work, using simple 'back of the envelope' calculations, estimated the M&A-related losses incurred by European firms following the crash of the ICT equity price bubble.[11] These calculations suggest that more than 30 per cent of the total effective value of initial euro area M&A investment in the US and the UK had been lost by the middle of 2002 as a consequence of the past decline in equity prices. This loss is larger if we focus only on the high-tech and telecommunications sectors where the decline of the same period is estimated to be 61 per cent (around €133 billion) and 67 per cent (€131 billion) respectively. These estimates are obtained using the changes in the foreign equity indices (see Figure 2.15) to

---

[11] See pp. 38–40 of ECB Occasional Paper No. 12 'Understanding the impact of the external dimension for the euro area: trade, capital flows and other macroeconomic linkages'.

calculate the variation in the value of cross-border M&A investment of euro area companies. Obviously there are many caveats to these simple calculations, not least the fact that we have no information as to whether firms that undertook such transactions still hold all of the shares involved in those deals. In addition, the stock market has also partly recovered from the declines of the early 2000s.

'Vertical' FDI channel

As mentioned in the previous section, the vertical FDI channel operates mainly through the impact on trade. Earlier it was hypothesised that vertical FDI and the internationalisation of production was behind the rising import content of euro area exports. Here we offer some more direct evidence of the impact of vertical FDI by reporting previously-published econometric evidence on the effects on trade of FDI to transition economies.[12] In particular, as shown in Table 2.8, German FDI to the transition economies had a significant positive impact on both German imports and exports for the low-medium and high-tech sectors. Moreover, the elasticity of German imports is higher than the elasticity of German exports, which is consistent with the fact that firms specialising in manufacturing electrical machinery, professional and scientific equipment or transport equipment have shifted production abroad in order to import intermediate manufacturing products.

At the euro area level, the above vertical FDI-related trade impacts resulted in a substantial increase in the CEECs share of euro area trade – particularly the new EU Member States – and was to some extent accompanied by declining intra-euro area trade, which affected mostly the larger euro area countries. Over the period 1985–2001, there was a significant decline in the share of the total (i.e. intra plus extra) imports of the euro area supplied by France, Germany, the Netherlands and Italy, while the share of the new EU Member States increased from just over one to almost five per cent. Meanwhile, in terms of purely extra-euro area imports, the share of the new EU Member States had increased to around 11 per cent by 2003.

The biggest transformation has occurred in trade between the new EU Member States and Germany. The share of the new EU Member States in total (intra plus extra) German imports increased from around two per cent in 1985 to around ten per cent in 2001, with the key trade partners being the Czech Republic, Hungary and Poland. Over the same

---

[12] ECB Occasional Paper No. 30 'Competitiveness and the export performance of the euro area'.

Table 2.8 *Impact of German inward and outward manufacturing FDI on bilateral trade with transition economies*

	Transition economies			
	low-med tech		high-tech	
	exports	imports	exports	imports
GDP	0.338	0.22	0.447	0.279
	[3.45]**	[1.74]	[3.57]**	[2.62]*
Distance	−0.392	−1.036	−0.259	−1.572
	[1.65]	[3.46]**	[1.07]	[4.61]**
FDI (out): low-med tech	0.213	0.285		
	[2.02]*	[3.89]**		
FDI (out): high-tech			0.372	0.667
			[6.21]**	[7.80]**
Constant	3.583	8.57	1.387	10.4
	[1.97]	[3.28]**	[0.95]	[3.68]**
Observ.	106	106	42	42
R2 – adj.	0.32	0.31	0.68	0.77
F-test	13.25	18.24	31.49	73.98
Prob>F	0	0	0	0

Source: Reproduced from ECB Occasional Paper No. 30 'Competitiveness and the export performance of the euro area'.
Note: Robust t-statistics in brackets; * significant at 5%; ** significant at 1%
Cross-section gravity model estimates based on 21 sectors and 16 'transition' economies for the year 2002.
[1] The 'transition economies' are the ten new EU Member States, Bulgaria, Croatia, Romania, Russia, Turkey and Ukraine.
[2] FDI stocks of the reforming countries in Germany are negligible and were therefore excluded.

period, the share of euro area countries in German imports decreased from around 50 to just below 45 per cent, with virtually all the decline occurring from the mid-1990s onwards. The major euro area countries accounting for this decline are France, Italy and the Netherlands. It is especially pronounced in sectors such as textiles, wood and wood products, fabricated metals, electrical machinery and transport equipment. To a large extent, this trade shift is due to the rising importance of new EU Member States' affiliates in German firms' production processes, which has entailed a rise in intra-industry trade of a vertical nature. However, some of the loss in market share by euro area countries in Germany was also due to increasing import penetration by Asian economies, particularly China.

2.3   Additional transmission channels and synchronisation

Starting in the second half of 2000, there was an almost-simultaneous deceleration in real GDP growth in the US and the euro area, accompanied by a sharp contraction in world trade. Given the relatively-closed nature of the euro area economy as measured by standard trade indicators, the extent to which euro area activity declined in line with the global downturn seems to have surprised some forecasters.[13] The subsequent upturn that began in 2001 has resulted in stronger growth rates of GDP for the US and Asia in comparison to the euro area. However, this does not necessarily mean that linkages between the world economy and the euro area have become less synchronised during 2001–2005, particularly as growth in the euro area over this period has benefited from the robust strength of foreign demand which has provided a substantial boost to euro area exports, while common shocks such as the oil price rises may have also increased synchronisation across countries.

Drawing from these episodes and others, the purpose of this section is to study how external shocks can, directly or indirectly, spill over and affect euro area growth via mechanisms additional to those already examined. In this context, a special emphasis in this section is given to possible additional links with the US, such as confidence linkages. Following this analysis, the section assesses whether global economic integration and international linkages have actually resulted in a greater degree of synchronisation of international activity at a global level, with a particular reference to the euro area. Equity market developments – which seem to be highly correlated across the world – provide another important linkage which may result in co-movement between the euro area and global economies given that stock markets can have substantial effects on economic activity as they are an important source of finance for investment and can affect consumption via wealth effects. However, these linkages are not examined in this chapter as a detailed analysis of the macroeconomic impact of equity market declines is presented in chapter 7.

2.3.1   Confidence channels

The events of 11 September 2001 in the US brought confidence to the fore as another potential channel for transmission of international disturbances. A key question, however, is whether confidence linkages between countries simply reflect real spillovers and common shocks rather than additional effects that are purely due to confidence effects. In previous

---

[13] See Anderton, di Mauro and Moneta (2004) p. 41 for further details of forecasts over this period.

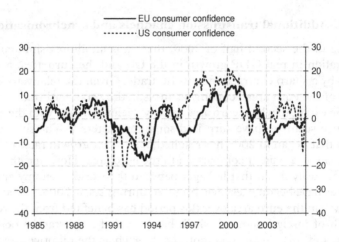

Figure 2.16. Consumer confidence in the euro area and the US (percentage balances, mean adjusted)

work using a VAR methodology, we found evidence of impacts of US confidence on euro area confidence even after taking out the impacts of real and nominal spillovers between the US and euro area, hence confidence effects seem to provide an additional transmission mechanism by which the US might affect the euro area.[14]

The following section takes a closer look at the possible linkages between the US and euro area originating from consumer confidence and business/industrial confidence. In general, one might expect the impact of consumer confidence to be on consumption while industrial confidence is likely to affect investment. Considering that the share of industrial output in overall euro area real GDP is only around one-quarter, while that of private consumption is around half, contagion effects via consumer confidence may be expected to be relatively-more important than those via industrial confidence. In the euro area, consumer confidence seems to be rather-closely aligned with total employment growth and unemployment changes, which, to a large extent, reflect factors in the domestic economy. Despite the relatively-larger importance of domestic factors, consumer confidence in the euro area follows a pattern that is rather similar to that in the US (see Figure 2.16).

External developments might also impact on euro area production growth via contagion effects in terms of business confidence. For

[14] See Box 8 in ECB Occasional Paper No. 12: 'Confidence spillovers: an empirical investigation'.

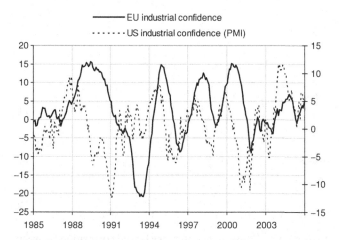

Figure 2.17. Industrial confidence in the euro area and the US (percentage balances, mean adjusted)
Source: European Commission, OECD and ECB calculations.
Note: Percentage balances – mean adjusted. PMI refers to Purchasing Managers Index.
Last observation refers to December 2005.

example, industrial confidence in the US may influence confidence in the euro area which, in turn, may impact on euro area industrial production growth. In this respect, the overall pattern of movements in business confidence in the euro area and the US shows, by contrast with the dissimilarity in the first half of the 1990s, a higher similarity in the second half of the 1990s, with further increases in the correspondence between the series in the early 2000s. Indeed, from 1995, the turning points in the Purchasing Managers Index for the US seem to lead those in the European Commission's industrial confidence indicator for the euro area by around two-quarters (Figure 2.17).

Figure 2.18 and Figure 2.19 show the correlation between the US and euro area confidence indicators. Overall, the confidence correlations have been increasing over time, although in the most recent years of the charts, the confidence correlations have fallen somewhat towards the end of the sample period. This limited evidence of a trend increase in the confidence correlations suggests that spillover effects from the US to the euro area may have increased and become more constant, perhaps not simply reflecting anymore the usual traditional business cycle linkages. This latter evidence can also be due to the recent boost of foreign demand and its impact on export performance as well as stronger FDI linkages

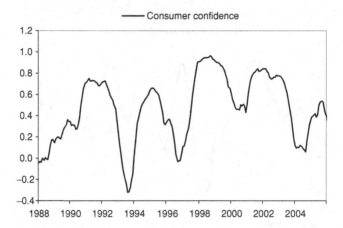

Figure 2.18. Consumer confidence lagged correlation between the euro area and the US
(rolling 3-year correlation window, US indicator 3-quarter lagged)

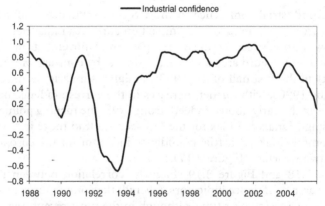

Figure 2.19. Industrial confidence lagged correlation between the euro area and the US
(rolling 3-year correlation window, US indicator 3-quarter lagged)
Source: European Commission, OECD and ECB calculations.
Note: Percentage balances – mean adjusted.
Last observation refers to December 2005.

between different countries. Conversely, it might be the case that the 'common shock' of the oil price rise during 1999–2005 is part of the reason for the sustained high level of the business confidence correlation over this period.

2.3.2   Is international activity now more synchronised?

The apparent increasing degree of economic interdependence across nations has stimulated a rather extensive literature studying the existence and characteristics of an 'international business cycle'. This section, begins by explaining the formation of the international business cycle – that is, the co-movements in the main macroeconomics variables across countries – paying specific attention to oil price shocks. This is followed by a discussion of the evidence as to whether the increased interdependence in trade and finance of recent years has raised the synchronisation of international activity.

This is a relevant issue for policy purposes. Indeed, if economic cycles are more closely synchronised, recessions and slowdowns in more countries are likely to reinforce each other. By contrast, when business cycles are unsynchronised, channels of international linkages can help to dampen economic fluctuations. Accordingly, if an economy is experiencing strong cyclical growth this will tend to stimulate activity in other economies where output growth is weaker. Moreover, the degree of synchronisation of business cycles can be a factor affecting price developments. Indeed, periods of desynchronisation may help to contain inflationary pressures, since excess demand can be redistributed across countries. In addition, if there is a common factor present in business cycles across countries, and this is found to be present systematically, policy makers would have to consider it when assessing developments in individual economies.

2.3.3   Determinants of business cycle synchronisation

Numerous contributions attempt to explain international business cycle co-movements and synchronisation. In a first theory, called 'business cycle transmission' or the 'locomotive' hypothesis, economic fluctuations originating in one country are transmitted to another country, usually from a large country to a smaller one, through the spillover channels which have been examined previously. In a second theory, the 'common shock hypothesis', business cycle synchronisation is caused by exogenous common shocks, such as the oil price shock of the 1970s (see Box 2.4).

Various empirical papers claim that the international linkages examined in this chapter and common shocks play a role in explaining the co-movement of business cycles. However, the impact of international linkages on the synchronisation of the business cycle is still not well understood.

On the one hand, Frankel and Rose (1998) find that an increase in trade flows between two countries causes a greater degree of synchronicity between their business cycles, since a higher level of trade will allow demand shocks to be more-easily spread across national borders or because of the increasing importance of intra-industry trade. In addition, international linkages examined in this chapter and elsewhere could produce a higher degree of business cycle synchronisation. For example, the chapter by Jansen and Stockman in this book finds that there is a positive relationship between the size of bilateral FDI positions and the degree of business cycle co-movement across countries. As noted previously, financial linkages could also result in a higher degree of business cycle synchronisation. Indeed, financial links also allow international wealth transfers as well as international risk sharing. Finally, particularly from the perspective of the speed of transmission, the confidence channel may strengthen the degree of business cycle synchronisation.

On the other hand, according to economic theory, trade flows and a more-integrated market can lead each country to specialise in the production of goods in which it has a comparative advantage. This increase in specialisation could therefore decrease the correlation of output across countries.

Box 2.4

Oil price shocks

One of the most important common shocks is an oil price shock and indeed the recent spike in oil prices has raised global concerns regarding its potential effects on the world economy. Oil consumption has increased since the early 1970s for the US, Japan and euro area economies, the increase being more important in the case of the US. However, the intensity of oil utilization (i.e. the ratio of oil consumption to real GDP) has been gradually decreasing since the 1970s (see Figure 2.20).

As shown in Figure 2.21, oil prices rose in 1999 before reaching around $32.4 per barrel in September 2000 – their highest level since the Gulf War – and declining to around $19.1 at the end of

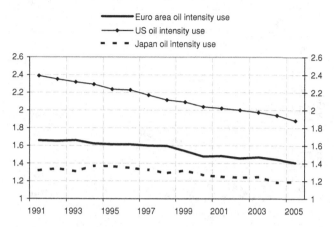

Figure 2.20. Intensity of oil utilisation
Source: International Energy Agency (IEA), Eurostat and Bloomberg.
Note: Last observation refers to December 2005.
The intensity of oil utilisation is computed as oil demand/GDP in real terms.

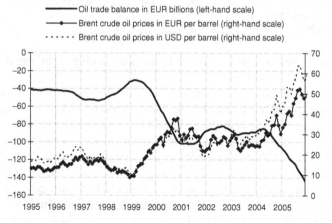

Figure 2.21. Euro area oil balance in values and oil Brent prices (monthly data, oil deficit is cumulated over twelve months)

2001. In 2002, the oil price started to rise again, with a further rapid acceleration from 2004 onwards before reaching in excess of $60 per barrel at the beginning of 2006. This represents one of the most prolonged oil price rises of recent times, reflecting the strength of the global economy, in particular the strong demand in China and the

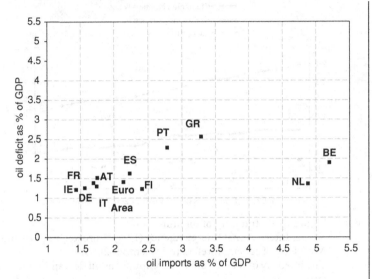

Figure 2.22. Oil imports and oil deficit as % of GDP
(Average 2000–2005; seasonally adjusted; quarterly data)
Source: Eurostat.
Note: Latest observation refers to December 2005.

United States, as well as fears of disruptions in oil production due to tensions in the Middle East.

The impact on the euro area's oil trade balance has been substantial, with the oil deficit increasing from around €7 billion per quarter at the end of 1998 to more than €40 billion per quarter at the start of 2006, resulting in a rise in the euro area's oil deficit to around €150 billion per annum which is equivalent to approximately two per cent of GDP (Figure 2.21). As oil prices are denominated in dollars, the deterioration in the oil deficit has been mitigated by the substantial bilateral appreciation of the euro against the US dollar between 2002–2005; hence the oil price increase in terms of euro has been significantly less than the dollar price increase. In absolute terms, the oil imports of the euro area at the end of 2005 were around 2.8 per cent of GDP, while the oil deficit is marginally smaller at approximately 1.9 per cent of GDP. However, the oil dependency of the euro area countries is quite diverse, with oil imports for Belgium, the Netherlands and Greece significantly above the euro area average at just over 5.2, 4.8 and 3.2 per cent of GDP respectively (Figure 2.22). In the case of the Netherlands, the oil deficit at just over 1.4 per cent of GDP is significantly smaller than its oil imports due to the oil refining and exporting activities of large Dutch multinationals in the petroleum industry. Meanwhile, Ireland, Germany and France have notably smaller imports of oil than the euro area average at just close to 1.5 per cent of GDP. Overall, such heterogeneity across the euro area countries in terms of their degree of oil dependency implies that the impacts of an oil price rise can be quantitatively quite different between the individual countries.

There are various mechanisms by which an oil price hike may affect growth. On the demand side, an oil price rise may reduce real income and thereby put downward pressure on consumption. It can also have a negative impact on investment via a reduction in profitability, particularly if the oil shock is expected to be relatively persistent. On the supply side, there may also be negative effects as the increased cost of oil will reduce profit margins which may lead to reductions in both output and employment. In addition, since oil price hikes are inflationary, some central banks could adopt a tighter monetary policy which may induce a downward adjustment in activity.

However, the impact of the recent oil price shocks on output and inflation seems so far, to have been significantly weaker than in previous episodes of oil price hikes.

2.3.4   Empirical evidence of synchronisation

In this section we explore whether the degree of business cycle synchronisation across countries has increased over time. In particular, from some of the previous analysis, it seems that the transmission of international disturbances may have strengthened, thereby increasing the co-movement of the euro area economy with other major economies such as the United States. Moreover, common shocks such as the oil price shock from 1999–2006, or the global ICT shock associated with the downturn in 2000, also seem to play an important role, representing another factor which could increase the degree of synchronisation.

An OECD study (OECD, 2002a) suggests that the degree of business cycle divergence across countries, measured by the standard deviation of output gap, is decreasing over time. However, (Monfort et al., 2002), using a dynamic factor model, studied the co-movement of GDP and industrial production between the G7 countries for the period

1972–2002. Using Kalman filter techniques, the authors extract a common component from these variables and – by using the correlation between the common factor and GDP growth as a measure of synchronisation of international activity – found that the degree of synchronisation has declined over the past three decades in the G7 countries, although they also found an increase in correlation in recent years. This long-term negative trend in the co-movements of output is confirmed by Doyle and Faust (2002) who analyse the correlation between the output growth of the US and the other G7 countries. However, in line with historical evidence, they also note the recent increase in correlation particularly during periods of recession.

Nevertheless, the result of a long-term trend decline in synchronisation still appears quite puzzling. As examined earlier, the euro area is becoming increasingly interconnected with other main economies through trade, FDI, financial and confidence linkages. In addition, increases in trade over the past decade do not appear to have been associated with increases in sectoral specialisation (OECD, 2002b). By contrast, large countries appear to have become more similar in sectoral composition. In addition, as documented by Hummels *et al.* (2001) for 10 OECD and four emerging countries, trade is increasingly characterised by vertical specialisation, that is, by countries specialising in particular stages of a good's production sequence, rather than in producing the entire good. This type of trade is generally related to the internationalisation of production chains and should in principle increase the correlation of output across countries (see, e.g. Kose and Yi, 2001). However, this feature has increased the import content of exports. This affects the transmission of shocks and the synchronisation of business cycles. Indeed, the impact on output of an external shock transmitted by a reduction in exports is dampened, if at the same time, imports also drop. Therefore it seems, as examined previously, that in the literature the impact of international linkages on the international transmission of economic shocks is still not well understood. In particular, the evidence of the effects of these linkages on the synchronisation of business cycles is rather mixed.

In order to shed light on this issue and adopt a euro area perspective, we use the model of Monfort *et al.* to calculate the correlation between the euro area and a common factor obtained using GDP data up to 2005 for the US, Canada, UK and the euro area. The declining trend in the degree of synchronisation is still present, however the increase in synchronisation in the most recent period is more evident and pronounced (see Figure 2.23). Perhaps somewhat surprisingly, the degree of

Figure 2.23. Euro area: GDP growth common factor correlation
(correlation computed over a 4-year moving window)
Source: Eurostat, IMF and ECB calculations.
Note: Last observation refers to 2005Q2.

synchronisation seems to have remained high during the latest years of
the estimation period despite the relatively slower growth of the euro area
compared to, say, the USA. From a euro area perspective, this sustained
higher level of synchronisation may be partly due to the fact that the
strength of foreign demand has significantly contributed to GDP growth
by boosting euro area exports and has substantially more than offset the
negative impact of the euro appreciation on exports during 2002–2005.
At the same time, the significant and sustained rise in oil prices over this
period represents a common shock which probably accounts for a significant part of the apparent ongoing higher degree of synchronisation
across the major world economies.

It is also interesting to note that the lowest degree of synchronisation of euro area GDP growth using this common factor approach is
registered in the first half of the 1990s when two large idiosyncratic
shocks, related to German reunification, and the ERM crisis of 1992–
1993 affected the euro area economies and the UK. These shocks may
also be a major factor in causing the overall trend decline in synchronisation over the whole sample period. Comparing these results with those
of Montfort *et al.* also suggests that the behaviour of the euro area as
a whole might be somewhat different from that of the individual euro
area countries. For example, the degree of synchronisation between the
GDP of Germany, France and Italy and the other G7 economies may
be negatively affected by the growing intra-area trade of the three major
euro area countries. By contrast, measures of the co-movements of the

GDP of the euro area as a whole, and the other G7 economies are not affected by the increasing importance of internal trade within the euro area (as total intra-euro area trade does not contribute to euro area GDP). In summary, it seems that for the euro area as a whole, the evidence provided in this chapter of spillovers coming from economic shocks in major economies, combined with the presence of common shocks, might explain the increase in the degree of synchronisation in the most recent period. Moreover, this higher degree of synchronisation may explain the impact of the global slowdown on the euro area in 2000 – as discussed at the beginning of the section – which could be related to the fact that only traditional channels of transmission are usually considered in forecast models thereby overlooking other important channels documented in this chapter.

2.4   Conclusions

This chapter looks at three channels of transmission of external shocks to the euro area, namely: trade, capital flows and other linkages. Starting with trade, although the openness of the euro area is lower than that of the individual euro area countries, the euro area remains more open than the United States and Japan. However, it is important to note that the standard measures of openness provided in the first part of this chapter only provide a limited understanding of the 'external dimension' of the euro area and the degree of its international interdependences. The 'effective' trade openness of the euro area is rather more complex and is not fully captured by simple measures since external trade linkages frequently involve complex links working through third markets outside the euro area as well as trade interactions between the individual euro area economies. Furthermore, the impact of external shocks on the euro area also depends on the specific nature of the shock and how it relates to the product and geographical specialisation of euro area trade.

Meanwhile, non-trade channels of international spillovers seem to be increasing in importance, although they remain a rather uncharted territory for theorists as well as policy makers. For example, euro area capital flows have undergone considerable changes in recent years, corresponding with the global surge in cross-border capital flows, resulting in strong growth in the stocks of foreign assets and liabilities of the euro area. Accordingly, the potential magnitude of the impact of capital flows as a channel for the transmission of external shocks to the euro area may now be significantly larger than it was previously, particularly the FDI channel. 'Horizontal' FDI may be an important channel, particularly regarding the profits of euro area multinationals and how they may now be more exposed to fluctuations in US activity and profitability, while the increased presence of US multinationals in the euro area also strengthens the economic links between the two economies. At the same time, the changing value of the stock of euro area firms' foreign direct investments in the US highlights another channel for the international transmission of shocks. In particular, we highlighted the significant past losses in the value of euro area corporation's M&A investments in the US due to the fall in equity prices in the early 2000s, especially in the 'new economy' sectors, which may have had a negative impact on euro area employment and capital expenditure through the implied decline in the corporate wealth of the acquirer/parent company. Meanwhile, euro area 'vertical' FDI – particularly *vis-à-vis* the new EU Member States – seems to have amplified the external trade links of the euro area. This largely reflects the internationalisation of euro area production and has been associated with an increase in the import intensity of exports which may have implications for the value-added contribution of exports to GDP.

Finally, we looked at various international linkages, focusing on additional channels and the degree of synchronisation of economic activity across countries. As regards possible confidence linkages, our limited empirical work finds evidence of US confidence affecting euro area confidence and that these effects are in addition to those due to movements in real and nominal variables. Furthermore, the correlation between US and euro area industrial and consumer confidence seems to have been increasing over time, although it has fallen somewhat in more-recent years.

As regards the co-movement of output across countries, some measures of synchronisation of international activity reveal that the degree of synchronisation has shown a trend decline over the past three decades in the G7 countries, although there has also been an increase in synchronisation since the mid-1990s. In order to shed light on this issue, we examined the synchronisation of the euro area with the US, UK and Canada and found that the declining trend in the degree of synchronisation is still present, although there is an evident increase in synchronisation in the most-recent period which is pronounced and prolonged. In addition, the lowest degree of synchronisation of euro area GDP growth with the other G7 countries occurred in the first half of the 1990s when two shocks, related to German reunification and the ERM crisis of 1992–1993, affected the euro area. These shocks may also be a major factor in causing the overall trend decline in synchronisation over the whole sample period. Meanwhile, the subsequent increase in synchronisation might be due to a possible increase in the external linkages mentioned in this chapter, while common shocks, such as the oil price shock from 1999–2006, as well as the global ICT shock around 2000, may also provide part of the explanation.

In summary, this chapter showed that there is some evidence that the external linkages of the euro area may be increasing over time. However, in the case of the euro area, increasingly important factors that may be driving this process which are also common to other economies, such as globalisation, are compounded by the fact that the euro area is a new and still somewhat unfamiliar entity and therefore many structural and possibly some global changes are at play contemporaneously.

REFERENCES

Anderton, R., F. di Mauro and F. Moneta (2004), 'Understanding the impact of the external dimension on the euro area: trade, capital flows and other international macroeconomic linkages', European Central Bank Occasional Paper No. 12.

Anderton, R., B. Baltagi, F. Skudelny and N. Sousa (2005), 'Intra- and extra-euro area import demand for manufactures', European Central Bank Working Paper No. 532.

Anderton, R. (2003), 'Extra-euro area manufacturing import prices and exchange rate pass-through', European Central Bank Working Paper No. 219.

De Santis, R. Anderton, and A. Hijzen (2004), 'On the determinants of euro area FDI to the United States: the knowledge-capital – Tobin's Q framework', European Central Bank Working Paper No. 329.

Doyle, B. M. and J. Faust (2002), 'An investigation of co-movements among the growth rates of the G7 countries', *Federal Reserve Bulletin*, pp. 427–437, October.

Frankel, J. A. and A. K. Rose (1998), 'The endogeneity of the optimum currency area criteria', *Economic Journal*, 108, pp. 379–399.

Hummels, D., J. Ishii and K. Yi (2001), 'The nature and growth of vertical specialization in world trade', *Journal of International Economics*, Vol. 54, No. 1.

Kose, M. A. and K.-M. Yi (2001), 'International trade and business cycles: Is vertical specialization the missing link?' *American Economic Review*, Vol. 91(2), pp. 371–375.

Monfort, A., J. R. Renne, R. Rüffer and G. Vitale (2002), 'Is economic activity in the G-7 synchronized? Common shocks vs. spillover effects', European Central Bank Working Paper.

OECD (2002a), 'Ongoing changes in the business cycle', *OECD Economic Outlook*, 71.

OECD (2002b), 'International linkages and changes in the business cycle', Working Party No. 1 on Macroeconomic and Structural Policy Analysis, October.

Task Force of the Monetary Policy Committee of the European System of Central Banks (2005), 'Competitiveness and the export performance of the euro area', European Central Bank Occasional Paper No. 30.

3   Product variety and macro trade models: implications for the new EU Member States

Joseph Gagnon[1]

3.1   Introduction

Standard trade equations in multi-country macroeconomic models imply that rapidly-growing countries should have either declining trade balances or declining terms of trade.[2] In long-run equilibrium, intertemporal budget constraints prevent trade balances from declining indefinitely. Hence, for countries that are expected to grow faster than their trading partners for an extended period of time, standard models imply that the terms of trade should decline secularly.

The new EU Member States (NEUMS) to the European Union (EU) are expected to grow faster than the fifteen pre-2004 EU countries (EU-15) for the foreseeable future.[3] Given that the overwhelming majority of NEUMS trade occurs within the EU, standard macroeconomic models imply that NEUMS export prices should decline relative to NEUMS import prices. This conclusion has a potentially important implication for NEUMS monetary policy. A fixed exchange rate with other EU countries might be expected to have a deflationary effect on NEUMS economies – yet six of the NEUMS have already joined the Exchange Rate Mechanism linking them (plus Denmark) to the euro, albeit with fairly wide bands. All of the NEUMS have expressed their intention to join the euro area by the end of the decade.[4]

Will exchange-rate links to the euro doom the NEUMS to persistent export price deflation, with possible harmful consequences for

---

[1] Board of Governors of the Federal Reserve System.
[2] See, for example, the models described in Levin *et al.* (1997), Laxton *et al.* (1998), Le Fouler *et al.* (2001), and Chari *et al.* (2002).
[3] The European Commission Spring 2005 forecast calls for (unweighted) average growth in the NEUMS of 4.6% in 2005 and 4.7% in 2006, versus 1.9 and 2.2%, respectively, for the EU-15.
[4] Technically, the NEUMS are required by EU law to adopt the euro as soon as they meet the economic criteria laid down in the Maastricht treaty. The criteria are fiscal deficits below 3% of GDP, public debts below 60% of GDP, inflation rates and long-term interest rates close to or lower than those prevailing in the member countries, and exchange rates remaining within the normal bands of the exchange rate mechanism.

macroeconomic outcomes? This chapter argues that the answer is 'no' because the standard macroeconomic models have a serious misspecification of the trade sector. Previous research has shown that an alternative trade specification – derived from explicit consideration of the role of product variety – explains long-run trends in trade significantly better.[5] In this specification, rapidly-growing countries are able to have stable trade balances without a secular decline in the terms of trade. There is every reason to believe that this alternative specification is relevant for the NEUMS. Indeed, despite the rapid economic and export growth of the NEUMS over the past ten years, there has been no tendency for NEUMS export prices to fall relative to import prices.

The alternative trade model based on product variety does support one of the conclusions of a recent paper by Natalucci and Ravenna (2002), who argue that tight exchange links between the NEUMS and the euro area could lead to excessive inflation in the NEUMS. This result is based on the work of Balassa (1964) and Samuelson (1964). Balassa and Samuelson noted that productivity growth tends to be concentrated in the production of tradable goods and that this tends to cause a rise in the prices of non-tradable goods relative to the prices of tradable goods. If global competition equalises the prices of tradable goods across countries, and if a country with rapidly-growing productivity has a fixed exchange rate with a slower-growing region, then the rapidly-growing country would be expected to have a higher overall inflation rate than the slower-growing region. The relevance to the NEUMS is immediately apparent when one notes that GDP deflators in the seven largest of the NEUMS have risen relative to export deflators by an average of 2.9 per cent per year over the past ten years, whereas for the EU-15 GDP deflators have risen only 1.1 per cent per year relative to export deflators.

This chapter shows that the result derived by Natalucci and Ravenna (and the Balassa-Samuelson hypothesis more generally) is not sensitive to the restrictive assumption of perfect substitution among tradables produced in different countries. In particular, the more general trade model of this chapter also delivers a prediction of constant terms of trade, which is consistent with the recent evidence for the NEUMS countries. With constant terms of trade and a fixed exchange rate to the euro, the NEUMS would be expected to have GDP inflation around 1.8 percentage points higher than in the euro area if productivity trends continue as they have over the past ten years.

---

[5] See Gagnon (2003, 2004).

3.2   Trade linkages in macro models

The simplest specification of trade in a macroeconomic model is that of perfect competition. Exporters in each country are price-takers on the global market and goods produced in different countries are perfectly substitutable. Purchasing power parity (PPP) holds, and net exports are the residual between spending and production in each country. This is the specification assumed in Balassa (1964) and Samuelson (1964).

The perfect competition model is a good description for small commodity-exporters who do not dominate global production of the commodities they export. However, most trade is in differentiated manufactured goods and services. For these exports, there is abundant evidence that PPP does not hold. Movements in relative prices across countries do elicit increases in exports from low-cost producers and decreases in exports from high-cost producers, but these changes in trade volumes are far from the infinitely large changes that would be implied by the perfect competition model.

Armington (1969) proposed a simple export demand specification to model trade in imperfect substitutes. As shown in equation (1) export demand responds positively to foreign income, Y^*, and negatively to the price of exports, PX, relative to foreign prices, P^*, converted into exporter currency by the exchange rate, E.[6] (Asterisks denote foreign variables.) This equation has a long pedigree of empirical success for many countries and sample periods. The estimated coefficients almost always have the correct signs, are usually statistically significantly different from zero and usually not statistically significantly different from plausible economic magnitudes. For time-series data on aggregate trade flows, the income elasticity estimates, β, are centered between 1 and 2; the price elasticity estimates, γ, are centered between 0.5 and 1.[7]

$$\underline{\text{Armington Demand}} \quad \log(X) = \alpha + \beta \log(Y^*) - \gamma \log\left(\frac{PX}{E \times P^*}\right) \tag{1}$$

Less attention has been devoted to modeling export supply. Early studies typically found that export supply is highly elastic.[8] Thus, some models assume a perfectly elastic supply of exports at a price proportional to the overall output price of the exporting country. More recently, studies have examined price discrimination in trade that is linked to real exchange rate movements. These studies have inspired an alternative export supply

---

[6] In some formulations, foreign income is replaced by foreign expenditures.
[7] See Senhadji and Montenegro (1999) and Marquez (2002).
[8] See Goldstein and Khan (1985).

specification (shown in equation (2)) in which exports are perfectly elastically supplied at a price that is a weighted average of domestic and foreign output prices, P and E × P*, respectively. The older, more simple export supply equation is given by equation (2) with full pass-through, $\gamma = 1$. Estimated versions of equation (2) typically find values of λ around 0.75.[9]

Supply $$\log(PX) = \delta + \lambda \log(P) + (1 - \lambda) \log(E \times P^*) \quad (2)$$

One implication of equations (1) and (2) is that an acceleration of one country's income, Y, that is not matched by income in the rest of the world, Y*, will lead to an acceleration of its imports but not its exports. This is because its imports are other countries' exports, and other countries' exports depend, in part, on Y.[10]

Krugman (1989) argued that this implication of the Armington model is not empirically plausible. In particular, he noted that estimated income elasticities differ across countries roughly in proportion to their trend growth rates. Nothing in the Armington model predicts such a relationship, so Krugman posited that there is an omitted variable, namely the share of exporter output in world output. He showed how his alternative model could be derived from a highly-simplified version of his earlier work with Helpman on the role of product varieties and imperfect competition in trade.[11] Gagnon (2004) generalised Krugman's result to allow for variable real exchange rates and non-unitary income elasticities.

The basic building blocks of the Krugman model are a Dixit-Stiglitz 'love of variety' utility function and increasing returns to scale in the production of new varieties.[12] Under these conditions, consumers will buy a positive amount of all available varieties and the number of varieties will be limited by the fixed cost associated with producing each one. The number of varieties produced in each country will be proportional to that country's economic resources or potential income. Total consumer demand depends on consumer income, but the allocation of consumer demand across countries depends on the price of each country's goods relative to other countries' goods and on the number of varieties each country produces relative to the number of varieties produced in other countries. (Each variety is produced in only one country, so varieties

---

[9] See Goldberg and Knetter (1997).
[10] Here we have held prices and exchange rates constant. But, in a general equilibrium setting, this model implies that the acceleration of one country's income will lead to a secular decline in its output prices relative to foreign output prices, P/(E × P*), which, in turn, implies a secular decline in its terms of trade, PX/(E × PX*).
[11] See Helpman and Krugman (1985).
[12] The utility function is described in Dixit and Stiglitz (1977).

are different across countries.) Total export demand thus takes the form of equation (3). In the simplest version of the model, both the income elasticity, β, and the varieties elasticity, σ, equal unity. Under these conditions, equation (3) implies that an acceleration of one country's potential income (YP), will lead to a balanced increase in both its exports (due to increasing numbers of varieties) and its imports (due to increasing consumer income), regardless of whether that acceleration is shared by the rest of the world.[13]

$$\underline{\text{Krugman Demand}} \quad \log(X) = \alpha + \beta \log(Y^*) - \gamma \log\left(\frac{PX}{E \times P^*}\right)$$

$$+ \sigma \log\left(\frac{YP}{YP + YP^*}\right) \tag{3}$$

Comparison of equations (1) and (3) shows that Armington demand is a special case of Krugman demand in which $\sigma = 0$. Direct estimates of this coefficient in time series data are generally unsatisfactory because there is little variation in relative potential income. (And there is no consensus on how to estimate potential income.) Gagnon (2003, 2004) takes a cross-country approach in which growth rates of exports are regressed on growth rates of the explanatory variables. By using growth rates over long periods of time (up to forty years) one can make the assumption that potential income has grown about as much as actual income and one can avoid modelling dynamic adjustment. Gagnon (2003) shows that US imports from fast-growing countries tend to grow faster than US imports from slow-growing countries, even after controlling for relative cost shocks and potential reverse causality. Gagnon (2004) shows that multilateral exports of fast-growing countries tend to grow faster than exports of slow-growing countries, again with controls for cost shocks and reverse causality. Both papers find estimates of σ that are very highly significant and close to, but a bit larger than, unity.

3.3   Application to Europe

Of the NEUMS, only Hungary was included in Gagnon (2003, 2004) because it is the only one with sufficient historical data. About ten years of data exist for most of the rest of the NEUMS. I will focus here on the seven largest: Czech Republic, Estonia, Hungary, Latvia, Lithuania, Poland, and Slovakia, henceforth NEUMS. The data sample is too

---

[13] For a small country, the varieties effect works entirely through domestic exports because the analogous varieties term in foreign exports is essentially fixed at unity, i.e. the foreign share of world income is nearly 100% and is not measurably affected by domestic growth. For a large country, both exports and imports have a varieties effect, though the export effect is bigger as long as the country has less than half of world potential income.

short and the number of countries too small to estimate equation (3) for the NEUMS.

However, the Krugman model does explain the growth of exports very well among the EU-15. Equation (4) presents results from a regression of equation (3) in terms of growth rates over the period 1960–1980 across individual EU-15 countries.[14] Equation (5) shows that similar results have been obtained for the period 1980–2000. In both cases, the varieties coefficient (σ in equation (3)) is positive and significantly different from zero. In the 1960–1980 sample, the varieties coefficient is significantly greater than unity at the ten per cent level, but not at the five per cent level. In the 1980–2000 sample, it is not significantly greater than unity at any level.

1960–1980 $N = 14$

$$\Delta \log(X) = 1.83\Delta \log(Y^*) - 0.64\Delta \log\left(\frac{PX}{E \times P^*}\right)$$

$t - stat$ (19.57)   (1.57)

$$+ 1.71\Delta \log\left(\frac{Y}{Y + Y^*}\right) \quad R^2 = .79 \quad (4)$$

(4.98)

1980–2000 $N = 15$

$$\Delta \log(X) = 1.85\Delta \log(Y^*) - 0.50\Delta \log\left(\frac{PX}{E \times P^*}\right)$$

$t - stat$ (6.07)   (1.33)

$$+ 1.46\Delta \log\left(\frac{Y}{Y + Y^*}\right) \quad R^2 = .78 \quad (5)$$

(4.30)

Figure 3.1 shows that among EU-15 countries, long-run income growth is strongly correlated with long-run export growth. This correlation is present over the entire forty-year period, as shown, as well as over both twenty-year sub-periods, not shown. Figure 3.2 shows that long-run income growth is not correlated with long-run changes in the terms of trade. This finding holds true over the period 1960–2000, as shown, as well as over both sub-periods, not shown. Figure 3.3 shows that there is no tendency for long-run income growth to be associated with declining trade balances, a result that also holds true over the two sub-periods.

---

[14] The variables are all 20-year growth rates and each country is one observation. German data are not available for the 1960–1980 growth rates. Data are from World Development Indicators 2004. Exports are total goods and services. Foreign variables computed as world minus exporter.

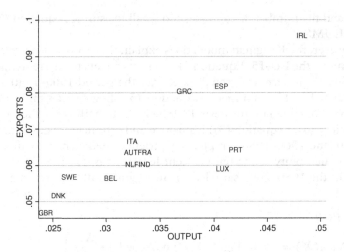

Figure 3.1. Export and output growth rates, 1960–2000 average

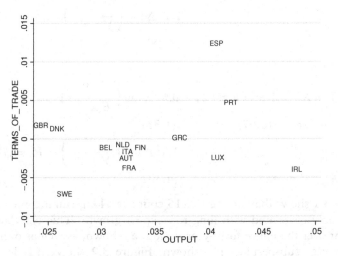

Figure 3.2. Change in terms of trade and output growth rate, 1960–2000 average

It is of particular interest to focus on two entrants to the EU in the 1980s that started out poorer than average and grew rapidly, namely Portugal (PRT) and Spain (ESP). Over both the forty-year period shown in Figures 3.1 and 3.2 and over the twenty-year period 1980–2000, Portugal and Spain each grew faster than the EU average, experienced more rapid

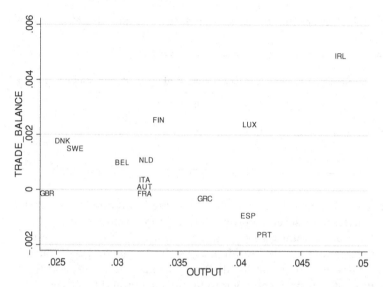

Figure 3.3. Change in trade balance/GDP and output growth rate, 1960–2000 average

export growth than the EU average and suffered no decline in their terms of trade. Indeed, they experienced rising terms of trade.[15]

Since there is no historical evidence that fast-growing EU-15 countries suffer either declining terms of trade or falling trade balances, it is reasonable to suppose that these results should apply to the NEUMS. Moreover, at the simplest level, it appears that NEUMS experience during the transition supports this conclusion.

Table 3.1 shows that all the NEUMS-7 had faster GDP growth and faster export growth than the EU-15 over the past ten years. Yet, in four of the NEUMS-7, the terms of trade rose on average during this period and in two of those that experienced declining terms of trade, the rate of decline was very close to zero. Thus, the experience of the NEUMS-7 over the past ten years is consistent with the empirical evidence for other countries over the past forty years, including the experience of the EU-15. Rapid growth of income does not doom a country to declining terms of trade.

Two recent papers have delved deeper into the experience of the transition economies by looking at more direct measures of varieties. Boeri

---

[15] Another relatively-poor recent entrant, Greece (GRC), has not experienced particularly-rapid output growth. Longstanding member Ireland (IRL) has experienced the most-rapid output growth of any of the EU-15 with only a modest decline in its terms of trade.

Table 3.1 *Average growth rates for selected macroeconomic variables,* *1995–2004*

	Czech Republic	Estonia	Hungary	Latvia	Lithuania	Poland	Slovakia	EU-15
Real GDP	2.1	5.7	3.5	6.0	5.2	4.0	4.1	2.1
Real exports	9.6	9.8	12.4	7.5	9.3	10.3	8.7	5.7
Real imports	10.7	10.0	12.1	8.8	11.0	12.3	10.1	5.9
Terms of trade	1.2	1.0	0.2	−0.9	−0.0	0.2	−0.3	0.1

and Oliveira Martins (2002) document the rise in production of differentiated varieties for several European transition economies during the 1990s. They use several measures of varieties, including (a) the number of enterprises per 1,000 residents; (b) the Feenstra (1994) variety indicator based on exports in highly disaggregated categories; and (c) a classification of industrial activity into homogeneous and heterogeneous sectors. For each of these measures, they find evidence of an increase in the number of varieties in production. But, Boeri and Oliveira Martins warn that growth in varieties appears to be slowing in several of the NEUMS and that there may be barriers to enterprise creation and diversification, particularly in the areas of infrastructure and finance. If such barriers prove to be detrimental to the proliferation of product varieties, they could potentially retard overall GDP and export growth. In the four years since the end of the Boeri and Oliveira-Martins sample, GDP and export growth in the NEUMS have held up well. One explanation may be that growth in varieties and output has occurred through new channels not well captured by their measures.

Funke and Ruhwedel (2005) employ an updated version of the Feenstra (1994) variety indicator applied to both exports and imports of several transition economies. They find evidence that proliferation of export varieties is associated with strong economic growth, whereas proliferation of import varieties is not highly correlated with growth.[16] This finding is consistent with the Krugman model's prediction that economic growth drives the production of new varieties, which are then available for export.

[16] Funke and Ruhwedel test two models of the role of varieties in growth. In one model, varieties are an input to the production process and greater variety of imports should lead to faster growth. In the other model, proliferation of export varieties is a path to export-led growth. The latter model is equivalent in many respects to the Krugman model.

3.4 Conclusions

This chapter shows both theoretically and empirically that there is no reason to fear that rapid growth of GDP and exports in the new EU Member States (NEUMS) will cause a secular decline in the terms of trade. It follows that tighter exchange rate links between the NEUMS and the euro should not give rise to deflationary pressures in the NEUMS. Indeed, the opposite risk seems more likely, namely that exchange rate stability against the euro could give rise to inflationary pressures in the NEUMS through the Balassa-Samuelson effect as recently suggested by Natalucci and Ravenna (2002). This effect operates through the prices of non-tradables in countries that are experiencing rapid productivity growth in the tradables sector. Based on the average productivity growth differential of the past ten years between the NEUMS and the EU-15, fixed exchange rates with the euro would be expected to cause overall (GDP) inflation in the NEUMS to be one to two percentage points higher than in the EU-15.

REFERENCES

Armington, P. S. (1969), 'A theory of demand for products distinguished by place of production', *IMF Staff Papers* 16, pp. 159–176.

Balassa, B. (1964), 'The purchasing-power parity doctrine: A reappraisal', *Journal of Political Economy* 72, pp. 584–596.

Boeri, T. and J. O. Martins (2002), 'Varieties, jobs and EU enlargement', *Rivista di Politica Economica* 92, pp. 139–178.

Chari, V. V., P. J. Kehoe, and E. R. McGrattan (2002), 'Can sticky price models generate volatile and persistent real exchange rates?' Staff Report No. 277, Federal Reserve Bank of Minneapolis.

Dixit, A. and J. Stiglitz (1977), 'Monopolistic competition and optimum product diversity', *American Economic Review* 67, pp. 297–308.

Feenstra, R. C. (1994), 'New product varieties and the measurement of international prices', *American Economic Review* 84, pp. 157–177.

Funke, M. and R. Ruhwedel (2005), 'Export variety and economic growth in East European transition economies', *Economics of Transition* 13, pp. 25–50.

Gagnon, J. E. (2003), 'Productive capacity, product varieties, and the elasticities Approach to Trade', International Finance Discussion Papers No. 781, Board of Governors of the Federal Reserve System.

Gagnon, J. E. (2004), 'Growth-led exports: Is variety the spice of trade?' International Finance Discussion Papers No. 822, Board of Governors of the Federal Reserve System.

Goldberg, P. and M. Knetter (1997), 'Goods prices and exchange rates: What have we learned?' *Journal of Economic Literature* 35, pp. 1243–1272.

Goldstein, Morris, and M. Khan (1985), 'Income and price elasticities in trade', in Jones and Kenen (eds.) *Handbook of international economics*, Vol. II, North-Holland, Amsterdam.

Helpman, E. and P. R. Krugman (1985), *Market structure and foreign trade: Increasing returns, imperfect competition, and the international economy*, The MIT Press, Cambridge, MA.

Krugman, P. (1989), 'Differences in income elasticities and trends in real exchange rates', *European Economic Review* 33, pp. 1055–1085.

Laxton, D. P. Isard, H. Faruqee, E. Prasad and Bart Turtelboom (1998), 'MULTIMOD Mark III: The core dynamic and steady-state models', Occasional Paper No. 164, International Monetary Fund.

Le Fouler, L. W. Suyker and D. Turner (2001), 'Trade linkages and the trade matrices in the OECD interlink model', Economics Department Working Papers No. 310, Organisation for Economic Cooperation and Development.

Levin, A. J. Rogers and R. Tryon (1997), 'Evaluating international economic policy with the Federal Reserve's global model', *Federal Reserve Bulletin* 83, October.

Marquez, J. (2002), *Estimating trade elasticities*, Kluwer Academic Publishers, Boston.

Natalucci, F. and F. Ravenna (2002), 'The road to adopting the euro: Monetary policy and exchange rate regimes in EU candidate countries', International Finance Discussion Papers No. 741, Board of Governors of the Federal Reserve System.

Samuelson, P. (1964), 'Theoretical notes on trade problems', *Review of Economics and Statistics* 46, pp. 145–154.

Senhadji, A. and C. Montenegro (1999), 'Time series analysis of export demand equations: A cross-country analysis', *IMF Staff Papers* 46, pp. 259–273.

4 Exchange-rate pass-through to import prices in the euro area

José Manuel Campa, Linda S. Goldberg and
José M. González-Mínguez[1]

4.1 Introduction

While exchange rate pass-through has long been of interest, the focus of this interest has evolved considerably over time. After a long period of debate over the law of one price and convergence across countries, beginning in the late 1980s exchange rate pass-through studies emphasised industrial organisation and the role of segmentation and price discrimination across geographically distinct product markets. More recently, pass-through issues play a central role in debates over appropriate monetary policies, exchange rate regime optimality in general equilibrium models and adjustment scenarios with respect to country external imbalances. These debates have broad implications for the conduct of monetary policy, for macroeconomic stability, international transmission of shocks and efforts to contain large imbalances in trade and international capital flows.

Another issue receiving attention in the recent macroeconomic debate is the stability of exchange rate pass-through rates over time. Taylor (2000), Goldfajn and Werlang (2000), Campa and Goldberg (2005), and Frankel, Parsley and Wei (2005), have argued that pass-through rates may have been declining over time in some countries. The Brazilian experience of the late 1990s is often cited. Here, consumer prices hardly responded to large home currency depreciation, in sharp contrast with past depreciation episodes. Campa and Goldberg (2005) caution against the assumption that pass-through has been declining over time across all OECD countries. While some countries have experienced reduced transmission of exchange rate changes into import prices, much of their measured declines are due to a change in the composition of their import bundle towards goods with lower pass-through elasticities. Other recent studies argue that declining pass-through has been more pervasive, at

[1] IESE Business School and CEPR, Federal Reserve Bank of New York and NBER and Banco de España, respectively.

63

least for the United States (Marazzi *et al*, 2005). However, measurement and interpretation issues leave these findings under debate. The issue posed in these and related studies is whether this decline in pass-through rates is statistically significant and if so, whether it stems from improved macroeconomic conditions in the importing countries, changing competitive conditions facing exporters, changes in the composition of imports or from some other economic changes.

The analysis of aggregate pass-through rates can be divided into two parts. The first part is a border phenomenon and addresses the extent to which there are changes in pass-through rates at the level of import prices. The second issue addresses the extent to which these border price changes are transmitted to consumers or even offset by anticipated current or future monetary policy changes. Our analysis specifically deals with the former question. This component of the question motivates an analysis that explicitly focuses on the pricing and invoicing decisions of the foreign exporter.

This chapter begins with a review of the conceptual underpinnings of exchange rate pass-through. While debates over pass-through elasticities seem to focus on estimates, theoretical analyses appropriately emphasise that there are clear structural forces at work in determining the sensitivities of prices to exchange rates (as well as the more general equilibrium determination of exchange rates). In Section 4.3 these lessons are applied to import prices for the euro area countries. We estimate short- and long-run pass-through elasticities and allow them to differ by country of destination and by industry. Short-run pass-through is incomplete and country- and industry-specific. In the long-run, elasticities are larger, although it can generally be rejected that they are equal to unity. Moreover, long-run pass-through rates are not statistically different for most industries in each country and for most countries given an industry. Finally, we perform tests of structural stability in the pass-through rates around the introduction of the euro. Although several arguments point towards a possible reduction in the rates of transmission of exchange rate movements to import prices after the start of EMU, there is only very weak statistical evidence in that direction.

4.2   Conceptual underpinnings

Pass-through of exchange rate movements into a country's import prices has been at the centre of macroeconomic debate over the past two decades. The increased openness of most developed economies and the incidence of large fluctuations in nominal exchange rates have led to a need for a better understanding of the determinants of the transmission of exchange rate changes into import prices.

In the purely statistical sense the relationship between import prices and exchange rates is the correlation between those two variables. We will call this relationship the 'statistical beta' $\beta = \text{cov}(\rho_m, e)/\text{var}(e)$, where p_m are the (log) import prices denominated in the currency of the importer, and e is the (log) nominal exchange rate expressed in terms of units of the importer currency per unit of the exporter currency. This purely statistical relationship between exchange rates and prices does not have a meaningful economic interpretation. First, exchange rates are by definition the relative prices of currencies. They are endogenous variables and their value gets determined within a general equilibrium context, along-side other asset prices. The effect of any movements in exchange rates on prices will therefore depend on three issues: (1) the underlying shock within the economy that induced the exchange rate to move; (2) the mechanisms within the model that lead to a relationship between the underlying shock, the exchange rate and import prices; and (3) the time frame of interest for understanding the relationship between exchange rates and import prices. The answer to the question of the effect that exchange rate changes have on import prices in any theoretical framework crucially depends on the approach taken on modelling these circumstances. These alternative approaches motivate the empirical specifications to be used in estimating exchange rate pass-through elasticities across countries and over time and shed light on the implicit assumptions behind the resulting estimates.

The initial research on this topic focused on the modelling of partial-equilibrium setups arising from the problem of a single exporter/importer or from the industrial organisation of one industry (Dornbusch, 1987). The approach ignores the view that exchange rates are endogenous economic variables and looks at the impact that an exogenous exchange rate movement has on the resulting equilibrium price in the industry. In this context, nominal exchange rates change the import price of the good according to the interaction of industry participants in oligopolistic markets. The micro-foundations of pricing behaviour by exporters are presented as a useful starting point for understanding the dynamics of exchange rate pass-through into import prices.[2] By definition, the import prices for any country, $P_t^{m,j}$, are a transformation of the export prices of that country's trading partners, $P_t^{x,j}$, using the exchange rate

---

[2] Some of the theoretical work in this literature is Froot and Klemperer (1989), Giovannini (1988), Marston (1990). Goldberg and Knetter (1997) provide a review of this literature.

E_t defined in units of the home (importing country) currency relative to the foreign (exporting country) currency:

$$P_t^{m,j} = E_t P_t^{x,j} \tag{1}$$

The export prices, in turn, are a markup $(mkup_t^x)$ over exporter marginal costs (mc_t^x). We rewrite equation [1] in logarithms as[3]

$$p_t^m = e_t + mkup_t^x + mc_t^x \tag{2}$$

The industrial organisation-based literature has a partial-equilibrium approach and takes the process of the exchange rate (e_t) as exogenous in the economy. Its focus is on the modelling of how the markup and the marginal cost of production, $mkup_t^x$ and mc_t^x, move with exchange rates. The markup response is often interpreted as an indicator of changes in the competitive conditions confronting foreign exporters in the destination market. In this case, the correlation between import prices and nominal exchange rates is different from one, $\beta \neq 1$. Estimated pass-through elasticities represent the summed effects of the unity translation effect on import prices from the exchange rate movement, the response of markup to offset some of this translation effect and any changes in marginal costs that are specifically attributable to exchange rate movements such as effects of imported inputs in production or wage sensitivity to exchange rates. Markup responsiveness will depend mainly on the market share of domestic producers relative to foreign producers, the form that competition takes place in the industry, and the extent of price discrimination possible in the industry. A general result in this literature is that a larger share of imports in total industry supply, a higher degree of price discrimination or a larger share of imported inputs in production in the destination country leads to higher predicted pass-through rates of exchange rates into import prices. Exchange rate pass-through may be higher if the exporters are large in number relative to the presence of local competitors.[4] Exchange rate variability and local monetary volatility could also matter as exporters compete for market share, as discussed in Froot and Klemperer (1989): exchange rate pass-through may be lower when exporters try to maintain local market share, even if nominal exchange rate variability is high.

The second strand of literature embeds a more general-equilibrium approach, whereby prices are sticky in one currency, that is set in advance

---

[3] In addition, the country superscript j has been dropped for simplicity.

[4] Dornbusch (1987). One approximation to this point is that pass-through elasticities might be inversely related to real GDP in the destination country. An alternative approach would be to also consider measures of sector-specific openness for countries.

of the realisation of the exchange rate by exporters. When prices are determined in the exporter's currency (producer currency pricing or PCP)
exchange rate pass-through tends to be much larger than when prices
are set in the importer's currency (local currency pricing or LCP). In the
extreme case of a purely-exogenous exchange rate shock, exchange rate
pass-through would be one under producer currency pricing and zero
under local currency pricing. As exemplified by the dialogue between
Devereux and Engel (2001) and Corsetti and Pesenti (2005), the assumptions made on the currency of export pricing generate radically different conclusions on optimal monetary, fiscal and exchange rate policies.
New models of international macroeconomics have imperfect competition and/or some form of price stickiness built in, as in Obstfeld and
Rogoff (1995), Corsetti and Pesenti (2005), and Corsetti, Dedola, and
Leduc (2004). These new micro-based open-economy general equilibrium models yield clear predictions for exchange rate behaviour, and for
pass-through into import prices as a function of the underlying shocks
in the economy and given the assumed specific competitive structures of
the industries involved.

Recent research in this area experiments with integrated production
activities and the interplay between producers and distributors in the
supply chain. Imperfect competition in the intermediate goods sector
and the local component value added of the final price both dampen the
pass-through of exchange rates into consumer prices. Corsetti and Dedola
(2002) provide a model of optimal international price discrimination in
a world with nominal wage rigidities and monopolistic competition in
production, in which upstream firms differentially price goods to retailers
in different locations. Bacchetta and van Wincoop (2003) expand upon
the Dornbusch (1987) insights that a pass-through disconnect may be
linked to the optimal pricing strategies of foreign exporting firms who sell
intermediate inputs to domestic firms producing final goods. Empirical
research attempts to quantify the importance of distribution margins for
pass-through and whether such margins are viewed as parameters, as
in Burstein, Eichenbaum, and Rebelo (2002), or whether distributors
also adjust such margins in response to exchange rate fluctuations, as in
Campa and Goldberg (2006).

Most recently this literature has evolved into endogenously determining the choice for currency of denomination of exports.[5] In much of
this research, price stickiness remains an essential part of the model, but

---

[5] See for instance Bacchetta and van Wincoop (2003, 2005), Corsetti and Pesenti (2002)
and Devereux, Engel and Storgaard (2004) for examples in this literature of different
ways to endogenise the pricing decision.

the decision by exporters to set prices in domestic or foreign currency is endogenous in the model. In so doing, exchange rate risk is considered *ex ante* and potentially optimally hedged. Engel (2005) and Goldberg and Tille (2005) show that optimal invoicing currency choice has a close analogue to optimally-chosen rates of exchange rate pass-through. Devereux and Engel (2001) and Devereux, Engel and Storgaard (2004) argue that in equilibrium, countries with low relative exchange rate variability and relatively-stable monetary policies would have their currencies chosen for transaction invoicing. All else being equal, exchange rate pass-through would be higher for importing countries with a more volatile monetary policy.[6]

An alternative argument, emphasised by Bacchetta and van Wincoop (2005) and Goldberg and Tille (2005), is that – even in the context of these models – the role of macroeconomic variability in currency invoicing choices may be limited. The industry composition of trade in particular, the dominance of trade in differentiated products, is needed for macroeconomic variability to drive invoice currency choices. If trade is largely in homogeneous or reference-priced goods, the role of macroeconomic variability in invoice currency choice is substantially damped. For these producers, the most important driver of invoice currency selection will be the need to have their goods priced in the same way as other competing producers price their products. This herding into a common invoicing currency will be more important that the volatility-hedging motives emphasised elsewhere in the literature.

This discussion has focused mainly on the relationship between movements in exchange rates and import prices into an economy. Yet another important observation is that the degree of pass-through into aggregate price indexes is substantially smaller than into import prices (Campa and Goldberg (2006), Bachetta and van Wincoop (2003)). Various explanations have been offered for these differences in the elasticity of prices to exchange rate changes. The most obvious, but still an incomplete explanation, is that tradable goods account for only a portion of consumption in the overall price indices. Burstein, Neves and Rebelo (2003), in considering the effects of large contractionary devaluations in developing countries, emphasise both the importance of distribution costs (transportation, wholesaling and retailing services) and the ability of

---

[6] Engel (2005) shows that, with flexible prices, an industry structure that leads to the variability of prices in the exporter's currency being larger than the variability of prices in the importer's currency will also result in an equilibrium exchange rate pass-through greater than $^1/_2$. This same condition will imply in a sticky-price model that the producer will prefer producer currency pricing to local currency pricing in invoicing exports. Therefore, an economic setting with pass-through being less than $^1/_2$ arising from an imperfect competition setup with flexible prices could be observationally equivalent to a setting with local-currency-pricing, regardless of whether prices are sticky or not.

consumers to substitute away from high quality imports towards lower quality domestically-produced goods. The distribution costs reduce the weight of the border price of imports in the aggregate CPI, since the imported goods ultimately consumed will contain value added from domestic distribution services.[7] The substitutability implies that the weight of foreign products and the overall quality mix of consumption are responsive to exchange rate fluctuations. Moreover, distributors also can adjust the profit margin that they receive, thereby further dampening the real effects of exchange rates (Hellerstein, 2004). One only-partially countervailing force arises through the use of imported inputs into production, which can introduce price sensitivity to exchange rates even among non-traded goods, as in Campa and Goldberg (2006).

Another explanation for the lack of CPI responsiveness hinges on a policy-reaction function by monetary authorities, as argued by Gagnon and Ihrig (2001) and Baily (2002). This line of research generates observed price insensitivity to exchange rates because an inflation shock arising through import prices due to domestic currency depreciation may trigger contractionary monetary policy. Thus, the prices of domestic non-traded goods will have to decline to offset the inflationary stimulus through traded goods prices. This research makes the point that CPI unresponsiveness is not because of a lack of pass-through of exchange rates into import or tradable prices. Rather, it is because central banks are so good at containing price pressures that they pursue policies that immediately insulate aggregate prices from these exchange-rate-induced pressures.

Overall, the degree of insensitivity of consumer prices to exchange rates still is unexplained, given the estimated sensitivity of import prices to exchange rates. This issue continues to receive attention from the research community. In our exploration of euro area issues below, however, we focus exclusively on import price sensitivity to exchange rates, leaving the aggregate CPI insensitivity issue to ongoing research.

4.3 Import price pass-through for the euro area

4.3.1 Introduction[8]

There have been large movements in exchange rates across euro area countries, with the euro strongly depreciating against the US dollar in

---

[7] Dornbusch (1987) argued that such distribution costs can help explain why comparable goods are more expensive in rich countries than in poor countries.

[8] This section is based on the methodology used in Campa and Goldberg (2005) and Campa and González-Mínguez (2006) and provides more-updated estimates for the euro area.

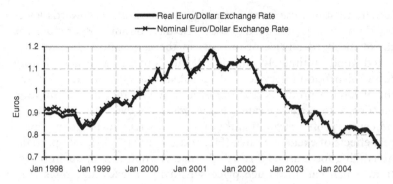

Figure 4.1. Euros per dollar, 1998–2004

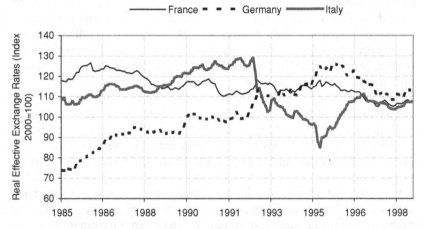

Figure 4.2. Real effective exchange rate, 1985–1998

1998–2001 and then appreciating between 2002–2004. As shown in Figure 4.1 which tracks both real and nominal exchange rates for the period through to the end of 2004, these realignments were not just a nominal phenomenon. Indeed, such swings in currency values are not unique to this period, as they were a regular feature of legacy currency valuations relative to the US dollar and baskets of currencies. Figure 4.2 shows the real effective exchange rates for sample legacy currencies – the German mark, the French franc, and the Italian lira – for the period 1985–1998. Cycles and sharp quarterly movements in exchange rates have occurred many times in recent history.

Such movements can put substantial pressures on producers and subsequently be reflected in pricing. In this section we explore these pricing consequences, estimating exchange rate pass-through into import prices for euro area countries (Austria, Belgium-Luxembourg, Finland, France, Germany, Greece, Ireland, Italy, Netherlands, Portugal and Spain). We use both aggregated and disaggregated data for this purpose. The aggregate import price data used for the analysis are monthly unit value indices for the period 1989:1 to 2004:5.[9] The disaggregated import price data for each country corresponds to the 1-digit level of disaggregation in the SITC classification for nine different industry categories.[10]

The aim in this exercise is twofold. First, we provide evidence on the degree of exchange rate pass-through observed and contrast these experiences across countries and product categories. Second, we explore the stability of the exchange rate pass-through (ERPT) relationships. Structural shifts in pass-through rates during the sample period could stem from the establishment of the euro or other environmental changes as motivated by the theoretical work surveyed in section 4.2. We conclude the section by comparing our results with existing evidence on pass-through rates to import prices from other studies (Campa and González-Mínguez (2006) and Anderton (2003)), including from a wider sample of 23 OECD countries (Campa and Goldberg, 2005).

The methodology for estimation draws heavily on Campa and González-Mínguez (2005), whose results are updated here. That analysis obtains estimates of pass-through of exchange rate changes into the prices of imports made by countries from outside the euro area for disaggregated product categories in each country of EMU. In the short run, pass-through rates are smaller than one and differ across industries and countries. In the long run neither full pass-through nor equality of pass-through rates across industries and countries can be rejected. These findings corroborate those for the broader group of OECD countries.

The rest of this section is organised as follows. Section 4.2 summarises the estimation strategy and presents the results, comparing them with those in the existing literature. Section 4.3.3 provides arguments for a structural shift in exchange rate pass-through among euro area countries due to the creation of the monetary union. The section also reports statistical evidence on the existence of such a structural shift for euro area imports.

---

[9] The source for these data is the database COMEXT produced by Eurostat. For Austria and Finland the import price series start only in 1995:1.

[10] There are no data for category 9 (goods considered as 'n.e.s.' or not elsewhere specified), which has a residual nature. The product disaggregation is as follows: 0. Food and live animals, 1. Beverages and tobacco, 2. Crude materials, inedible, 3. Mineral fuels, 4. Oils, fats and waxes, 5. Chemical products, 6. Basic manufactures, 7. Machines and transport equipment, 8. Miscellaneous manufactured goods.

4.3.2   Empirical estimation of exchange rate pass-through into import prices

Equation (2) expressed import prices as a function of exchange rates, exporter markup, and exporter marginal costs, forming the basis of our empirical implementation.

We start the implementation of the empirical set-up from equation [2] above:

$$p_t^m = \alpha_0 e_t + \alpha_1 mkup_t^x + \alpha_2 mc_t^x + \varepsilon_t \tag{3}$$

where ε_t is a regression residual, all variables are in logarithms. Pure currency translation effects generate the expectation of $\alpha_0 = 1$. The specification for markups and marginal costs determines if there are additional influences that would lead to exchange rate pass-through at levels below one. As in the empirical work of Campa and Goldberg (2005) or the theoretical analysis of Corsetti, Dedola and Leduc (2004), exporters operating in a given industry decide to what extent they pass-through exchange rate variations into their prices expressed in the importing country currency. These firms may decide that this pass-through is complete, in which case their mark-ups are insensitive to the exchange rate and producer currency pricing occurs. Alternatively, exporters may decide not to vary prices in terms of the destination currency, in which markups fully absorb the exchange rate movements and local currency pricing occurs. Thus, mark-ups in the industry can be broken down into two components: an industry-specific fixed effect exogenous to exchange rate changes whose value depends on the specific structure of competition in each industry and a second component which is correlated with exchange rate movements:

$$mkup_t^x = \phi + \Phi e_t \tag{4}$$

in which case we expect $\phi > 0$ and $\Phi < 0$. An additional influence on import price sensitivity could enter through marginal costs, as earlier discussed in the context of imported inputs or commodity prices. We assume that exporters marginal costs of production are increasing as a positive function of demand conditions in the destination country, y_t, and of marginal costs of production (wages) in the exporting country, w_t^x, and commodity prices denoted in foreign currency cp_t^x. If commodity prices are determined in world markets (with invoicing typically in US dollars) then commodity price effects on import prices may differ, since the wage changes may be exporter-specific while commodity price changes could have effects common to the exporter and his competitors. This suggests specifying marginal costs as in (5) where the effect of exchange rates on marginal costs (including the effect on commodity prices) enters through the c_2 parameter and the residual commodity price effects enter through c_3.

$$mc_t^x = c_0 y_t + c_1 w_t^x + c_2 e_t + c_3 c p_t^x \tag{5}$$

Substituting 4 and 5 into 3:

$$p_t^m = \alpha_1 \phi + (\alpha_0 + \alpha_1 \Phi + \alpha_2 c_2) e_t + \alpha_2 c_0 y_t + \alpha_2 c_1 w_t^x + \alpha_2 c_3 c p_t^x + \varepsilon_t \tag{6}$$

where $\beta = \alpha_0 + \alpha_1 \Phi + \alpha_2 c_2$ is the pass-through rate.[11] In empirical specifications, one can allow for delayed effects of exchange rates and marginal costs on import prices by introducing a more dynamic specification, for example through also including lags on right hand side variables.

Equation 6 forms the basis of our empirical model. Empirical implementation requires specification of the appropriate proxy for foreign costs of production (w_t^x and cp_t^x) and the evolution of domestic demand. Campa and González Mínguez (2006) test for alternative specifications of the appropriate market to model pass-through into euro import prices. The cost of serving the domestic market is a function of the opportunity cost of allocating those same goods to other customers. In markets integrated worldwide, this opportunity cost is reflected in the world price of the product, while in more-segmented markets the opportunity cost may vary. For European markets, they conclude that the model that best describes the data is that of an integrated world market for the product. This implies that the appropriate measure proxy of the opportunity cost of exporting is the world market price of the product.

One obvious critique of equation (6) is the endogeneity of variables on both sides of the regression equation. Basic purchasing power parity and arbitrage arguments hold that import prices, exchange rates and foreign prices should be cointegrated, that is that a linear combination of these variables should be a stationary process. While hardly contestable on theoretical grounds, on empirical grounds we test the validity of the single equation approach of (6), and explore the possibility of specifying a vector error correction model accounting for a long-run cointegration relationship between import prices, exchange rates and foreign prices. Augmented Dickey Fuller tests on the original series (import unit values, exchange rates and foreign prices) revealed that the null hypothesis of a unit root could not be rejected for about two thirds of all series.

---

[11] The exchange rate operating on commodity prices is likely to be a bilateral exchange rate relative to US dollars – the currency used for pricing most commodities. In general, this choice may differ from the effective exchange rate appropriate for the marginal cost considerations, which is a weighting of exchange rates relative to export partners for a particular industry and country.

Different specifications of the Johansen tests to check for the number of cointegrating vectors failed to reject the hypothesis of no cointegration for a large majority of industries.[12] This evidence against the presence of a cointegrating relationship leads us to perform the analysis in a single equation framework without introducing biases in our associated parameter estimates.[13]

The empirical model estimated is:

$$\Delta p_t^{ij} = c^{ij} + \sum_{k=0}^{4} a_k^{ij} \Delta e_t^{ij} + \sum_{k=0}^{4} b_k^{ij} \Delta f p_t^{ij} + v_t^{ij} \tag{7}$$

where the superscripts i and j refer, respectively, to an importing country and to an industry. We denote as p_t^{ij} the (log) import unit value index (denominated in local currency) of industry j in country i, $e_t^{i,j}$ is the nominal exchange rate for industry j of country i expressed in terms of units of domestic currency per unit of foreign currency. Finally, fp_t^{ij} stands for the price index of products of industry j into country i in the countries of origin of these imports and expressed in foreign currency. The presumption is that pricing to market occurs at the level of industries and countries, in part in relation to local demand elasticities, as in Corsetti, Dedola and Leduc (2004). The US dollar price of the imports coming from outside the area is taken as the proxy for the foreign price and the bilateral exchange rate between the domestic currency and the US dollar is used as our exchange rate measure.[14] First-differenced variables enter the equation in order to control for the possibility of non-stationarity, given the existence of unit roots in some of the time series variables contained

---

[12] To be more precise we find that a cointegration relationship cannot be rejected in 34% of all combinations of import prices, exchange rates and foreign prices for the nine products and eleven countries in our sample. The cointegration tests were performed in a set-up in which the original series do not have a linear trend and the cointegration equations have intercepts. Lengthening and broadening the sample in comparison with Campa and González-Mínguez (2006) resulted in stronger evidence of cointegration, which in that case could not be rejected just for 14% of all instances.

[13] As a further robustness check, we perform the error correction models on the cases where cointegration could not be rejected. The resulting pass-through parameter estimates were not qualitatively different even in these cases.

[14] Campa and González-Mínguez (2006) tested for alternative specifications of industry structure that may best describe these euro area markets, yielding the specification used here. It implies that international markets are integrated, meaning that there exists a single market for each product, regardless of its origin, destination or currency of denomination. This leads to selecting, as appropriate measures of the foreign price and the exchange rate, a proxy of the world price in a common currency and the bilateral exchange rate between the currency in which the foreign price is denominated and the home currency (as opposed to measures for the bilateral exchange rate and the foreign price which are contingent, for a given destination country, on the countries in which these imports originate).

in this specification. In the estimation of equation 7, we include a correction for first-order autocorrelation, given the existence of residual autocorrelation in many industries when estimating by OLS.

Estimation yields short-run (one month) and long-run (four months) pass-through elasticities for all the different industry/country combinations, where short-run exchange rate pass-through elasticities are given by the estimated coefficients a_0^{ij} while long-run elasticities are defined as the sum of the pass-through coefficients for the contemporaneous exchange rate and its first four lags – that is $\sum_{i=0}^{4} a_k^{ij}$. We will focus on two benchmarks of pass-through estimates: (1) zero pass-through, in which there is no reaction from exchange rate movements into import prices, sometimes interpreted as local currency pricing, and (2) complete pass-through, which is consistent with producers pricing exports in their own currency and sometimes called producer currency pricing. Two other sets of tests are reported in this section. First, we estimate short-run and long-run pass-through elasticities when the restriction imposed is that these elasticities are the same for all industries within a given country. Second, we estimate while imposing the restriction that exchange rate pass-through rates are the same for a given industry across the eleven countries in the sample.

The results from these various procedures are reported in Table 4.1, which reports the point estimates for the unrestricted estimates and LCP and PCP tests, Table 4.2 which reports the tests of restrictions that elasticities are the same across all industries within a country and Table 4.3 which reports the results under the restriction that industry elasticities are the same across euro area countries. Columns (3) to (6) in Tables 4.2 and 4.3 summarise in a more tractable way the results for all the different industry and country combinations contained in Table 4.1 by reporting summary statistics of the estimated short- and long-run elasticities for the different industries within a country (Table 4.2) and for the different countries given an industry (Table 4.3).

A number of strong results are generated. The main results can be summarised as follows. First, the transmission of exchange rate movements to import prices is incomplete, in the short run – defined as the month contemporaneous to the exchange rate movement. Unweighted average rates by country and by industry are, respectively, 0.66 and 0.56. The evidence that transmission is high, but incomplete in the short run is supported by the rejection *in all cases* of the hypothesis that the estimated elasticities in the first column in Tables 4.2 and 4.3 are one or zero.[15]

---

[15] The exception is Spain, for the hypothesis that ERPT is equal to one.

Table 4.1 *Elasticities of exchange rate pass-through into import prices in the short run and long run*

Country/Industry		France	Belgium – Luxembourg	Netherlands	Germany	Italy	Ireland	Greece	Portugal	Spain	Finland	Austria	Pool
0	Short run	0.72*+	0.61*+	0.55*+	0.60*+	0.49*+	0.22+	0.28+	1.12*	0.58*+	0.48*+	0.32**+	0.54*+
	Long run	0.73*+	0.98*	0.85*	0.96*	0.89*	0.43*	0.55+	0.57	1.02*	0.87*	0.77*	0.78*+
1	Short run	0.23+	0.44*+	0.21+	0.15*+	0.70+	0.16+	0.78**	0.52*++	2.47*+	0.19+	0.51**++	0.56*+
	Long run	0.37+	0.55*+	0.33**+	0.26*+	0.85*+	-0.08+	0.50	0.78*	2.15*+	0.17+	0.46	0.64*+
2	Short run	0.73*+	0.92*	0.65*+	0.65*+	0.58*+	0.35*+	0.07+	0.69*+	0.78*+	0.57*+	0.43*+	0.57*+
	Long run	1.03*	1.07*	0.85*	0.87*	1.06*	0.81*	0.73*	0.94*	1.09*	0.82*	0.71*+	0.93*
3	Short run	1.07*	0.60*+	1.26*+	0.83*+	0.92*	0.64*	0.68	0.81*	0.77*+	0.98*	0.57*+	0.85*+
	Long run	1.12*	0.93*	0.84*	0.94*	1.03*	1.10*	1.52*	0.89*	1.08*	0.97*	0.71*+	1.02*
4	Short run	0.88*	0.52*+	0.78*++	0.62*+	0.49*+	0.24+	0.82*	0.54	1.18*	0.63*	0.22+	0.64*+
	Long run	0.83*	0.74*	1.06*	0.88*	0.98*	0.46	0.75	1.08*	1.00*	0.39	0.43	0.84*
5	Short run	0.61*+	0.72*+	0.58*+	0.97*	0.85*	1.25*	-0.42+	0.58**	0.48*+	0.43*+	0.50*+	0.62*+
	Long run	0.85*	1.03*	0.74*	1.09*	0.94*	0.97	0.48	0.18	0.78*+	0.76*	0.62	0.78*+
6	Short run	0.58*+	0.62*+	0.71*+	0.42*+	0.56*+	0.61*+	0.35**+	0.36*+	0.51*+	0.24*+	0.31*+	0.50*+
	Long run	0.89*	0.97*	1.11*	0.73*+	1.07*	0.58*+	0.85*	0.94*	0.98*	0.66*+	0.56*+	0.87*+
7	Short run	0.60*+	0.46*+	0.91*	0.58*+	0.56*+	1.04*	0.04+	0.22*++	0.36*+	0.34*+	0.14+	0.51*+
	Long run	0.58*+	0.92*	1.07*	0.81*	0.99*	1.26*	0.18+	0.65*++	0.75*+	0.76*	0.04+	0.76*+
8	Short run	0.62*+	0.60*+	0.76*+	0.60*+	0.65*+	0.51*+	0.08+	0.58*	0.58*+	0.18*+	0.23*+	0.50*+
	Long run	0.62*+	0.84*	1.02*	0.74*+	0.84*	0.55	0.19+	0.91*	0.76	0.39*+	0.23+	0.64*+

*(**) the null hypothesis H_0: $a_0 = 0$ (short run) or $\sum_{i=0}^{4} a_i = 0$ (long run) is rejected at 95% (90%) level. +(++) the null hypothesis H_0: $a_0 = 1$ or $\sum_{i=0}^{4} a_i = 1$ is rejected at 95% (90%) level.

The product disaggregation is as follows: 0. Food and live animals, 1. Beverages and tobacco, 2. Crude materials, inedible, 3. Mineral fuels, 4. Oils, fats and waxes, 5. Chemical products, 6. Basic manufactures, 7. Machines and transport equipment, 8. Miscellaneous manufactured goods.

Table 4.2 *Differences in rates of exchange rate pass-through into import prices by country*

| Country | Pass-through rates by country | | Percentage of total industries for which the specified hypothesis can be rejected (a) | | | |
| | | | Short-run | | Long-run | |
	(1) Short-run	(2) Long-run	(3) Pass-through rate is zero	(4) Pass-through rate is one	(5) Pass-through rate is zero	(6) Pass-through rate is one
France	0.77 *+	0.79 *+	0.89	0.78	0.89	0.44
Belgium-Luxembourg	0.58 *+	0.83 *+	1.00	0.89	1.00	0.11
Netherlands	0.76 *+	0.79 *+	0.89	0.89	1.00	0.11
Germany	0.63 *+	0.75 *+	1.00	0.89	1.00	0.33
Italy	0.69 *+	0.94 *	0.89	0.78	1.00	0.00
Ireland	0.50 *+	0.56 *+	0.67	0.67	0.56	0.22
Greece	0.47 *+	0.78 *+	0.33	0.67	0.33	0.33
Portugal	0.80 *+	0.82 *	0.89	0.44	0.78	0.11
Spain (b)	0.81 *	1.04 *	1.00	0.88	0.88	0.25
Finland	0.75 *+	0.77 *+	0.89	0.78	0.78	0.33
Austria	0.54 *+	0.77 *+	0.78	1.00	0.44	0.56
Average	0.66	0.81				

Sources: Eurostat (Comext database) and own calculations.
(a) The total number of industries is 9.
(b) Excluding beverages and tobacco.
*/+: It can be statistically rejected at 5% level that the pass-through rate is zero/one.

Table 4.3 *Differences in rates of exchange rate pass-through into import prices by industry*

Industry	Pass-through rates by industry		Percentage of countries for which the specified hypothesis can be rejected (a)					
			Short run			Long run		
	(1) Short run	(2) Long run	(3) Pass-through rate is zero	(4) Pass-through rate is one	(5) Pass-through rate is zero	(6) Pass-through rate is one		
Food and live animals	0.54 *+	0.78 *+	0.82	0.91	0.82	0.18		
Beverages and tobacco (b)	0.31 *+	0.44 *+	0.50	0.90	0.50	0.60		
Crude material, inedible	0.57 *+	0.93 *	0.91	0.91	1.00	0.09		
Mineral fuels	0.85 *+	1.02 *	0.91	0.45	1.00	0.09		
Oils, fats and waxes	0.64 *+	0.84 *	0.73	0.55	0.64	0.00		
Chemical products	0.62 *+	0.78 *+	0.91	0.64	0.64	0.09		
Basic manufactures	0.50 *+	0.87 *+	1.00	1.00	1.00	0.36		
Machines and transport equipment	0.51 *+	0.76 *+	0.82	0.82	0.82	0.36		
Miscellaneous manufactured goods	0.50 *+	0.64 *+	0.91	0.91	0.73	0.45		
Average	0.56	0.79						

Sources: Eurostat (Comext database) and own calculations.
(a) The total number of countries is 11.
(b) Excluding Spain.
*/+: It can be statistically rejected at 5% level that the pass-through rate is zero/one.

Second, in the long run, average elasticities of transmission are larger than in the short run, with values of around 0.8 across countries (column 2 in both Tables 4.2 and 4.3). More importantly, the hypothesis that the transmission is complete in the long run is rejected for a majority of countries and products. More precisely, this hypothesis is not supported by the data in eight out of eleven economies and six out of nine products. It is interesting to realise that those cases for which this hypothesis is not rejected coincide with economies which have traditionally moved along a path of higher inflation (Italy, Portugal and Spain) and with industries in which commodity imports predominate, consistent with tendencies suggested *a priori* by theoretical models.

Third, the results of the tests of zero and full transmission when the same elasticity is imposed for all industries in each country, or for all countries in a given industry, are replicated quite closely when the pass-through coefficients are allowed to vary by country or by product (columns 3 to 6 in Tables 4.2 and 4.3). It is remarkable that only for one country (Austria) and for one industry (beverages and tobacco) full transmission in the long run is rejected in a majority of cases. The hypothesis that pass-through is either zero or one in the short run can be rejected for a vast majority of industries in most countries (columns 3 and 4 in Table 4.2), as can the hypothesis that pass-through is zero in the long run. The hypothesis that the pass-through is complete in the long run can be rejected in less than one-third of all industries in every country but Austria and France.

The last four columns in Table 4.3 show (as a counterpart to the columns in Table 4.2) that, in the short run, the hypothesis that industry-specific pass-through is either zero or one is rejected for a vast majority of countries. In the long run, zero pass-through is again rejected for most industries, but full pass-through is rejected in a minority of industries.

Finally, we perform tests for the equality of pass-through rates across countries and industries, both in the short and the long run (Table 4.4). In general, one can reject that ERPT rates in the short run are equal for all industries within a given country and for a given industry across the eleven countries in our sample. In the long run, the equality of the elasticities of transmission among the different industries of a country can be rejected only in the cases of Germany and Spain. The equality of industry pass-through across countries is rejected in only two of the nine industries: basic manufactures and machinery and transport equipment. The latter result supports the idea that exporter's price discriminates to a larger extent in manufacturing than in commodities, since these industries are more likely to show product differentiation and, thus, different degrees of pass-through in different countries. This finding is consistent with

Table 4.4. *Test of the equality of short- and long-run pass-through estimates (p-values)*

This table reports the p-values from a test of the restrictions that the estimated short-run and long-run pass-through elasticities are the same for all industries within each country (left panel) and that they are constant for a given industry in the eleven countries in the sample (right panel).

Country	Equality across industries within each country		Industry	Equality across countries within each industry	
	Short run	Long run		Short run	Long run
France	0.00	0.11	0. Food and live animals	0.00	0.28
Belgium–Luxembourg	0.43	0.39	1. Beverages and tobacco	0.54	0.52
Netherlands	0.00	0.45	2. Crude material, inedible	0.00	0.52
Germany	0.00	0.00	3. Mineral fuel	0.13	0.83
Italy	0.00	0.98	4. Oils, fats and waxes	0.21	0.89
Ireland	0.01	0.08	5. Chemical products	0.00	0.73
Greece	0.19	0.45	6. Basic manufactures	0.02	0.02
Portugal	0.47	0.86	7. Machines and transport equipment	0.00	0.02
Spain	0.00	0.00	8. Miscellaneous manufactured goods	0.04	0.20
Finland	0.00	0.40	% of rejections (at 5% level)	66.7%	22.2%
Austria	0.72	0.78			
% of rejections (at 5% level)	63.6%	18.2%			

the theoretical predictions of Bacchetta and van Wincoop (2005) and Goldberg and Tille (2005).

The estimated pass-through elasticities reported here are in line with previous estimates reported in the literature. Campa and Goldberg (2005) find elasticities of ERPT into aggregate import prices for a sample of 23 OECD countries which average 0.46 and 0.64 in the short and long run, respectively. The corresponding average elasticities for the ten euro area countries reported in this broader sample (all but Greece and Luxembourg) are, respectively, 0.47 and 0.70. These reported estimates of ERPT are slightly lower, but not significantly different, from those reported in Table 4.1 of 0.66 and 0.80 respectively. These latter estimates are the same as those reported in Campa and González-Mínguez (2005) for the same countries but a shorter time period (1989:1 to 2001:3). The average unweighted elasticities for the euro area countries reported in that paper are 0.66 and 0.81 in the short and long run, respectively.[16] Anderton (2003), using a somewhat different approach, estimates an average long-run ERPT between 0.5 and 0.7 for the aggregate manufacturing sector in the euro area. This slightly-lower estimate is not surprising given that the estimation explicitly excludes commodity industries for which pass-through rates are expected to be substantially larger.[17]

The difference between average elasticities reported here and the aggregate elasticities reported in Campa and Goldberg (2005) highlights the importance of the different point estimates across importing industries and the importance of each industry in the aggregate imports of the countries. The weighted average pass-through elasticities for each country computed using the disaggregated industry elasticities reported in Table 4.2 are significantly lower. The average of these weighted elasticities for the eleven EU countries is 0.52 in the short run and 0.72 in the long run.[18] These weighted estimates are very close to the 0.47 (0.70) reported in Campa and Goldberg for the short run (long run) euro area countries in their sample. As that study demonstrated, pass-through elasticities differ by industry and estimates of aggregate pass-through elasticities are dependent on the industry structure of imports of each country.

---

[16] The averages without Greece, in order to make comparable these figures with those in Campa and Goldberg (2005) are 0.68 and 0.81, respectively.

[17] Anderton (2003) focuses on a model of imperfect competition among euro and non-euro area producers in which foreign exporters to the euro area set their prices partly as a mark-up on their production costs (which represents the degree of ERPT) and partly holding them in line with those of their euro area competitors (pricing-to-market). The paper focuses on industries where imperfect competition may exist and thus chooses to exclude from the estimation commodity industries for which the law of one price is more likely to hold.

[18] For these calculations we have used the import share for each industry in 1998.

4.3.3   The euro and the stability of the exchange rate pass-through

The literature suggests several reasons why the rate of pass-through may have changed for the euro area members as a result of the introduction of the euro. Firstly, the process of monetary union has entailed some convergence of average inflation rates in euro area Member States towards the levels of countries with historically-lower inflation. Since higher inflation levels and volatility contribute, theoretically, to higher exchange rate pass-through, the countries that have experienced the largest declines in inflation and nominal volatility may have seen the largest reductions in pass-through elasticities.

Secondly, EMU induced changes in the pattern of trade could influence exchange rate pass-through into import prices. The creation of EMU has resulted in a higher proportion of trade being done in the common currency. Thus, a smaller proportion of industry output is exposed to the exchange rate fluctuations associated with trade with non-euro area countries. Some recent research suggests that the creation of EMU might have stimulated intra-area trade at the expense of that taking place with the rest of the world (Faruqee, 2004). Such trade diversion could have led to a change in the transmission of exchange rate movements to import prices by reducing the market power of exporters from outside the euro area. From a pure accounting perspective, the transmission of exchange rates into import prices would have declined as the proportion of final demand of the area satisfied with extra-EMU imports diminished. Likewise, the transmission from exchange rates to import prices is lower the larger the share of imports denominated in local currency. To the extent that the creation of a large-scale monetary union, such as the EMU, has favoured an expansion of the euro as a currency of denomination of its external trade, ERPT rates to import prices would have tended to reduce. The European Central Bank (2005) reports that the proportion of extra-euro trade denominated in euro has increased for all EU members. This change in currency invoicing is particularly apparent with respect to former accession countries like Poland and Estonia. We discuss each of these arguments in more detail.

4.3.3.1 Convergence in inflation rates
As previously indicated, one of the reasons for differences across countries in ERPT has been the inflation history of the country. Those countries which are currently members of EMU and which experienced higher nominal inflation and larger exchange rate depreciations during the eighties and nineties had larger ERPT rates, especially in the short run. To the extent that these countries now share the same currency, it could be

the case that the differences among their short run pass-through rates have tended to attenuate. In order to explore this hypothesis, we performed separate estimations for two sub-periods (1989:01 to 1997:12 and 1998:1 to 2004:5) and then correlated the change in average inflation between the two periods for each country with the change in the ERPT. The results of this exercise show that changes in both variables are basically uncorrelated.[19] The correlation across countries between changes in average short term (long term) pass-through rate and changes in inflation was −0.34 (−0.09). This is a crude exploration that neither takes into account the significance in the estimated changes in pass-through nor introduces other control variables. Nevertheless, the results are consistent with changing inflation regimes not being a primary driver of changes in rates of exchange rate pass-through into import prices.

4.3.3.2 Changes in the share of extra-EMU imports
The introduction of the single European currency has resulted in a change in the respective shares of trade exposed to exchange rate fluctuations. Trade among EMU economies is increasingly conducted in the same currency, although evidence on the pervasiveness of this phenomenon across manufactured goods versus commodities is largely lacking. Furthermore, the elimination of the risk associated with the fluctuations in nominal exchange rates in intra-EMU flows or the reduction in transaction costs suggest that monetary union might have stimulated trade among EA Member States at the expense of trade with non-EMU countries (*trade diversion*), or even net of any diversion effect. For instance, small-sized firms for which the existence of the transaction costs associated with multiple currencies posed barriers to their participation in international trade might have decided to enter euro area markets after the beginning of EMU (*trade creation*). A lower share of foreign currency imports in total industry supply should lead to higher pass-through rates.

Evidence accumulated since the inception of the euro does not show extensive changes in the composition of import flows into the area according to the country of origin (Faruqee, 2004). Indeed, observed changes seem to run in the opposite direction. In particular, as shown in Figures 4.3 and 4.4, the share of imports coming from outside the area has increased in seven of the eleven Member States, whether measured as a

---

[19] The selection of 1997:12 as the break point between subsamples is somewhat arbitrary. Disinflation was a common feature in current euro area members since 1996. This was not only the result of policies in inflation-prone countries as a result of efforts to fulfil the corresponding convergence criterion, but also a more general phenomenon related to the negative oil price shock at the time.

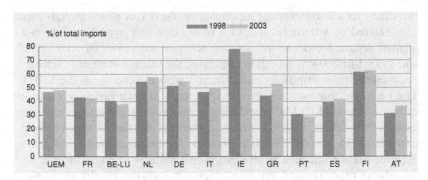

Figure 4.3. EMU. Imports of goods from outside the euro area in percentage of total imports
Source: Eurostat and National Statistics.

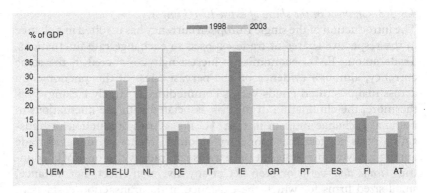

Figure 4.4. EMU. Imports of goods from outside the euro area in percentage of GDP
Source: Eurostat and National Statistics.

proportion of total imports or a proportion of GDP by country.[20] The ratio of extra-EMU imports to GDP has increased in all Member States except Ireland and, to a lesser extent, Portugal.

Even if the total share of imports coming from the rest of the world into the euro area has not changed significantly, changes in the product composition of those flows could have occurred. In this way, if transmission elasticities from exchange rate variations into import prices were to differ substantially by product categories, possible modifications in the structure of imported goods since the start of EMU might significantly alter overall ERPT rates as observed for the broader OECD countries

---

[20] Belgium and Luxembourg are treated as a single country in these data.

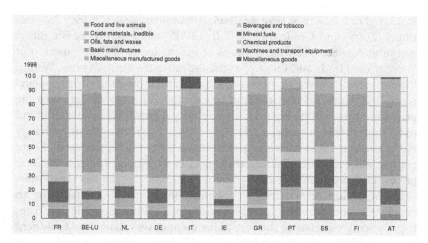

Figure 4.5. Composition by product of extra EMU imports of goods in 1998
Source: Eurostat and National Statistics.

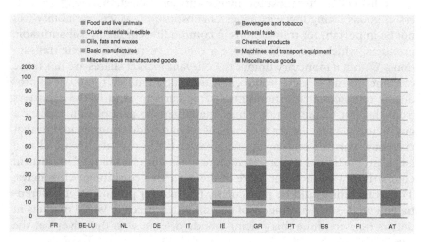

Figure 4.6. Composition by product of extra EMU imports of goods in 2003
Source: Eurostat and National Statistics.

since the 1970s. While possible, Figures 4.5 and 4.6 demonstrate that the size of such variations in the structure of imports according to the type of product has been relatively limited since the start of EMU. In particular, the shares of energy products and, to a lesser extent, machinery and transport equipment within total imports have increased, while those of food, other commodities and basic manufactures have declined.

4.3.3.3 The currency of price denomination in international trade

Engel (2005) and Goldberg and Tille (2005) show that there is a direct mapping between the determinants of the currency of denomination of international trade and those of exchange rate pass-through rates. Within the euro area, if foreign exporters tend to fix their prices in their own currency, the degree of transmission of exchange rate movements into the prices in euros will be high. If, alternatively, extra-EMU exporters tend to fix their prices in euros, a relatively-reduced transmission of exchange rate movements into euro area prices and activity will be observed. There are two key factors explaining the currency in which exporters fix their prices: hedging exchange rate and cost volatility and the degree of market competition or elasticity of substitution in foreign demand for an exporter's goods which influences a producer's willingness to deviate from the invoicing patterns of the rest of his competitors. Based on Goldberg and Tille (2005) and Bacchetta and van Wincoop (2005), the choice of invoice currency is expected to differ across industries, even in trade transactions between common partner countries. The role of macroeconomic variability will matter most for invoice currency selection among producers of goods facing low elasticities of substitution. Macro variability will not be important for transactions in commodities or highly-substitutable products, which may even choose a vehicle currency for their transactions. Within a monetary union, the relevant market shares are not those of domestic and foreign producers within each country, but those of producers of all countries sharing the same currency and of the exporters from the rest of the world. Thus, the larger the area of influence of a given currency, the larger the share of foreign trade denominated in that currency. For this reason, the creation of EMU probably resulted in a larger proportion of imports denominated in euro within total imports in comparison with the joint share of the euro area constituent currencies. This argument would be particularly relevant for producers of differentiated goods, since producers of commodities priced in world markets in dollars may continue this pricing standard, even with the advent of the euro.

Existing evidence regarding the use of the euro as the currency of denomination of international trade is incomplete. Since the beginning of EMU, data shown in Table 4.5 points to an increase in the share of imports coming from (and share of exports going to) outside the area with prices denominated in euros. An increased use of the euro as the currency of denomination has been observed in trade in both goods and services.[21]

---

[21] In the case of France, a decrease was recorded between 2002 and 2003 in the shares of euro-denominated imports of both goods and services and euro-denominated exports of goods.

Table 4.5 *Share of the euro as the currency of denomination of EMU trade with the rest of the world (as a % of the total) (a)*

	Imports								Exports							
	Goods				Services				Goods				Services			
	2000	2001	2002	2003	2000	2001	2002	2003	2000	2001	2002	2003	2000	2001	2002	2003
Belgium (b)	43.6	47.2	53.6	57.0	44.4	44.4	57.7	64.3	42.0	46.7	53.5	55.3	45.4	–	55.5	64.4
France	35.0	39.8	46.8	45.1	47.6	54.6	54.7	51.7	48.0	49.2	55.3	52.4	57.3	60.4	56.9	57.9
Germany	–	–	48.0	55.2	–	–	–	–	–	–	49.0	63.0	–	–	–	–
Greece	–	29.3	35.8	39.6	–	15.3	16.8	20.1	–	23.5	39.3	47.3	–	11.3	13.3	16.3
Italy	–	40.8	44.2	44.5	–	49.9	56.1	62.9	–	52.7	54.1	58.2	–	50.7	57.0	62.1
Luxembourg	–	–	35.3	41.7	–	–	28.5	36.0	–	–	51.5	52.7	–	–	40.4	43.0
Portugal	47.0	53.6	57.5	60.2	53.7	55.6	58.3	64.3	40.1	43.5	48.4	54.6	37.4	37.4	44.1	48.6
Spain	44.0	49.7	55.8	60.3	42.4	45.3	49.4	54.6	49.0	52.0	57.5	60.8	50.5	52.9	59.5	63.8

Source: ECB (2003 and 2005).

(a) Data refer to the use of the euro as a settlement currency, except for Germany (invoicing currency).

(b) Data for 2000 and 2001 for Belgium refer to Belgium and Luxembourg.

This finding is consistent with an expectation of lower exchange rate pass-through into EMU country import prices.

It is useful to note, however, that the creation of EMU may have had different effects on different industries. In commodity markets and for 'reference-priced goods', goods with a large degree of homogeneity are traded. For these goods, a single world market exists, in which imports into the area are denominated neither in euros nor in the exporters' currency, but usually in dollars (Goldberg and Tille, 2005). These markets are characterised by the fact that the location of buyers and sellers is irrelevant as far as the price of transactions is concerned. In this case, it is unlikely that the creation of EMU has caused, so far, relevant changes in invoicing patterns. Consequently, reductions in exchange rate pass-through into import prices in EMU countries might be more a feature of differentiated goods than of highly substitutable goods.

4.3.3.4 Evidence on the existence of a structural break

To determine whether evidence exists that a break took place around the time of the decision to fix permanently the exchange rates among the euro countries, we perform tests on the time stability of the estimated pass-through elasticities. Alternatively, a break might have occurred with the actual adoption of the euro among these countries. We perform two types of tests for the time stability of the estimated parameters. First, we follow the approach by Andrews (1993) and Andrews and Ploberger (1994) to detect endogenously structural changes in the pass-through relationship assuming that the break point is unknown. This procedure essentially searches for the strongest break point any time during the sample period. It is an appropriate test mainly to the extent that structural breaks in the data are large and discrete (Elliott and Muller 2005). For each estimation (i.e. for every pair-wise combination of country and industry), we perform two tests of structural breaks: a test that the contemporaneous coefficient on the exchange rate is stable (i.e. that short-run pass-through is stable) and a test that the sum of all coefficients on the exchange rate is stable (i.e. that there is a structural break in long-run pass-through).

We find little evidence in favour of the existence of a (statistically significant) structural break in the transmission of exchange rate movements into import prices across euro area countries. Table 4.6 reports those instances in which the null hypothesis of no structural break is rejected. In those instances, the p-value of the tests appears in parenthesis and the suggested break date is reported in italics. An empty cell means that, for that combination of product and country, the hypothesis of absence of a structural break cannot be rejected either in the short or the long run. There is very little evidence in favour of the alternative hypothesis that

Table 4.6 *Structural break tests (a)*

Product\Country	0 Food and live animals	1 Beverages and tobacco	2 Crude materials, inedible	3 Mineral fuels	4 Oils, fats and waxes	5 Chemical products	6 Basic manufactures	7 Machines and transport equipment	8 Miscellaneous manufactured goods
France	SR-C						SR-C	SR-C	SR-C
Belgium–Luxembourg	SR-C LR-C				LR-S 1992:9 (0.10)		SR-C	SR-C LR-C	SR-C
Netherlands					LR-S 1998:12 (0.10)		SR-C	SR-C	
Germany	SR-C LR-C						SR-C	SR-C LR-C	SR-C
Italy	LR-C						SR-S 1991:10 (0.03)	SR-C	
Ireland							LR-S 1993:1 (0.02)	LR-S 1993:3 (0.00)	
Greece	SR-C		SR-C						
Portugal	SR-C								
Spain		SR-C							
Finland			LR-S 2002:10 (0.02) LR-C	LR-S 1998:9 (0.07)					
Austria						SR-C			

(a) SR-S (LR-S) stands for a rejection of the null hypothesis of absence of an endogenous structural break in the short (long) run. The break takes place at the date shown. In parenthesis, p-value of the test. SR-C(LR-C) stands for a rejection of the null hypothesis of absence of a structural break in May 1998 in the short (long) run.

the transmission is not stable (7 out of 198 cases). This evidence is concentrated in the estimated long-run elasticities. Only two of the identified structural breaks took place around the dates of the creation of the euro (oils, fats and waxes in the Netherlands, and mineral fuels in Finland). The two breaks detected in the case of Ireland might be linked to pricing policies of British exports after sterling left the ERM. For the remaining instances, it is more difficult to find any plausible explanation.

Given the low power of the Andrews and Ploberger tests in small samples and the large confidence intervals around indicated structural break points (Elliott and Muller, 2005), we also perform Chow tests of the hypothesis that a structural break took place at the time of the adoption of the euro. We select May 1998, the month on which the parities among currencies replaced by the euro were announced, as the date for the break. Those cells in Table 4.6 where either SR-C, LR-C, or both appear represent those combinations of industry and country for which this test rejects the stability of transmission rates, both in the short run, in the long run or both.

The Chow test results do not systematically reject the hypothesis of stability of rates of transmission of exchange rates into European import prices. The test rejects stability, in the short run, for twenty out of the ninety-nine combinations of industry and country. Stability is rejected more frequently among manufacturing industries (basic manufactures, machinery and transport equipment, and other manufactures), which is consistent with the expectation that changes in ERPT should be rather expected in industries producing differentiated goods. Across countries, the stability is rejected more frequently (in three or four industries) for the countries which composed the core of the EMS (France, Germany, Belgium-Luxembourg and the Netherlands). As far as long-run elasticities are concerned, the stability of the relationship can only be rejected in six out of ninety-nine cases. This is, approximately, what should be statistically expected at a five per cent confidence level. Jointly considered, this evidence suggests that a significant change in transmission rates has not taken place as a result of the introduction of the euro. Tendencies toward instability are more prevalent within manufactured goods.

The results reported in Table 4.6 do not provide evidence on whether this change in pass-through has implied an increase or a decline in pass-through rates. The point estimates strongly suggest that a decline in pass-through rates may be taking place. Estimated short-run (long-run) pass-through rates were lower in the post-euro period for sixty nine (61) out of ninety-nine cases. This evidence would be consistent with the arguments put forward in Section 4.3.3 of a decline in pass-through. As discussed above, this evidence is not statistically significant in most cases.

What is more revealing is that the change in pass-through is negative in all but one of the instances where the Chow test rejects stability.[22]

4.4   Conclusions

This chapter has performed an empirical analysis of transmission rates from exchange rate movements to import prices of the countries in EMU. It has estimated short- and long-run elasticities for all euro countries, allowing them to change according to the type of product imported. The results obtained confirm that this transmission is high, although incomplete, in the short run and different across industries and countries. Long-run elasticities are higher, although estimated elasticities are still lower than unity, except for the traditionally more-inflationary economies and for commodities. In general, the equality of pass-through elasticities among the different industries in each country or for the different countries given an industry cannot be rejected in the long run.

One of the aims of this chapter has been to evaluate to what extent the start of the monetary union has implied a structural break in the transmission of exchange rate movements in the currencies of Member States to their import prices. Several reasons point towards the possibility that a change might have taken place. These reasons include the move to an environment characterised by higher macroeconomic stability and lower inflation rates for several Member States, a hypothetical increase in the share of intra-EMU trade at the expense of trade with countries outside the euro area, possible modifications in the competitive structure of the markets for tradable products and the impact that the creation of the euro might have had on the currency of denomination of imports coming from the rest of the world. Some of these factors may be occurring. Average inflation rates have declined and the share of trade in goods and services against third countries whose prices are fixed in euros has increased substantially for all euro area countries. The evidence is not so clear for other predictions. The creation of the euro has not implied a decline in the share of extra-EMU imports within total imports.

We have tested for structural changes in pass-through rates since the introduction of the euro. There is an apparent decline in the estimated point elasticities for two-thirds of the industries. However, this evidence is not statistically significant. At this point, we find that there is a statistically significant trend towards lower pass-through rates for manufacturing

---

[22] More precisely, in the short run, in 19 out of the 20 cases for which the pass-through rate is significantly different between both periods, point estimates indicate a reduction in pass-through. This is also the case for five of the six statistically-significant changes in long-run pass-through.

Table 4.7 *Vector error correction model results for exchange rate pass-through elasticities in the import price equation*

Industry		France	Belgium-Luxembourg	Netherlands	Germany	Italy	Ireland	Greece	Portugal	Spain	Finland	Austria
0. Food and live animals	Short run											
	Long run											
1. Beverages and tobacco	Short run					0.61	0.52		0.70			
	Long run											
2. Crude material, inedible	Short run					0.56	−0.04		0.85			
	Long run					1.12						
3. Mineral fuel	Short run		0.73		0.05	1.57		0.56	1.05	0.77	0.25	
	Long run		0.96		1.04	1.07		1.15	1.03	1.11	0.94	
4. Oils, fats and waxes	Short run						0.01	0.95			−0.11	0.53
	Long run						0.74	0.01			0.25	0.70
5. Chemical products	Short run				0.09	0.33	−0.06	0.44	0.10	0.25		
	Long run				1.05	0.84	1.18	0.11	0.33	0.92		
6. Basic manufactures	Short run											
	Long run											
7. Machines and transport equipment	Short run	−0.01	0.35	0.11	0.39	0.39		0.35	0.27	0.39		
	Long run	1.08	1.06	0.92	1.07	0.90		0.31	0.70	0.72		
8. Miscellaneous manufactured goods	Short run	0.62			0.06			0.54	−0.15		0.13	
	Long run	1.32			1.00			1.62	0.65		0.42	

Note: Estimation results are shown only for those cases in which it can be rejected that there is no cointegration. VECM are specified assuming that (i) there is only one cointegration equation, (ii) there is no linear trend in the series, (iii) the cointegration relationships include an intercept, (iv) two lags of the first differences of the variables are included in the specification.

industries. Tests for structural break are known to have very low power, especially in short samples like the recent history of the creation of the euro. A wider decline in pass-through may be taking place, but it is too early to ascertain whether this change is taking place and too early to determine the structural explanations for such declines. Exchange rate changes continue to lead to large changes in import prices across euro area countries. While pass-through is clearly incomplete, on average it remains more than 60 per cent one quarter after exchange rate moves and 80 per cent over the course of a year.

REFERENCES

Andrews, D. W. K. (1993), 'Tests for parameter instability and structural change with unknown change point', *Econometrica* 61, pp. 821–856.

Andrews, D. W. K. and W. Ploberger (1994), 'Optimal tests when a nuisance parameter is present only under the alternative', *Econometrica* 62, pp. 1383–1414.

Anderton, R. (2003), 'Extra-euro area manufacturing import prices and exchange rate pass-through', ECB Working Paper No. 219, March.

Bacchetta, P. and E. van Wincoop (2003), 'Why do consumer prices react less than import prices to exchange rates', *Journal of the European Economics Association* 1, pp. 662–670.

Bacchetta, P. and E. van Wincoop (2005), 'A theory of the currency denomination of international trade', *Journal of International Economics*, 67, pp. 295–399.

Baily, M. N. (2002), 'Persistent dollar swings and the US economy'. In *Dollar overvaluation and the world economy*, C. Fred Bergsten and John Williamson (eds.) Washington: Institute for International Economics.

Burstein, A., M. Eichenbaum and S. Rebelo (2002), 'Why are rates of inflation so low after large devaluations?' NBER Working Paper No. 8748 (February).

Burstein, A., J. Neves and S. Rebelo (2003), 'Distribution costs and real exchange rate dynamics during exchange rate based stabilisations', *Journal of Monetary Economics* 50, pp. 1189–1214.

Campa, J. and L. Goldberg. (2005). 'Exchange rate pass-through into import prices'. *Review of Economics and Statistics* 87(4), pp. 679–690.

Campa, J. and L. Goldberg (2006), 'Distribution margins, imported inputs, and the insensitivity of the CPI to exchange rates'. NBER Working Paper 12121.

Campa, J. and J. M. González-Mínguez (2005), 'Differences in exchange rate pass-through in the euro area', *European Economic Review*, 50(1), pp. 121–145.

Corsetti, G. and L. Dedola (2002), 'Macroeconomics of international price discrimination' European Central Bank Working Paper No. 176.

Corsetti, G., L. Dedola and S. Leduc (2004), 'Pass through and exchange rate fluctuations in a DGSE model of price discrimination'. Manuscript.

Corsetti, G. and P. Pesenti (2005), 'International dimensions of optimal monetary policy', *Journal of Monetary Economics*, Vol. 52, No. 2, pp. 281–305.

Devereux, M. (2001), 'Monetary policy, exchange rate flexibility and exchange rate pass-through'. In *Revisiting the case for flexible exchange rates* (Bank of Canada) pp. 47–82.

Devereux, M. and C. Engel (2001), 'Endogenous currency of price setting in a dynamic open economy model.' NBER Working Paper No. 8559.

Devereux, M., C. Engel and P. Storgaard (2004), 'Endogenous exchange rate pass-through when nominal prices are set in advance', *Journal of International Economics*, Vol. 63, No. 2, July, pp. 263–291.

Dornbusch, R. (1987), 'Exchange rates and prices', *American Economic Review* 77, pp. 93–106.

Elliott, G. and U. Muller (2005), 'Confidence sets for the date of a single break in linear time series regressions', manuscript, Princeton University.

Engel, C. (2005), 'Equivalence results for optimal pass-through, optimal indexing to exchange rates, and optimal choice of currency for export pricing', NBER Working Paper No. 11209.

European Central Bank (2003), 'Review of the international role of the euro', December.

European Central Bank (2005), 'Review of the international role of the euro', January.

Faruqee, H. (2004), 'Measuring the trade effects of the EMU', International Monetary Fund Working Paper WP/04/154.

Frankel, J., D. Parsley and S. J. Wei (2005), 'Slow pass-through around the world, a new import for developing countries?' NBER Working Paper No. 11199.

Froot, K. and P. Klemperer (1989), 'Exchange rate pass-through when market share matters', *American Economic Review* (September), pp. 637–654.

Gagnon, J. and J. Ihrig (2001), 'Monetary policy and exchange rate pass-through'. Board of Governors of the Federal Reserve System, International Finance Discussion Papers No. 704 (July).

Giovannini, A. (1988), 'Exchange rates and traded goods prices', *Journal of International Economics* Vol. 24, pp. 45–68.

Goldberg, P. and M. Knetter (1997), 'Goods prices and exchange rates: what have we learned?', *Journal of Economic Literature*, Vol. 35, pp. 1243–1292.

Goldberg, L. and C. Tille (2005), 'Vehicle currency use in international trade', NBER Working Paper No. 11127, February.

Goldfajn, I. and S. R. da C. Werlang (2000), 'The pass-through from depreciation to inflation: a panel study.' Banco Central do Brasil, Working Paper No. 5.

Hellerstein, R. (2004), 'Who bears the cost of a change in the exchange rate? The case of imported beer', Staff Reports No. 179 (February), Federal Reserve Bank of New York.

Marazzi, M., N. Sheets, R. Vigfusson, J. Faust, J. Gagnon, R. Martin, J. Márquez, T. Reeve and J. Rogers (2005), 'Exchange rate pass-through to US import prices: some new evidence,' International Finance Discussion Papers No. 833 (April), Federal Reserve Board of Governors.

Marston, R. (1990), 'Pricing to market in Japanese manufacturing'. *Journal of International Economics*, Vol. 29, pp. 217–236.

Obstfeld, M. and K. Rogoff (1995), 'Exchange rate dynamics redux', *Journal of Political Economy* 103, pp. 624–660.

Taylor, J. B. (2000), 'Low inflation, pass-through, and the pricing power of firms', *European Economic Review*, June Vol 44, No. 7, pp. 1389–1408.

5   The international equity holdings of euro area investors

Philip R. Lane[1] and Gian Maria Milesi-Ferretti[2]

5.1   Introduction

The integration of euro area financial markets since the launch of the euro in 1999 has been at the centre of attention in policy debate and academic literature. This chapter complements this much-explored line of research by examining a subject that has attracted much less attention – namely, the characteristics of the euro area's external portfolio investment, and particularly the geographical allocation of the international equity portfolios held by euro area investors.[3]

The geography of the euro area's external equity holdings is important for several reasons. First, the level of holdings in each international market is a direct determinant of the euro area's exposure to external financial shocks. Second, it is also useful to assess whether international investment provides diversification against internal risks. Third, differences in the composition of international portfolios between the euro area and other major economic blocs (e.g. the United States and Japan) may generate asymmetric responses to international financial crises or global shocks, which in turn may pose a challenge for coordinated management of the international financial system.

Our empirical work is made possible by the release of the International Monetary Fund's Coordinated Portfolio Investment Survey (CPIS). This dataset, described more in detail in section 5.2, provides a unique perspective on the geographical patterns of international portfolio holdings for most major international investors, including the entire euro area.

We analyse the international equity holdings of euro area investors from several different perspectives, and examine the external holdings of the aggregate euro area, as well as those of individual euro area members. We first ask the question of whether (all else equal) euro area members

[1] IIS and Economics Department, TCD; and CEPR.
[2] International Monetary Fund and CEPR.

[3] See Baele *et al.* (2004) on the current state of financial integration within the euro area and Anderton *et al.* (2004) for a general review of the euro area's external financial linkages.

are more likely to invest in each other, then investigate whether member countries have significantly different investment patterns in terms of extra-euro area holdings. The former exercise is a simple test of whether the move to a single currency has led (at least so far) to increased intra-union equity market integration; if the latter reveals substantial heterogeneity across Member States, this may be a source of asymmetric wealth dynamics across the euro area.

Our main findings can be summarised as follows. At the end of 2001, the euro area was already a major portfolio equity investor – larger than the United States if intra-euro area equity holdings are not netted out. With regard to bilateral investment holdings, some interesting patterns emerge: in particular, the importance of Luxembourg as both an international portfolio investor and the recipient of significant portfolio equity investment from some euro area countries (e.g. Belgium, Germany, and Italy).

Holdings by euro area countries outside the euro area appear to be associated with the host countries' stock market size, bilateral trade links, and proxies for 'cultural proximity'. We also find evidence that, in comparison with other OECD countries, euro area countries tend to invest in each other substantially more than underlying trade patterns and other fundamentals would suggest.

As discussed later in the chapter, this contribution applies underlying conceptual and empirical frameworks developed by Lane and Milesi-Ferretti (2004). A number of other recent papers have also examined the pattern of bilateral portfolio equity investment. For example, Yildrim (2003) focuses on the role of various corporate governance indicators to explain bilateral investment patterns. Bertaut and Kole (2004) underline the fact that most countries are 'underweight' in their holdings of US stocks, as compared to other international asset holdings, while Aviat and Coeurdacier (2004) jointly study trade in goods and assets in a simultaneous equations framework, using bilateral data on bank loans as well as portfolio holdings. Finally, Vlachos (2004) explores the importance of regulatory harmonisation for bilateral patterns in portfolio holdings.

Some other papers have focused more specifically on the bilateral investment patterns of individual countries: the United States (Ahearne, Griever, and Warnock (2004), Mann and Meade (2002); Dahlquist *et al.* (2003)) and Ireland (Honohan and Lane (2000)). We discuss their findings in section 5.4, when presenting the results for the determinants of bilateral investment patterns for the euro area as a whole.

The structure of the rest of the chapter is as follows. Section 5.2 reviews the theoretical literature. Section 5.3 briefly describes the dataset, and section 5.4 provides some stylised facts on the geographical distribution of international portfolio equity holdings. Section 5.5 presents the empirical analysis, focusing first on the geographical allocation of aggregate euro area holdings, and then on the determinants of bilateral portfolio equity holdings by euro area countries outside the euro area, as well as on the determinants of equity holdings by the entire set of OECD countries. Section 5.6 provides some concluding remarks.

5.2   Theoretical framework

In laying out a theoretical framework, we follow the analysis in Lane and Milesi-Ferretti (2004). We first discuss an approach that highlights frictions in product markets rather than capital markets in explaining asymmetric portfolios, before turning to theories that rather attribute heterogeneous portfolios to financial and informational frictions.

Regarding the former, Obstfeld and Rogoff (2001) construct a two-country model showing that the existence of trading costs (or, equivalently, heterogeneous preferences) in product markets naturally generates a home bias in equity positions, even if global financial markets are complete. Subsequently, Lane and Milesi-Ferretti (2004) have extended this model to an N-country setting. The intuition is that such trade frictions in product markets generate differences in consumption patterns across countries which, in turn, imply that investors face heterogeneous country-specific risk profiles: an investor in country A cares much more about a productivity shock in country B than in country C, if her consumption relies on imports from country B but not on imports from country C. Moreover, under certain conditions, the optimal hedge is to tilt national portfolios towards those countries that feature most prominently in the basket of imports.

In terms of frictions in asset markets, Cooper and Kaplanis (1986) and Martin and Rey (2004) develop models in which investment costs vary on a bilateral basis.[4] A natural interpretation is that such cost variation is generated by informational barriers that vary across country pairs, due to differences in factors such as language, cultural linkages and institutional commonalities.

Another form of asset market imperfection relates to the inability to hedge all types of risk. Davis et al. (2001)focus on domestic labour income as a form of endowment risk that cannot be directly laid off in financial markets. In such an environment, differences in the pattern of labour

---

[4] See also the application in Martin and Rey (2000). The working paper version of Ahearne et al. (2004) provides a useful account of the model originally developed by Cooper and Kaplanis (1986).

income risk across countries imply that investors will optimally select different international portfolios, since the covariances between domestic income and the returns on the various international stockmarkets will be a key determinant of portfolios.

These theoretical contributions provide a guide to our empirical work. Overall, they suggest that bilateral equity holdings should be related to the size of source-country imports from the destination country, to proxies for informational and institutional barriers to bilateral asset trade, and to the pattern of covariances between source-country income and stock market returns in the destination countries.

5.3   The coordinated portfolio investment survey

5.3.1   The dataset

Our data on asset holdings are drawn from the Coordinated Portfolio Investment Survey (CPIS) that is managed by the International Monetary Fund.[5] This dataset reports portfolio holdings for 1997, 2001 and 2002 for each participating country, with the geographical decomposition across 218 destination countries/territories. We focus on the 2001 data, since the 1997 survey was a based on a narrower set of investor nations, while the 2002 data are in some cases derived from an extrapolation of the 2001 benchmark survey data rather than representing truly 'new' data.

While the CPIS represents a major advance in availability of data on bilateral investment positions, Lane and Milesi-Ferretti (2004) highlight a number of limitations that are relevant for the euro area. First, there may be under-reporting of assets by CPIS participants. For example, the German survey did not cover holdings by households. As a result, the portfolio assets reported in the CPIS survey (US$800 billion), are over US$200 billion lower than those reported in the International Investment Position (which are estimated making use of flow data, therefore include household holdings as well). Under-reporting is also likely to occur, more generally, for assets held in offshore centres for tax shelter reasons. Second, the bilateral data can be distorted by third-party holdings, by which a resident in country A holds securities in country B through an institution residing in country C. This intermediation is filtered out of the data if the end investors are surveyed; however, there will be mis-measurement if the surveys are based on custodians. Third, the CPIS

---

[5] The data are available at http://www.imf.org/external/np/sta/pi/datarsl.htm.

Table 5.1 *The largest portfolio equity investors* (US billion)*

	CPIS	Estimates
	2001	2003
Euro area (including intra-area holdings)	1,739	2,486
United States	1,613	1,972
Euro area (external holdings)	894	1,332
United Kingdom	558	750
Switzerland	247	294
Japan	227	274
Canada	201	306
Total reported holdings	5,169	. . . .

* *Sources:* IMF Coordinated Portfolio Investment Survey, and Lane and Milesi-Ferretti (2005).

is still in its infancy and it is surely the case that not all countries have successfully implemented best-practice collection methods.

5.3.2   The major investor nations

Table 5.1 lists the largest foreign investors as reported by the 2001 survey, as well as some estimates of portfolio equity holdings at the end of 2003. Focusing first on the 2001 data, the total recorded level of portfolio equity investment in the CPIS was US$5.16 trillion. If intra-euro area holdings are included, the total portfolio equity holdings of the euro area exceed those of the United States. If we exclude intra-euro area holdings (over US$800 billion) the euro area becomes the second largest foreign portfolio equity investor, with portfolio equity assets equal to about 15 per cent of euro area GDP (as opposed to 16 per cent of GDP in the United States).

As shown in the second column of Table 5.1, these general patterns also apply to the stocks of aggregate portfolio equity holdings at the end of 2003 (as captured in the International Investment Position data) – once again, total euro area equity assets are larger than US holdings if intra-euro area holdings are not netted out and are equivalent to around 30 per cent of the area's GDP.

5.3.3   Portfolio equity holdings by euro area countries

The total holdings of individual euro area countries are listed in the first column of Table 5.2. In particular, the size of Luxembourg's portfolio

Table 5.2 *The euro area's international equity holdings at end-2001**

	Total value ($bn)	Per capita value ($000)	Intra-euro area	Extra-euro area
Euro area	1739	5.7	48.6	51.4
Austria	31	3.9	53.5	46.5
Belgium	106	10.3	78.9	21.1
France	202	3.4	51.1	48.9
Germany	381	4.6	59.7	40.3
Italy	239	4.1	64.4	35.6
Luxembourg	319	725.2	37.1	62.9
Netherlands	235	14.7	26.5	73.5
Finland	20	3.9	31.1	68.9
Greece	1	0.1	50.1	49.9
Ireland	136	35.3	25.5	74.5
Portugal	8	0.8	66.0	34.0
Spain	59	1.4	54.2	45.8
Max	381	725.2	25.5	74.5
Min	1.4	0.1	78.9	21.1
Range	380	725.1	46.6	53.4

Source: IMF Coordinated Portfolio Investment Survey 2001.
* *Note:* End-2001 equity holdings in billions of US dollars. Intra-euro-area refers to the fraction of total holdings that is allocated to other members of the euro area. Extra-euro area is the fraction that is allocated to non-euro-area countries.

equity holdings, associated with this country's role as a financial centre, is remarkable – they are the second largest in the euro area and the fourth largest among the world's reporting countries. The second column in Table 5.2 shows average per capita values for international portfolio equity investment: for the euro area as a whole, the average per capita value is $5,700. However, this obscures a considerable range, from a maximum of $725,000 for Luxembourg to a minimum of just $100 in Greece. The last two columns show the allocation of international equity holdings between fellow euro area members and extra-euro area destinations. The extent of 'euro area bias' is considerable: 49 per cent of cross-border equity investments by euro area members are in other member countries. Again, there is considerable cross-country heterogeneity: the euro area bias is 79 per cent for Belgium but only 25 per cent for Ireland.

When studying the geographical allocation of portfolio equity investment of individual euro area countries, it is important to keep one key factor in mind – namely, the remarkable importance of investment in small financial centres, particularly Luxembourg. For example, assets

Table 5.3 *Summary statistics on stock market size and foreign ownership (2001)*

Variable country	Domestic stock market cap. in per cent of world stock market cap.	Per cent of domestic stock market cap. owned by foreign portfolio investors	Domestic GDP in per cent of world GDP
Euro area	15.9	37.4	19.6
Japan	9.3	16.7	13.4
United Kingdom	8.9	35.6	4.6
United States	48.9	12.9	32.3
Other	17	N.A.	30.1

Note: Reproduced and updated from Lane and Milesi-Ferretti (2004). World stock market capitalisation is calculated as the sum of stock market capitalisation of 71 countries in the sample. In this calculation, holdings of shares by residents of one euro-area country in another are considered domestic holdings.

held in offshore and financial centres are over 40 per cent of total portfolio equity assets for Belgium and Italy, and over 25 per cent in Germany (almost entirely reflecting holdings in Luxembourg).[6] Clearly these centres are not the ultimate destination of investment; rather, they serve as intermediaries. It follows that the measured geographical allocation of portfolio equity investment by countries investing heavily in financial centers is unavoidably distorted. Interestingly, Belgium, Germany, and Italy emerge from Table 5.2 as countries with a strong 'euro area bias', while Luxembourg's investment is skewed towards countries outside the euro area. This suggests that part of the intra-euro area portfolio equity investment by Belgian, German, and Italian residents may actually have countries outside the euro area as the ultimate destination. More generally, devising methods to allocate, albeit roughly, equity investment in offshore centres to their ultimate destination is an important, if difficult, research objective.

5.3.4 *Portfolio equity investment, country size, and stock market capitalisation*

Table 5.3 (reproduced from Lane and Milesi-Ferretti (2004)) provides a brief summary of the size of economies, their stock markets and the share of domestic stocks owned by non-residents for major international investors. A couple of interesting stylised facts emerge from this

[6] Indeed, Luxembourg is the primary destination for portfolio equity investment undertaken by Belgian, German, Greek, Italian and Portuguese residents.

Table 5.4 *Foreign portfolio equity investment: actual and predicted shares*

Source country Host country		Euro area	Japan	United Kingdom	United States
Euro area	Theor. share		17.5%	17.5%	31.1%
	Actual share		16.8%	43.5%	28.6%
Japan	Theor. share	11.0%		10.2%	18.1%
	Actual share	7.4%		9.9%	10.6%
United Kingdom	Theor. share	10.6%	9.8%		17.4%
	Actual share	22.4%	13.0%		21.7%
United States	Theor. share	58.1%	53.8%	53.6%	
	Actual share	45.8%	54.4%	24.3%	
Rest of the world	Theor. share	20.3%	18.8%	18.7%	33.4%
	Actual share	24.5%	15.8%	22.3%	39.1%

* Reproduced and updated from Lane and Milesi-Ferretti (2004). Predicted share: ratio of host country's stock market capitalisation to the stock market capitalisation of the world minus the source country. Actual share: ratio of source country's equity investment in host country to total source country foreign equity investment.

table. First, at end-2001 exchange rates and prices, the United Kingdom and the United States' stock market capitalisation largely exceeded their aggregate weight in world GDP, while the aggregate weight of the euro area in world GDP exceeded its relative stock market capitalisation. Second, the fraction of the domestic stock market held by non-resident portfolio investors was substantially higher in the euro area and the United Kingdom (over a third) than in the United States and Japan (13 and 17%, respectively).[7]

Table 5.4, also reproduced from Lane and Milesi-Ferretti (2004), summarises the geographical distribution of portfolio equity investment among the main advanced economies by comparing the share of foreign equity investment in the host country with the share of the host country's stock market capitalisation in the rest of the world's stock market capitalisation. We use the latter as a simple predictive benchmark for the allocation of foreign portfolio equity investment. Japan's foreign equity investment is the most-closely aligned with the benchmark, while the least closely aligned is the UK, which invests much more in the euro area than in the US. The euro area has higher-than-predicted investment in the rest

[7] Note that Table 5.4 only reports domestic shares owned by portfolio equity investors (who by definition hold participations below 10 per cent). Adding the shares held by direct investors would increase the measured size of non-resident ownership of domestic shares.

Table 5.5 *Regional allocation of extra-euro area holdings*

	United States	United Kingdom	Japan	Asia	Latin America
Euro area	45.8	22.4	7.4	5.2	1.6
Austria	48.2	18.8	5.9	2.2	0.3
Belgium	44.8	24.5	7.0	2.9	1.4
France	42.5	25.9	7.4	2.3	0.6
Germany	45.5	28.9	3.8	2.0	0.8
Italy	44.8	19.0	12.1	5.2	3.3
Luxembourg	42.7	15.3	10.3	7.6	2.9
Netherlands	54.6	16.9	5.2	9.3	0.6
Finland	31.8	16.9	5.4	1.2	0.0
Greece	40.0	34.4	1.5	0.9	1.8
Ireland	46.8	31.7	6.1	4.5	0.6
Portugal	41.3	19.0	3.1	2.1	7.9
Spain	32.4	39.7	13.1	0.2	4.7
Max	54.6	39.7	13.1	9.3	7.9
Min	31.8	15.3	1.5	0.2	0.0
Range	22.8	24.4	11.6	9.1	7.9
Mkt Cap	58.1	10.6	11.0	7.0	1.8

Note: Allocation shares of extra-euro-area holdings. Mkt Cap is the share of each country/region in extra-euro-area aggregate stock market capitalisation (based on Datastream indices). Asia is the sum of holdings in China, Hong Kong SAR, India, Indonesia, Korea, Malaysia, Philippines, Pakistan, Singapore, Sri Lanka, Taiwan province of China, and Thailand. Latin America is the sum of holdings in Argentina, Bolivia, Brazil, Chile, Colombia, Mexico, Peru and Venezuela.

of the world, especially in the UK, and lower-than-predicted investment in Japan and the US. Finally, the US is 'overweight' in the UK and the rest of the world, but underweight in the euro area and especially in Japan.

5.3.5 Geographical allocation of euro area portfolio equity investment

Tables 5.5 and 5.6 focus on portfolio equity assets held by euro area residents outside the euro area. Table 5.5 presents the geographical allocation across major regions. Relative to the shares in non-euro area aggregate stock market capitalisation (the final row in the table), the portfolios of euro area members show considerable deviations. For the aggregate euro area, there is under-investment (relative to the benchmark) in the US, Japan and the rest of Asia and over-investment in the UK and Latin America. The Netherlands is closest to the benchmark allocation but Greece, Ireland and Spain have heavily-skewed portfolios, with these

Table 5.6 *Extra-euro-area holdings: country details*

	Mkt cap	Euro area	Max	Min	Range
United States	58.08	45.5	54.6	29.6	25.0
United Kingdom	10.57	22.2	39.5	15.3	24.1
Switzerland	2.96	8.2	14.0	3.9	10.1
Japan	11.04	7.4	13.0	1.5	11.5
Hong Kong SAR of China	2.27	2.3	6.7	0.0	6.7
Sweden	1.07	2.2	29.6	0.6	29.0
Australia	1.07	0.9	1.6	0.0	1.6
Korea, Republic of	0.91	0.9	1.6	0.0	1.6
Brazil	0.77	0.7	6.9	0.0	6.9
Canada	2.68	0.6	1.1	−0.3	1.4
Taiwan Prov. of China	1.15	0.5	1.3	0.0	1.3
Mexico	0.59	0.5	1.0	0.0	1.0
Denmark	0.39	0.5	3.1	0.0	3.1
Singapore	0.52	0.4	0.7	0.0	0.7
India	0.54	0.4	0.8	0.0	0.8
Norway	0.31	0.3	1.3	0.1	1.2
Russian Federation	0.35	0.3	0.6	0.0	0.6
South Africa	0.35	0.3	4.3	0.0	4.3
Malaysia	0.44	0.2	0.4	0.0	0.4
Israel	0.28	0.2	0.4	0.0	0.4
Hungary	0.05	0.2	2.5	0.0	2.5
Poland	0.12	0.2	1.6	0.0	1.6
Thailand	0.13	0.2	0.6	0.0	0.6
China, P. R.	0.80	0.2	0.3	0.0	0.3
Turkey	0.20	0.1	0.7	0.0	0.7
Venezuela	0.01	0.1	0.5	0.0	0.5
Argentina	0.09	0.1	1.1	0.0	1.1

Note: Allocation shares of extra-euro-area holdings. Mkt cap is the share of each country in extra-euro-area aggregate stock market capitalisation (based on Datastream indices).

countries in particular over-weighting the UK. It is also noteworthy that the Iberian countries are the heaviest investors in Latin America.

A more detailed breakdown of the destination of the euro area's external investments, which includes all countries with at least 0.1 per cent of the aggregate euro area portfolio of extra-euro area holdings, is provided in Table 5.6. This table highlights the strong bilateral variation in the data. For instance, Sweden accounts for portfolio shares that range from 0.6 per cent (Greece) to a remarkable 29.6 per cent (Finland), while the Swiss share ranges from 3.9 per cent (Ireland) to 14.0 per cent (Germany). Among the emerging market destinations, Portuguese holdings in Brazil and South Africa are especially high at 6.8 per cent and

4.2 per cent respectively of its total external portfolio, while Austria is heavily invested in Central and Eastern Europe.[8]

Taken together, the patterns highlighted so far demonstrate that the composition of the euro area's international portfolio cannot be simply explained by the cross-country distribution of stock market capitalisations. Moreover, it is clear that there is considerable heterogeneity in the international portfolios of the individual euro area member countries. The next section investigates the determinants of these spatial patterns using regression analysis.

5.4   Econometric analysis

We focus on a single cross-sectional observation for the structure of external equity portfolios for the year 2001.[9]

5.4.1   Determinants of the international equity holdings of the aggregate euro area

We begin the empirical analysis by investigating the determinants of the spatial pattern in the international equity holdings of the aggregate euro area. The empirical specification is given by

$$\log(x_j^{euro}) = \alpha + \sigma \log\left(IMP_j^{euro}\right) + \gamma F_j^{euro} + \varepsilon_j^{euro} \qquad (1)$$

where x_j^{euro} is the aggregate level of equity investment by euro area countries in destination country j, IMP_j^{euro} is the aggregate level of euro area imports from country j and F_j^{euro} is a vector of other country characteristics that influences the level of euro area investment in country j. As discussed in Section 5.2, Lane and Milesi-Ferretti (2004) develop a framework in which the level of bilateral trade plays an important role in the design of optimal portfolios; trade also plays a role as an informational variable. The vector F_j^{euro} comprises a set of variables that may proxy for financial and informational frictions.

The results are given in Table 5.7. As a benchmark, the specification in column (1) just includes stock market capitalisation as a regressor: if spatial allocations just reflected each country's share in global market capitalisation, this variable should enter with a unitary coefficient and have complete explanatory power. In this simple regression, it turns out

---

[8] See also Bertaut and Kole (2004) on the Austrian data.
[9] As noted in the introduction, the 1997 survey refers to a much smaller set of source countries; the newly-released results for end-2002 are highly correlated with the end-2001 positions.

Table 5.7 *Determinants of the euro area's international equity holdings*

	(1)	(2)	(3)	(4)	(5)
Stock market capitalis.	1.0	0.67	0.56	0.6	0.57
	(10.9)***	(7.2)***	(4.2)***	(4.78)***	(3.29)***
Imports		0.69	0.8	0.78	0.77
		(2.9)***	(2.74)***	(2.74)**	(2.6)**
Distance			0.17	0.1	0.09
			(0.92)	(0.58)	(0.46)
Euro_culture			0.59	0.37	0.54
			(1.57)	(1.2)	(1.49)
Financial centre			0.8	0.8	0.94
			(2.55)***	(2.4)**	(2.73)**
Sharpe				3.34	2.87
				(2.69)**	(2.22)**
Correl. in growth rates					0.78
					(1.1)
Correl. in stock returns					−0.98
					(1.23)
Observations	38	38	38	36	36
Adjusted R^2	0.82	0.88	0.90	0.90	0.91

Note: the dependent variable is log of portfolio equity holdings of the source country in the host country. T-statistics reported in parenthesis. *, **, *** indicate statistical significance at the 10%, 5%, and 1% confidence levels, respectively.

the simple elasticity of bilateral holdings with respect to market capitalisation is indeed unitary, highly significant, and with substantial explanatory power – the adjusted R^2 is 0.82.[10]

Regressions in columns (2)–(5) add additional controls that may help explain the remaining proportion of the cross-sectional variation. In column (2), the volume of euro-area imports from the destination country is added to the specification. Bilateral trade may matter for a variety of reasons. Following the theoretical discussion in section 5.2, purchasing the equity of a trading partner may act as a hedge against consumption risk emanating to shocks to imports from that country. However, more generally, trade linkages may also increase familiarity with a given destination, influencing portfolio decisions for informational reasons. The estimates in column (2) indeed show that imports are significant in explaining the spatial allocation of euro area investment; the inclusion of imports also

[10] The results are essentially unchanged if the largest destination country (the United States) is dropped from the sample.

leads to a reduction in the point estimate and significance level for the stock market capitalisation variable. These results remain stable in the broader specifications in columns (3)–(5).[11]

The specification is further extended in column (3) to include two informational proxies (distance and a 'euro culture' dummy), plus a dummy for financial centre destinations.[12] The 'euro culture' dummy takes the value 1 if a major European language is in widespread use in the destination country and/or if the destination was in a colonial relationship with a European country and 0 otherwise. The results in column (3) show that the financial centre dummy is quite significant, but neither distance nor the 'euro culture' dummy variables are individually significant. The results for these variables are broadly similar in columns (4) and (5).

Column (4) adds the Sharpe ratio for the destination country to the specification: if returns are expected to persist, a history of a high return-risk ratio may boost inward investment. Indeed, the estimates in both columns (4) and (5) support this notion, with the Sharpe variable turning out to be significant. Finally, the correlation in output growth rates and the correlation in stock market returns between the destination country and Germany (as a proxy for the euro area) are also included in the specification in column (5).[13] Allocations that are driven by a diversification motive should be reflected in a negative sign on these correlation variables: while the stock market correlation variable enters negatively, the output correlation is significantly positive (but neither is individually significant).

Overall, Table 5.7 does a good job of explaining the spatial pattern in the aggregate euro-area's portfolio of external equity holdings, capturing 90 per cent of the variation. In particular, deviations from the cross-country distribution of stock market capitalisation are largely explained by trade linkages, a destination's status as a financial centre, and the Sharpe ratio.[14]

Other papers focusing on single-country portfolio holdings have used somewhat different specifications. For example, Ahearne et al. (2004)

[11] The estimated coefficient is in the range (0.95–0.99) in columns (2)–(5), which is close to the unitary coefficient predicted by the model of Lane and Milesi-Ferretti (2004).

[12] We also investigated two further distance-related variables: a dummy for European Union membership (i.e. picking up Denmark, Sweden and the UK) and the difference in time zones (i.e. the time difference between the destination and Central European time). Neither variable was significant and their inclusion did not alter any of the other results.

[13] We also tried the correlation between the foreign stock market return and the German output growth rate: this was insignificant and did not affect the results for the other regressors.

[14] Other potential regressors (capital controls; restrictions on foreign ownership; financial trading costs) were found not to be important. Such variables are likely highly correlated with the level of stock market capitalisation that is included in all specifications.

use as dependent variable the degree of home bias, defined as one minus the ratio of the share of foreign equities in the United States' and world portfolios. They find that the portion of a country's portfolio that is listed in the US is a key determinant of that country's weight in US portfolios. Dahlquist *et al.* (2003) find instead that the share of a country's equity in the US portfolio is much-more-strongly correlated with that country's weight in the world 'float' portfolio (shares available to investors who are not controlling shareholders) than with the weight in the standard 'world' portfolio.[15] Finally, Honohan and Lane (2001) show that the geographical pattern of Ireland's international portfolio investment matches Irish trade patterns more closely than the destination countries' financial market size.

5.4.2   *International holdings by individual euro area countries*

We turn next to the exploration of possible heterogeneity across euro area members in terms of their external investment patterns. To this end, we employ the specification developed by Lane and Milesi-Ferretti (2004):

$$\log(x_{ij}) = \phi_i + \phi_j + \sigma \log(IMP_{ij}) + \gamma F_{ij} + \varepsilon_{ij} \qquad (2)$$

where the set of source countries $\{i\}$ is restricted to the euro area member countries. Relative to the previous section, the panel nature of this setup allows us to include a double set of fixed effects (source- and host-country dummies), in addition to variables that vary along the bilateral dimension. The inclusion of source dummies means that we are not trying to explain why euro area member countries may vary in the aggregate scale of their external holdings; we only focus on the geographical distribution of such holdings. The host dummies control instead for those characteristics of the destination countries that make a given country more or less generally attractive to all investors, regardless of origin. As such, this 'double fixed effects' specification targets the reasons why particular bilateral portfolio shares may vary across the euro area. Since this specification means that only explanatory variables that have variation along both sample dimensions can be included in the regression, the effect of variables such as stock market capitalisation, income per capita and country size are soaked up by the source and host country dummy variables.

---

[15] In common with the Ahearne *et al.* (2004) study, these authors study the US portfolio in 1997. We do not have updated data on the 'free float' market capitalisation for the countries in our study.

All regressions in this and later sections exclude source and host off-shore and small financial centres.[16] These centres act primarily or exclusively as intermediaries, rather than being true sources or final destinations of investment. Ideally, we would wish to 're-allocate' the funds invested by source economies in financial centres to their ultimate destination. However, this type of exercise is also fraught with uncertainty, given the limited available information on the pattern of investment of these centres.[17] Nevertheless, to the extent that every dollar invested by a source country in a financial centre is invested by the financial centre in the same way as the average dollar invested abroad by the source country, the exclusion of such centres has no implications for the empirical analysis. This is the case since re-allocating holdings in offshore centres to their ultimate destinations would affect bilateral holdings only up to a common factor of proportionality. Given that the regressions are run in log form, this factor of proportionality would be soaked up by the fixed source-country effects. Be that as it may, the exclusion of several financial centres is unavoidable, given the lack of data on macroeconomic variables, bilateral trade, stock market capitalisation and returns.

Table 5.8 displays the regression results. Panel least squares estimates are reported in columns (1) and (2); the results from the Tobit estimator are shown in columns (3) and (4). The Tobit estimates are included, since many of the observed bilateral observations are equal to zero and we want to allow for the possibility that these zero values reflect censoring. The specification in columns (1) and (3) includes the following bilateral variables: the level of imports by the source country from the host country; distance between the two countries; a common language dummy; a colony dummy; a tax treaty dummy; and the correlation in output growth rates.[18]

The specification in columns (2) and (4) is expanded to include some bilateral financial correlations (the correlation in stock market returns

---

[16] Among the euro area source countries, we exclude Luxembourg. According to a decomposition by the Irish Central Statistical Office, a sizable fraction of Irish portfolio investment (close to 80% in 2001) is also undertaken in the International Financial Services Centre. Excluding Ireland as well among source countries yields very similar results. A complete data appendix with a list of host countries and territories for each sample is available from the authors upon request.

[17] An exception is Luxembourg, which reports in detail its international equity holdings.

[18] See Lane and Milesi-Ferretti (2004) for a detailed discussion of this choice of explanatory variables. Relative to the specification in that paper, we do not include the time zone difference between source and destination countries, since there is very little difference in time zones across euro area member countries. We also drop a currency union dummy since there are no available observations for those destination countries that are in monetary unions with euro-area member countries.

Table 5.8 *International equity holdings by euro area member countries*

	(1)	(2)	(3)	(4)
	Panel FE	Panel FE	Tobit	Tobit
Avg. imports, 1997–2001	0.17	0.24	0.39	0.24
	(4.80)**	(2.24)*	(5.23)**	(2.38)*
Log distance	−0.85	−0.25	−0.88	−0.21
	(5.78)**	(0.91)	(3.82)**	(0.83)
Common language	0.16	0.33	0.32	0.28
	(1.33)	(1.20)	(1.30)	(1.11)
Colony dummy	0.50	1.16	1.06	1.20
	(2.77)**	(2.82)**	(3.14)**	(3.16)**
Tax treaty	−0.03	−0.22	0.04	−0.25
	(0.35)	(1.03)	(0.20)	(1.29)
Correl. in growth rates	0.22	0.27	0.51	0.28
	(1.30)	(0.65)	(1.47)	(0.71)
Correl. in stock returns		2.29		2.47
		(2.68)**		(3.08)**
Correl. growth-stock ret.		0.07		−0.04
		(0.18)		(0.11)
Common legal origin		0.15		0.24
		(0.89)		(1.49)
Observations	1035	285	1035	285
No. of host countries	146	31	146	31
No. of source countries	11	11	11	11
Adjusted R^2	0.86	0.86		

Note: The dependent variable is log of 1+ portfolio equity holdings of the source country in the host country. Regressions include fixed source and host country effects. T-statistics reported in parenthesis. *, **, *** indicate statistical significance at the 10%, 5%, and 1% confidence level, respectively.

and the correlation between output growth in the source country and the stock market return in the destination country), plus a dummy variable that scores one if source and host countries share legal systems with common origins and zero otherwise. This broader specification comes at the price of a substantial decline in the number of available observations: restrictions on data availability mean that the number of these countries drops from 146 to 31 (and observations from 1,035 to 285) with the addition of the financial correlation variables in columns (2) and (4). However, as shown in Table 5.9, the substantial reduction in sample size entails only a very modest reduction in the total size of equity holdings

Table 5.9 *Investment by euro area countries outside the euro area. Summary statistics*

	Total holdings (billions US$)	Source	Host	Total observations	Observations = 0
Total	894	12	223	1657	981
excluding Luxembourg	687	11	223	1451	890
in regressions (1) and (3)	668	11	146	1036	595
in regressions (2) and (4)	663	11	31	286	11

in the regression sample (less than 1 per cent) – close to 600 of the 750 lost observations feature equity holdings equal to zero.

A number of patterns are evident across the specifications in columns (1)–(4) of Table 5.5. First, the variation in portfolio allocations by euro area member countries is significantly correlated with the relative importance of the various destination countries as trading partners: euro area members systematically hold larger equity stakes in those extra-union countries that supply a lot of imports to them. This holds true even though a number of gravity-type variables are included in the regression, which are highly collinear with the pattern of bilateral trade.

Second, there is general support for the notion that informational variables are also important. Beyond the familiarity interpretation for the role of trade in determining portfolio decisions, the information hypothesis is also supported by the significantly-negative effect of distance (in columns (1) and (3)) and especially the positive effect of the colony dummy, which is statistically and economically significant in all specifications.[19] However, neither the common language dummy nor the tax treaty dummy offer any additional explanatory power.

Among the bilateral correlation variables, only the stock market correlation is significant. However, it is in fact significantly positive, which goes against a diversification motive for the determination of portfolio allocations. The evidence tends therefore to suggest that countries invest in hosts that have a more-similar economic structure. The coefficient on the common legal origin dummy is not estimated precisely and is statistically insignificant.[20]

---

[19] The fact that distance is significantly negative only in the wider sample, where over half of the total observations are zero, suggests that distance helps explain whether euro area countries invest or not in a specific destination, but is less helpful in explaining the amount of investment.

[20] The coefficient on common legal origin increases in size and becomes statistically significant if Ireland is excluded from the sample.

In summary, the results in Table 5.8 show that the heterogeneity in the international portfolio allocations by euro-area member countries can be related to structural differences in the relations between individual member countries and the various destination countries. A robust pattern is that financial linkages are positively associated with trade linkages, with additional explanatory power provided by informational variables (distance, colonial history).

5.4.3   *Do euro-area members invest disproportionately in each other?*

In order to address this question, we expand the sample in two directions. First, we include all industrial countries in the set of source countries $\{i\}$. Second, we include all available country pairs in the specification: that is, cross-border investments within the euro area in addition to extra-euro area holdings. In addition, we slightly adapt our specification

$$\log(x_{ij}) = \phi_i + \phi_j + \beta \, EURODUM_{ij} + \sigma \log(IMP_{ij}) + \gamma \, F_{ij} + \varepsilon_{ij}$$

$$(3)$$

where $EURODUM_{ij}$ is a dummy variable that takes the value 1 if both source and destination countries are members of the euro area and 0 otherwise. If this dummy turns out to be significant, it will indicate that (controlling for the other factors in the regression) euro-area members indeed invest disproportionately in each other.

Table 5.10 reports the results for this specification, as adapted from the original estimates in Lane and Milesi-Ferretti (2004). As in Table 5.5, we report panel OLS regressions with fixed source and host effects in columns (1)–(2), while columns (3)–(4) report Tobit regressions. (In fact, it turns out that that the choice of estimator makes little difference in terms of the significance and value of the euro-area dummy variable.) As was the case for the sample in Table 5.8, adding stock market correlations and the index of legal origin curtail the sample size considerably, with the number of host countries dropping from 157 to 42 and over 1,400 lost observations. However, as shown in Table 5.11, most of the lost observations have equity holdings equal to zero (over 1,000) and the cumulative value of equity holdings in the other lost observations is tiny (less than 1%) compared to total equity holdings in the sample.

The results show that euro-area dummy variable is not significant in the broader sample in columns (1) and (3) but that it is quite significant in the regressions in columns (2) and (4). The difference is not attributable to the inclusion of extra regressors: rather, it is the reduction in sample size that is important. Since it is that smaller destination countries that are excluded from the regressions in columns (2) and (4) by virtue of not

Table 5.10 *Bilateral portfolio equity holdings*

	(1)	(2)	(3)	(4)
	Panel FE	Panel FE	Tobit	Tobit
Euro-area dummy	0.14	0.41	0.00	0.39
	(1.01)	(2.61)**	(0.01)	(2.57)**
Avg. imports, 1997–2001	0.17	0.24	0.34	0.26
	(7.38)***	(4.71)***	(7.84)***	(5.04)***
Log distance	−0.40	−0.07	−0.40	−0.05
	(6.32)***	(0.69)	(3.93)***	(0.48)
Time difference	0.04	−0.03	0.03	−0.04
	(3.02)***	(1.72)*	(1.35)	(1.91)*
Common language	0.22	0.27	0.44	0.27
	(3.05)***	(2.20)**	(3.39)***	(2.26)**
Colony dummy	0.33	0.25	0.60	0.27
	(2.81)***	(1.34)	(3.11)***	(1.46)
Tax treaty	−0.05	−0.27	0.03	−0.25
	(0.74)	(2.48)**	(0.32)	(2.29)**
Correl. in growth rates	0.22	0.10	0.35	0.03
	(2.59)**	(0.61)	(2.12)**	(0.22)
Correl. in stock returns		0.78		0.79
		(1.68)		(1.72)*
Correl. growth-stock ret.		−0.06		−0.15
		(0.37)		(0.92)
Common legal origin		0.18		0.20
		(2.05)**		(2.37)**
Observations	2426	790	2426	790
No. of host countries	157	42	157	42
No. of source countries	23	22	23	22
Adjusted R^2	0.89	0.89		

Note: Reproduced from Lane and Milesi-Ferretti (2004). The dependent variable is log of 1+portfolio equity holdings of the source country in the host country. Regressions include fixed source and host country effects. t-statistics reported in parenthesis. *, **, *** indicate statistical significance at the 10%, 5%, and 1% confidence level, respectively.

having stock market data, it may be argued that it is these results that are relatively more interesting.

The point estimate for the euro-area dummy in both columns (2) and (4) is 0.48. This is a quantitatively large effect: it implies that equity investment in a euro-area partner country is 162 per cent larger than in a non-euro-area partner country, controlling for the other factors in the

Table 5.11 *Portfolio equity investment of OECD countries. Summary statistics*

Sample	Total holdings (billions US$)	Source	Host	Total observations	Observations = 0
Total	4781	24	223	3541	2017
Excluding offshore countries (Table 5.10, regressions (1)–(3))	3847	23	157	2426	1291
No offshore countries (Table 5.10, regressions (2)–(4))	3820	23	42	792	27

regression. This is a striking result in view of the fact that the regression includes many variables (such as trade and distance) that might be expected to mop up the euro-area effect.

One issue we have not discussed so far is the possible endogeneity of product trade to the degree of bilateral financial integration. In Lane and Milesi-Ferretti (2004) we present estimation results using instrumental variables, treating the level of imports; the correlation of GDP growth rates; the correlation of stock returns; and the correlation between domestic GDP growth and the foreign stock return as endogenous variables.[21] Results still show a strong and statistically significant effect of imports on equity holdings, with the colony dummy also retaining a statistically- and economically-significant coefficient.

5.5   Concluding remarks

This chapter has provided a number of stylised facts concerning the size and geographical distribution of euro zone portfolio equity holdings. It has shown that the euro area is a major portfolio equity investor, with aggregate holdings second only to those of the US – even larger if intra-euro-area holdings are not netted out.

For euro-area countries, about half of international portfolio equity investment occurs outside the euro area and relative to stock market capitalisation, is particularly high in the UK. Some other interesting geographical patterns emerge – namely, the large portfolio equity investment

---

[21] Our instrument list consists of: distance; the time difference; a border dummy; the lagged correlation in GDP growth rates; the lagged correlation in stock returns; and the lagged correlation between domestic GDP growth and the foreign stock return. In related work (but using a different empirical specification), Aviat and Coeurdacier (2004) find that the causality between bilateral asset holdings and trade in goods runs in both directions, with statistically and economically significant effects.

by Austria in Central and Eastern Europe, and the significant share of Iberian investment that is allocated to Latin America. We also showed the remarkable importance of investment in financial centres – particularly Luxembourg – for a number of euro area countries.

More formal econometric analysis shows the pattern of investment of equity holdings for the euro area is strongly related to the size of host country characteristics such as stock market capitalisation, bilateral trade ties and its status as a financial centre. With regard to bilateral equity holdings of individual euro area countries with destinations outside the euro area, again we find a strong link with trade ties and a common culture. Finally, in a sample of OECD investor countries we find evidence that intra-euro-area equity investment is larger than that predicted on the basis of 'fundamentals' such as trade ties, distance, and co-movements in key macroeconomic variables. As data become available for later periods, it will be interesting to examine whether the intra-euro-area equity holdings are rising more than proportionately relative to external holdings.

Appendix 5.1

Countries and regions participating in the 2001 Coordinated Portfolio Investment Survey:

Argentina, Aruba, Australia, Austria, the Bahamas, Bahrain, Belgium, Bermuda, Brazil, Bulgaria, Canada, Cayman Islands, Chile, Colombia, Costa Rica, Cyprus, Czech Republic, Denmark, Egypt, Estonia, Finland, France, Germany, Greece, Guernsey, Hong Kong SAR of China, Hungary, Iceland, Indonesia, Ireland, Isle of Man, Israel, Italy, Japan, Jersey, Kazakhstan, Republic of Korea, Lebanon, Luxembourg, Macao SAR of China, Malaysia, Malta, Mauritius, Netherlands, Netherlands Antilles, New Zealand, Norway, Panama, Philippines, Poland, Portugal, Romania, Russian Federation, Singapore, Slovak Republic, South Africa, Spain, Sweden, Switzerland, Thailand, Turkey, Ukraine, United Kingdom, United States, Uruguay, Vanuatu, Venezuela.

Variables: sources and definitions

Bilateral portfolio equity holdings: Portfolio equity instruments issued by host country residents and held by source country residents. Source: 2001 Coordinated Portfolio Survey.

Source-country imports: Imports of goods by source countries from host countries (average 1997–2001). Source: International Monetary Fund, Direction of Trade Statistics.

Log distance: Logarithm of Great Circle distance in miles between the capital cities of source and host country. Source: Rose and Spiegel (2004).

Correlation of stock returns: Correlation between the stock market returns of the host and source country, expressed in US dollars. Source: Authors' calculations based on returns data from Datastream and Morgan Stanley Capital International.

Correlation in growth rates: Correlation between the GDP growth rate in the source and host country. Source: Authors' calculations based on World Bank, World Development Indicators.

Log domestic stock market capitalisation: Log of the domestic stock market capitalisation in US dollars as of end-2001. Sources: Datastream, Morgan Stanley Capital International, national sources.

Financial centre dummy: Dummy variable taking the value of 1 if the country or territory is a 'large' international financial centre.

Sharpe ratio: Average excess return of the country stock market relative to world returns, divided by the standard deviation of the excess return's variability. Source: Authors' calculations based on Datastream and Morgan Stanley Capital International.

Common legal origin: Dummy variable taking the value of 1 if source and host countries have a legal system with a common origin (common law, French, German, or Scandinavian). Source: Authors' elaborations based on La Porta *et al.* (2003).

Tax treaty: Dummy variable taking the value of 1 if the source and host country have a tax treaty enacted prior to 1999. Source: Authors' elaborations based on treaty data taken from www.unctad.org.

Common language: Dummy taking the value of 1 if source and host country share a common language. Source: Rose and Spiegel (2004).

Colony dummy: Dummy taking the value of 1 if source and host country ever had a colonial relationship. Source: Rose and Spiegel (2004).

Correlation growth-stock return: Correlation between GDP growth in the source country and real stock returns in the host country, 1980–1999. Source: Authors' calculations based on Datastream, Morgan Stanley Capital International and World Development Indicators.

REFERENCES

Ahearne, A. B., W. Griever and F. Warnock (2004), 'Information costs and the home bias', *Journal of International Economics* 62, pp. 313–336.
Anderton, R. F. di Mauro and F. Moneta (2004), 'Measuring financial integration in the euro area', ECB Occasional Paper No. 14, May.

Aviat, A. and N. Coeurdacier (2004), '*The geography of trade in goods and assets*', mimeo, Delta.

Baele, L. A. Ferrando, P. Hördahl, E. Krylova and C. Monnet (2004), 'Measuring financial integration in the euro area', ECB Occasional Paper No. 12, April.

Bertaut, C. and L. Kole (2004), 'What makes investors overweight or underweight? Explaining international appetites for foreign equities', *Federal Reserve Board Bulletin* 90, No. 1 (Winter), pp. 19–31.

Cooper, I. and E. Kaplanis (1986), 'Costs to crossborder investment and international equity market equilibrium'. In Jeremy Edwards, Julian Franks, Colin Mayer and Stephen Schaefer (eds.), *Recent developments in corporate finance.* Cambridge University Press, Cambridge, pp. 209–240.

Coval, J. D. and T. J. Moskowitz (1999), 'The geography of investment: Informed trading and asset prices', *Journal of Finance* LIV, pp. 2045–2073.

Dahlquist, M., L. Pinkowitz, R. M. Stulz and R. Williamson (2003), 'Corporate governance and the home bias', *Journal of Financial and Quantitative Analysis* Vol. 38, No. 1.

Davis, S. J. Nalewaik and P. Willen (2001), 'On the gains to international trade in risky financial assets', mimeo. Chicago Graduate School of Business.

Honohan, P. and P. R. Lane (2000), 'Where do the Irish invest?', *Irish Banking Review*, Autumn, pp. 12–23.

International Monetary Fund (2000), *The Results of the 1997 Comprehensive Portfolio Investment Survey*, Washington, DC.

Lane, P. R. and G. M. Milesi-Ferretti (2004), 'International Investment Patterns', IMF Working Paper 04/134, July.

Lane, P. R. and G. M. Milesi-Ferretti (2005), 'The external wealth of nations Mark II: Revised and extended estimates of external assets and liabilities', mimeo. Trinity College Dublin and International Monetary Fund.

La Porta, R. F. Lopez-de-Silanes, and A. Shleifer (2003), 'What works in securities laws?' mimeo. Harvard University, July.

Mann, C. and E. Meade (2002), 'Home bias, transaction costs, and prospects for the euro: a more detailed analysis', mimeo. Institute for International Economics and Centre for Economic Performance, LSE.

Martin, P. and H. Rey (2000), 'Financial integration and asset returns', *European Economic Review* 44, pp. 1327–1350.

Martin, P. and H. Rey (2004), 'Financial super-markets: size matters for asset trade', *Journal of International Economics* 64, December, pp. 351–381.

Obstfeld, M. and K. Rogoff (2001), 'The six major puzzles in international macroeconomics. Is there a common cause?' NBER Macroeconomics Annual 15, pp. 339–390.

Portes, R. and H. Rey (2005), 'The determinants of cross-border equity flows', *Journal of International Economics* 65 No. 2, March, 269–296.

Rose, A. K. and M. Spiegel (2004), 'A gravity model of sovereign lending: trade, default and credit', *International Monetary Fund Staff Papers* 51 No. 4 (Special Issue), pp. 50–63.

Yildrim, C. (2003), 'Informational asymmetries, corporate governance infrastructure and foreign portfolio equity investment', mimeo. Tilburg University.

6   Global linkages through foreign direct investment

W. Jos Jansen and Ad C. J. Stokman[1]

6.1   Relevance

Over the past decades, national economies have become more integrated through ever-intensifying foreign trade relations and international financial relations (Figure 6.1). For example, cross-border holdings of stocks and bonds have grown spectacularly in the past twenty years due to sharply-lower transaction costs and the worldwide trend towards capital account liberalisation and financial sector deregulation. An important aspect of international economic integration is the larger role of foreign direct investment (FDI) in the economy. FDI has grown at rates far greater than those of international trade or output since the late 1980s, especially among the industrialised countries. Estimates by UNCTAD (2002) put the total stock of FDI capital at 17.5 per cent of global GDP in 2000, more than double the size in 1990 (8.3%). A direct consequence of the greater presence of foreign-owned firms is the internationalisation of production. Currently, about 11 per cent of global production is accounted for by companies that are under control of foreign investors.

The rise in international economic interdependence means that economic conditions in one country have become increasingly sensitive to disturbances occurring in others. The 'traditional' channel through which economies may affect each other is formed by international trade flows.

Furthermore, it is widely recognised that the increase in international capital mobility has boosted the importance of financial markets as a conduit for the cross-border transmission of disturbances. Correlations among the major stock markets have greatly increased in the past twenty years (Berben and Jansen 2005). As a consequence, international trade flows and financial asset prices serve as the main linkages among economies in the macro-econometric models that are currently used for making forecasts and conducting policy analyses by national and international policy makers.

---

[1] Ministry of Social Affairs and Employment resp. De Nederlandsche Bank (Netherlands).

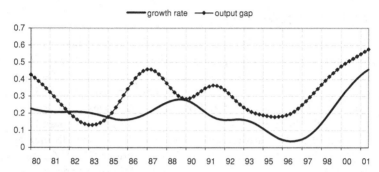

Figure 6.1. Average output co-movement among G7 countries
Note: Unweighted average of the bilateral correlations of quarterly real GDP growth rates and output gaps respectively, for all possible pairs among the United States, Japan, Germany, France, the United Kingdom, Italy and Canada. Before averaging across the 21 country pairs, correlations were smoothed using asymmetric rolling 40-quarter window, using a Gaussian kernel.

By contrast, comparatively little is known about the role of FDI and multinational firm behaviour in the transmission of disturbances from one country to the next at the aggregate level. The empirical literature on the impact of FDI mainly deals with supply-side effects on host economies in the longer run – focusing on the transfer of technology, management techniques and business models – rather than business cycle issues. Jansen and Stokman (2003) recently found that countries maintaining comparatively intense FDI relations also have business cycles that are more correlated (see section 6.4). Next to foreign trade flows and financial flows, FDI thus appears to be a separate, third channel through which economies may affect each other in an economically-significant fashion. This finding naturally raises the question of how the FDI channel operates. What are the underlying mechanisms at work? We take the labour market as example. As foreign-owned firms' shares in employment and output are substantial in quite a number of countries, their behaviour may be an important determinant of wage and employment outcomes in host countries (section 6.5).

Before getting into this, the following section offers a short description of the main trends in FDI positions over the past twenty years and their geographical composition in a number of industrialised countries. It also presents some figures on the significance of foreign affiliates for host-economy output and employment. Next, we briefly discuss the companies' motives for direct investment in section 6.3. Section 6.6 summarises our main findings and draws some policy conclusions.

6.2   Who is investing where?

Stocks and flows of FDI have grown rapidly across the OECD area since the mid-1980s, with a marked acceleration since 1995. FDI has also increased faster than international trade. The outward FDI position of Germany and France is currently around 25 per cent of GDP, four to five times the level of 1985. For traditional investor countries like the UK and the Netherlands, positions are much larger, 55 and 80 per cent respectively. The outward investment position of the US increased from five per cent of GDP in 1985 to 13 per cent in 2000. As outward and inward FDI positions tend to move in tandem over time, gross positions have grown much faster than net positions. The increase in FDI ties among the industrialised countries can thus be characterised as a process of diversification. The Japanese experience does not fit in with the general picture. Japanese corporations even reduced their presence abroad in the second half of the 1990s, while Japan's stock of inward FDI is very small (1% of GDP in 2000).

To gain some insight into where countries undertake FDI projects, Table 6.1 presents data on the geographical distribution of the stocks of inward and outward FDI for Canada, France, Germany, Netherlands, the UK and the US for the years 1985 and 2000. The most intensive FDI link is that between Canada and the US. In 1985 75 per cent of total Canadian inward FDI originated from the US, while in 2000 this was still 63 per cent. In general, the US is a major source and destination of FDI. In 2000, the UK was the largest direct investor in the US (17.6% of the US total), followed by Japan (13.5%) and the Netherlands (12.1%). The UK, Canada and the Netherlands received the largest amounts of American FDI. France, Germany and the Netherlands have established intensive FDI relations with EU countries, both as investors and as hosts. The overall trend towards diversification is also visible in the geographical distributions of the FDI positions, which have become more even over time. Finally, shares in the inward FDI portfolio and shares in the outward FDI portfolio are positively correlated. Inward and outward FDI move together, not only at the aggregate level, but also bilaterally. This observation confirms that the FDI process between two countries typically involves capital flows of comparable size in both directions, through which countries swap claims on their capital stocks.

The presence of foreign investors means that part of domestic output is produced by firms controlled by foreigners. Comprehensive data on the share of output accounted for by foreign affiliates are scarce. In Table 6.2 we have collected some data, taken from several sources, that may give an impression of the weight of foreign-owned companies in the

Table 6.1 *Bilateral FDI positions, 1985–2000*

	1985						2000					
	Canada	France	Germany	N'lands	UK	US	Canada	France	Germany	N'lands	UK	US
	Inward foreign direct investment position (% of total)											
Australia	0.1	0.0	0.1	0.0	4.7	1.8	0.5	0.0	0.0	0.2	3.4	1.7
Belgium	0.4	9.5	2.2	5.4	1.7	1.4	1.2	15.5	33.1	18.7	1.4	5.6
Canada		0.5	0.9	0.2	2.9	9.3		0.5	0.3	0.2	3.2	9.4
France	1.7		6.1	4.4	4.4	3.6	9.9		7.2	5.2	16.7	10.8
Germany	2.9	13.5		7.7	2.4	8.0	2.4	11.4		13.8	8.9	10.3
Italy	0.0	4.3	1.4	0.1	0.5	0.7	0.3	4.0	1.2	0.4	0.8	0.5
Japan	2.5	0.5	5.8	2.6	2.2	10.5	2.6	1.9	1.8	3.5	3.6	13.5
Netherlands	2.2	17.1	12.7		18.0	20.1	4.7	19.2	19.7		14.1	12.1
Sweden	0.4	1.0	2.1	2.1	1.5	1.3	0.8	2.3	1.7	2.5	1.3	1.8
Switzerland	1.7	10.3	14.0	11.2	6.3	5.7	2.0	7.9	4.9	4.8	3.1	5.7
UK	9.6	13.7	8.9	14.1		23.6	7.3	13.7	7.1	15.7		17.6
US	75.1	23.1	37.6	34.3	51.2		63.2	15.0	17.5	21.6	34.4	
Total (% of GDP)	18.6	5.6	4.6	12.1	12.1	4.4	28.4	19.5	23.8	64.6	30.9	12.4

(*cont.*)

Table 6.1 (*cont.*)

	Outward foreign direct investment position (% of total)											
Australia	2.1	0.5	1.3	0.7	9.6	3.8	1.3	0.6	0.6	0.8	1.3	2.7
Belgium	0.2	11.9	9.2	7.0	1.7	2.5	1.0	13.8	7.7	12.1	9.9	3.5
Canada		2.0	3.8	3.3	6.8	20.4		7.0	1.1	1.8	1.7	10.0
France	0.3		8.3	5.6	2.9	3.3	1.3		5.0	6.1	3.6	3.0
Germany	1.1	8.9		9.3	4.2	7.3	1.1	5.6		10.5	3.9	3.9
Italy	0.3	4.2	3.8	1.4	0.9	2.6	0.9	3.2	3.4	1.8	0.6	1.7
Japan	0.5	0.9	1.5	1.0	1.0	4.0	1.6	1.7	1.7	0.4	0.8	4.6
Netherlands	0.9	7.0	6.1		5.2	3.1	2.3	9.0	13.2		30.4	9.1
Sweden	0.0	0.1	0.5	0.3	0.6	0.4	0.3	0.6	1.4	0.8	3.2	1.8
Switzerland	1.0	16.3	7.4	5.6	1.3	6.8	1.5	4.0	3.1	4.9	1.1	4.3
UK	7.7	6.5	4.9	5.8		14.3	10.4	12.7	10.4	10.7		18.7
US	69.2	24.2	29.7	41.3	35.2		48.3	25.4	28.0	25.7	23.5	
Total (% of GDP)	11.8	4.6	6.6	29.6	21.7	5.5	32.0	32.8	24.9	79.8	63.3	13.2
Correlation in-out	1.00	0.82	0.91	0.94	0.94	0.47	0.98	0.71	0.57	0.91	0.68	0.75
same, excl US	0.90	0.69	0.44	0.67	0.32		0.51	0.78	0.68	0.95	0.52	

Sources: OECD (2002), Deutsche Bundesbank (2002), Statistics Canada (2002), Sparling (2002), Banque de France (2002), UK National Statistics (2002), Borga and Yogarson (2002) and Borga and Mataloni (2001).

Table 6.2 *The role of foreign affiliates in host economies*

	share in host country GDP of US affliates (%)		estimated share in host country GDP of all foreign affiliates (%)		share in host country man. employment of all for affiliates (%)	p.m. US share in host country of all FDI stock (%)	
	1989	1999	1989	1999	1998	1989	1999
Australia	4.9	4.7	18.7	10.8		26.3	43.6
Belgium	5.6	5.1					
Canada	9.5	10.0	14.5	14.4		65.6	69.5
France	2.3	2.6	12.0	15.0	27.8	19.1	17.3
Germany	3.0	2.9	9.3	12.0	7.2	32.4	24.2
Ireland	12.4	16.8			36.8		
Italy	1.9	2.0	12.7	15.0	14.0	15.0	13.3
Japan	0.5	0.7	1.0	1.7	1.8	50.5	40.5
Netherlands	5.8	4.5	21.4	17.7	21.9	27.1	25.4
Sweden	1.2	2.6	12.2	19.6	26.8	9.9	13.2
Switzerland	2.9	3.3	12.3	10.3		23.6	32.0
UK	6.2	7.0	14.7	14.9	27.3	42.1	47.0
US			4.1	5.6	13.4		

Sources: columns 1 and 2: Borga and Yogarson (2002); US data: Zeile (2002); columns 3 and 4; own calculations; column 5: UNCTAD (2002) and OECD (2002); columns 6 and 7: UNCTAD (2002).

manufacturing sector and the total economy in thirteen host countries in 1989 and 1998–1999. Table 6.2 shows the output produced by majority-owned foreign affiliates (MOFA) of US companies as a percentage of host country GDP in 12 countries.[2] In 1999, US MOFAs alone were responsible for seventeen per cent of Irish GDP, ten per cent of Canadian GDP and seven per cent of UK GDP. In Australia, Belgium and the Netherlands their output share was around five per cent. We combine this information with the share of the US in the host country's inward FDI position, if available, to arrive at a back-of-the-envelope estimate of the output share of all foreign affiliates taken together.[3]

Our, admittedly rough, estimates indicate that between ten and twenty per cent of GDP could be accounted for by foreign-owned firms, pointing to a potentially substantial role for foreign affiliates in the domestic economy. Because the US economy is so large, foreign affiliates still account for a relatively small part of US GDP (5.6% in 1999 and 6.0% in 2000

[2] US FDI in MOFAs is approximately 85% of total outward FDI.
[3] We computed the estimated output share of all foreign affiliates by dividing the US MOFA output share by the US share in inward FDI (as reported by the host country).

(Zeile 2002)). Still, this represents a substantial increase from the level ten years ago (4.1%). Table 6.2 also reports, depending on availability, the share in employment in the manufacturing sector accounted for by foreign affiliates in 1998. These data, too, are suggestive of an important role of foreign firms in their host economies.

6.3   Why do companies invest abroad?

FDI is much too complex to single out just a few dominant motives of investment. In earlier studies on FDI, the presence of raw commodities, cheap labour, market imperfections and the desire to expand market power were considered to be decisive to a direct investor. Nowadays, explanations of FDI focus more on firm-specific advantages, owing to product or process superiority, superior marketing and distribution networks. Typically, firm-specific assets cannot be split and often have a large and costly research content. FDI ensures protection of such intangibles and produces benefits through economies of scale and scope. When firm-specific advantages are strong enough to outweigh the costs of setting up or taking over a production unit abroad, FDI might be attractive. Other relevant determinants of FDI are market size, the quality of the infrastructure and political and economic stability (Moran 1998).

Alternative explanations of FDI focus on regulatory restrictions like tariffs, quotas and so on, which hinder exports or imports, and might therefore be a reason to invest inside the country or free trade area (jumping the tariff). Although countries have been deregulating their home markets for quite some time, national borders are still formidable barriers to trade in goods and services (Obstfeld and Rogoff 2000). As to the connection with international trade, a distinction between vertical and horizontal FDI is meaningful. With horizontal FDI, the investment involves the complete production process. Horizontal FDI is likely to be a substitute for foreign trade, as the underlying motive is better serving local markets. With vertical FDI, different parts of the production process are located in different countries, in order to reduce production costs. This type of investment is likely to be trade-creating, as intermediate products at different stages have to be moved cross-border from one location to another. In most cases, FDI projects combine aspects of both types, which might explain why empirical studies have found mixed results. A quick-and-dirty inspection of international trade trends does not suggest that in general foreign trade relations have been replaced by direct investments. On the contrary, foreign trade shares for countries like Germany, France and the Netherlands were growing substantially during the merger and acquisition (M&A) wave in the second half of the 1990s.

Perhaps this could be explained by vertical direct investment, perhaps by EMU benefits from further integration and the disappearing of exchange rate risk.

Theories of managerial discipline predicting that inefficient domestic firms will be taken over by foreigners and the surviving plants will perform better, post-acquisition, find little empirical support (Ravenscraft and Scherer 1989). FDI motivated by a desire to acquire operational efficiency is more common (McGuckin and Nguyen 1995). Harris and Robinson (2002) show that the British plants picked by foreign MNCs performed above-average compared to other manufacturing firms. This is an interesting observation, because it suggests that firm-specific spillover effects may go in both directions.

Greenfield investments are, generally speaking, expected to produce higher returns than M&A brownfield investments. Some tend to qualify M&As as just re-labelling companies. In developed countries a relatively high proportion of direct investments consist of M&As, especially in the second half of the 1990s. Barrell and Pain (1997) warn that it would be wrong to suggest that the benefits of FDI must be limited in developed countries because of the high M&A content. They produce evidence that technology transfers from foreign-owned firms to the UK and Germany has stimulated the rate of technical progress in these two countries.

To sum up, direct investment is more then a cross-border (portfolio) investment. To quote Dunning (1970, p. 4): '. . .This might simply be informal managerial or technical guidance; on the other hand it could incorporate the dissemination of valuable knowledge and/or entrepreneurship in the form of research and development, production technology, marketing skills and so on; *none of which usually accompanies investment*' (emphasis added).

6.4   What are the international spillover effects of FDI?

Supply-side effects

Theoretically, positive growth effects from FDI can be explained by more recent developments in growth theory, which highlights the importance of improvements in technology, efficiency and productivity in stimulating growth (Ewe-Ghee Lim 2001). Empirically, there is firm evidence that positive spill-over effects on economic activity do exist, but there is disagreement on the magnitude (Blomström, Globerman and Kokko 2000). For developed countries, the available evidence suggests that productivity of domestically-owned companies is positively related to the presence of foreign firms. The magnitude of these supply-side effects is largely dependent on the ability of the host economy to absorb foreign technology. If there is a large difference in technological level between direct investor and host country, domestic companies will have difficulty in adopting the new technology and so the positive spillover on the economy will be limited. This explains why FDI is highly concentrated in developed countries.

Demand-side effects

Apart from affecting the supply side in the longer run, FDI (inward as well as outward) may make the domestic economy more sensitive to economic disturbances abroad in the short run. The macroeconomic vulnerability related to outward FDI has to do with the consequences that disturbances abroad might have for the financial position of the investing domestic firms. Unfavourable developments abroad may reduce the value of their overseas investment projects and thus the value of the domestic firms. This reduction of net worth may lead to lower stock prices and greater difficulties for domestic firms in securing external finance for planned domestic investment projects, both in the capital market and with banks. Domestic investment may thus be hurt via the balance sheet channel and the stock market channel (Tobin's q). The fall in stock prices may adversely affect domestic consumption via wealth effects, balance sheet effects and confidence effects. These types of effects are outside the scope of this chapter, however, as financial asset prices play a crucial part in the transmission of shocks.

As the inward position represents imported capital, the host country always runs the risk that foreign investors, for whatever reason, may want to withdraw their money. More generally, a deterioration of the economic conditions in the foreign investor's home country may weaken the financial health of the parent company, which in turn may lead the multinational to decide to lower employment, wages and investment at affiliates in host countries. As explained in the next section, international rent sharing within multinational companies may be at the root of this type of vulnerability. Within a multinational corporation, firm-specific assets are a joint input, giving economies of scale at the company level rather than at the level of the individual plant. Global profits and losses may be shared (with a lag) with affiliates and their workers. Due to the trend towards a greater presence of foreign firms, domestic wages and employment may thus increasingly reflect international factors in addition to local economic conditions (Blanchflower, Oswald and Sanfey, 1996; Budd, Konings and Slaughter 2002).

International business cycle co-movement

In this section we investigate whether there is a positive relationship between the size of bilateral foreign direct investment positions and the degree of business cycle co-movement among countries. If two countries have invested a lot in each other, do their output cycles tend to move in a more synchronised way? In addition we examine whether this relationship has changed over time.

Taking a bilateral perspective, we focus on the experience in the past twenty years of Canada, France, Germany, the Netherlands, the UK and the US. For these countries bilateral FDI positions (both inward and outward) that are consistently measured across time are available for a long period, including estimates for the year 2001.[4] We will refer to these six countries as the reporting countries, since the FDI positions are measured from their perspective. We look at the bilateral linkages of the six reporting countries among themselves and with six other countries (Australia, Belgium, Italy, Japan, Sweden and Switzerland). These latter six countries are selected because of their size and their importance as an importer and exporter of FDI. Taken together, our twelve countries represent seventy per cent of the outstanding stock of FDI at the end of 2000. For each reporting country we thus distinguish bilateral links with eleven countries, which we will refer to as its partner countries.

The data on the FDI positions are available on an annual basis and reflect the state at the end of the year. We define the bilateral FDI position of country R versus country P as the sum of R's stock of direct investments in P and P's stock of direct investments in R, as reported by country R (in R's currency). We take the sum of both the inward and the outward position as our measure of the bilateral FDI link, as disturbances in country P may affect economic conditions in country R via both types of exposure. For instance, an unfavourable shock in country P may reduce the value of domestic firms' investment projects located in P, depressing their stock prices. This in turn may negatively affect domestic consumption and investment via wealth effects, confidence effects and balance sheet effects. Alternatively, companies in P may react to the worsening situation in their home country by reducing their presence abroad,

---

[4] Data on bilateral FDI positions for the US, Germany and Canada are available for the years 1982–2001, for France for 1988–2001, for the Netherlands for 1984–2001 and for 1984 and 1987–2001 for the UK. Missing observations have been estimated on the basis of bilateral FDI flows. Sources are OECD (2002a), Banque de France (2002), Deutsche Bundesbank (2003), Statistics Canada (2002), Sparling (2002), Borga and Yorgason (2002) and Borga and Mataloni (2001). Recent data are also available on the websites of Statistics Canada, the Deutsche Bundesbank, the Banque de France, De Nederlandsche Bank, the UK Office of National Statistics and the US Department of Commerce.

cutting back employment and/or reducing investment at their affiliates in country R and other countries.

In the absence of a well-established definition of international output co-movement, we distinguish five measures of the degree of output co-movement. The first measure is the correlation of the quarterly growth rates of real GDP. The second measure is the correlation of the quarterly output gaps, the log difference between actual real GDP and its trend level. The third measure is the business cycle coherence on a quarterly basis, which is based on business cycle dating by the IMF (2002).[5] It equals the fraction of time that two countries are in the same business cycle phase (expansion or recession). The fourth and fifth co-movement measures are the correlation of the annual growth rates of real GDP and the correlation of the annual output gaps respectively. The correlations derived from annual data may also pick up spillover effects that occur with a delay of one or more quarters.

Figure 6.1 offered an impression of the average degree of business cycle co-movement among the G7 countries (the United States, Japan, the United Kingdom, Germany, France, Italy and Canada) in the years 1980–2001, based on our first two measures. The graph first of all shows that the degree of output co-movement has been high by historical standards in recent years. Moreover, its behaviour over time differs from period to period. In the 1980s the average correlation of real GDP growth rates was fairly constant, in the first half of the 1990s it substantially declined, while in recent years it sharply increased. This non-monotonic time profile underscores the importance of time-variation in the mixture of common and idiosyncratic shocks. Given that the time profile of FDI linkages (and other measures of interdependence) is strictly increasing, Figure 6.1 makes clear that any link between FDI and business cycle co-movement must be hidden in the cross-section of countries.[6]

Our estimation method has to take into account that time variation in the mix and size of disturbances may obscure the relationship between FDI positions and output correlations. For this reason, cross-section regressions for each reporting country are the natural estimation design. Due to the limited number of observations (11) per country, we have pooled the cross-section regressions for the six reporting countries into

---

[5] The IMF (2002) dated business cycle peaks and troughs for the level of real GDP on the basis of the Bry-Boschan algorithm for twenty-one industrial countries using quarterly data for the years 1973–2000. We use this dating of (level) recessions and expansions to calculate the coherence for each pair of countries, which is defined as the fraction of time the two countries are in a recession or an expansion simultaneously.

[6] Recent empirical evidence on increasing business cycle co-movement is provided by Artis and Zhang (1999), Luginbuhl and Koopman (2003), Lumsdaine and Prasad (2003) and Carvalho and Harvey (2003), among others.

a single one.[7] To find out whether more intensive FDI linkages are associated with a greater degree of output co-movement, we estimate the following regression equation

$$\rho(i, j) = \alpha_0 + \alpha_1 D_1 + \alpha_2 D_2 + \alpha_3 D_3 + \alpha_4 D_4 + \alpha_5 D_5 + \beta FDIP(i, j) \quad (1)$$

where D_i indicate country-specific dummies, which are one if the observation refers to reporting country i, and zero otherwise. $\rho(i, j)$ denotes the measure of business cycle co-movement between reporting country i and partner country j (11 countries) over a certain time-span, while $FDIP(i, j)$ is the average strength of the corresponding FDI link. Eq. (1) assumes that the intercept differs across countries, but that β is the same for each country. Differences in intercepts take into account fixed differences across countries and may also correct for methodological differences between national FDI statistics. The parameter β measures the sensitivity of output co-movement to variations in the intensity of FDI relations. We conduct diagnostic tests to see if the data support the implied restriction that all countries have the same β.

If the sample period for which we compute output co-movement measures and FDI exposures happens to be characterised by a preponderance of common shocks, all $\rho(i, j)$ will tend to be large, which will translate into high estimates of the intercepts $\alpha_0 + \alpha_i$ in eq. [1]. By contrast, if the sample period is dominated by idiosyncratic shocks, all $\rho(i, j)$ will tend to be small, resulting in low estimates of $\alpha_0 + \alpha_i$. However, conditional on the mixture of shocks, differences in $\rho(i, j)$ for a given country i vis-à-vis its partners could still be explained by differences in the intensity of the bilateral economic relations. The coefficient β can thus be interpreted as the effect of a unit increase in FDI exposure given the mixture and size of shocks in the years over which output co-movement and FDI positions have been measured.

The average vulnerability through bilateral FDI linkages – denoted by $FDIP(i, j)$ – over a certain time-span is calculated as follows. Since both inward and outward FDI make a country more sensitive to outside developments, we first compute, for each year, the total FDI position (both inward and outward) of country i vis-à-vis country j, as recorded by country i (in the currency of country i). To calculate the vulnerability of reporting country i and partner country j that is associated with this amount, we express it as a percentage of GDP of country i and j, respectively. Since a correlation is a symmetric concept, we take the simple average of both vulnerability measures as our annual observation of the

---

[7] We have also estimated separate cross-section regressions for each reporting country. These results are available from the authors upon request.

exposure associated with the bilateral FDI link.[8] $FDIP(i, j)$ is the average of the annual observations over the time-span under consideration.

Simple pooling of six cross-section regressions into a single one renders sixty-six observations, which implies some sort of double counting of the observations relating to the links among the six reporting countries. Although there are sixty-six independent observations on FDI exposures, there are only fifty-one unique observations on the correlations. Observations relating to links among the six reporting countries thus get double weight in the sum of squares, once with $FDIP(i, j)$ according to country i's statistics and once with $FDIP(i, j)$ according to country j's statistics. Note that estimation of six separate cross-section equations would implicitly involve the same double counting. For this reason we always report two sets of estimation results: the first one is based on OLS (66 observations), the second one on weighted least squares (WLS). Observations relating to links among the six reporting countries are assigned a weight of $\frac{1}{2}$, all other observations a weight of 1, so that all observations on $\rho(i, j)$ receive equal weight in the sum of squares. The effective number of observations in case of estimation by WLS is 51.[9]

Table 6.3 reports the empirical results for the complete sample period 1982–2001 and three subperiods, 1982–1989, 1990–1994 and 1995–2001. This particular split-up of the sample is based on the work by Helbling and Bayoumi (2003), who studied business cycles in the period 1973–2002 for the G7 countries. They found that the years 1990–1994 were characterised by an atypical pattern of business cycle linkages, probably because of the aftermath of German reunification and the collapse of the Japanese asset market bubble. Moreover, FDI grew very rapidly in the period 1995–2001.

The empirical results provide supportive evidence for a link between bilateral FDI patterns and output co-movement patterns.

---

[8] Note that the same dollar amount may imply vastly different vulnerabilities because GDPs differ greatly across countries. For example, the Dutch FDI position versus the US at the end of 2000 amounted to 35% of Dutch GDP or 1.6% of US GDP. We use purchasing power parity exchange rates to convert partner country GDPs into reporting country currencies. Assigning the two individual vulnerability measures the same weight in the calculation of FDIP is supported by the data. When we included both measures in eq. (1) as separate explanatory variables, the hypothesis of equal slope coefficients could not be rejected at the usual significance levels. Note that the use of the bilateral position implicitly assumes that indirect exposures via third countries are relatively unimportant.

[9] FDIP may possibly be endogenous. For example, FDI location decisions may partly be driven by the desire to insure against national business cycle risks. This argument implies a negative association between output correlations and FDI intensity. Our working hypothesis is that the association is positive, however. To the extent risk diversification motives play a part, some downward bias may be introduced, which will tend to make it more difficult to obtain a positive estimate that is statistically significant. Consequently, significant positive estimates cannot be attributed to this kind of endogeneity bias.

Table 6.3 *Pooled cross-section regression of output co-movement on FDI positions*

	OLS-estimates				WLS-estimates			
	estimate beta	t(beta)	p-value test a(i) = a	p-value test b(i) = b	estimate beta	t(beta)	p-value test a(i) = a	p-value test b(i) = b
(a) quarterly growth rate of real GDP								
1982–2001	0.014	2.83	0.321	0.165	0.020	4.01	0.135	0.331
1982–1989	0.018	2.10	0.367	0.393	0.023	2.62	0.257	0.356
1990–1994	0.025	2.32	0.664	0.504	0.030	2.78	0.393	0.486
1995–2001	0.019	5.36	0.088	0.612	0.023	6.30	0.011	0.721
(b) quarterly output gap (HP filter)								
1982–2001	0.021	2.93	0.331	0.328	0.022	2.97	0.224	0.428
1982–1989	0.026	2.44	0.028	0.503	0.018	1.66	0.007	0.394
1990–1994	0.027	2.08	0.242	0.651	0.027	2.17	0.046	0.887
1995–2001	0.016	2.71	0.125	0.476	0.025	3.83	0.150	0.657
(c) business cycle indicator (coherence)								
1982–2001	0.448	2.97	0.225	0.843	0.361	2.01	0.373	0.847
1982–1989	0.083	0.43	0.942	0.286	0.063	0.28	0.932	0.047
1990–1994	1.319	2.48	0.274	0.842	0.874	1.49	0.359	0.658
1995–2001	0.325	1.85	0.054	0.998	0.365	1.70	0.086	0.990
(d) annual growth rate of real GDP								
1982–2001	0.023	3.10	0.184	0.367	0.024	3.12	0.159	0.475
1982–1989	0.021	2.06	0.000	0.594	0.017	1.69	0.000	0.407
1990–1994	0.048	2.64	0.245	0.727	0.043	2.30	0.078	0.783
1995–2001	0.017	3.06	0.102	0.982	0.020	3.23	0.158	0.907
(e) annual output gap (HP filter)								
1982–2001	0.024	2.79	0.226	0.643	0.022	2.36	0.205	0.494
1982–1989	0.025	3.04	0.120	0.921	0.019	2.05	0.183	0.910
1990–1994	0.021	2.34	0.181	0.759	0.020	2.20	0.111	0.871
1995–2001	0.021	2.81	0.416	0.979	0.027	2.92	0.539	0.967

Contemporaneous correlations of quarterly growth rates are significantly higher for economies that have intensive investment relations than for countries that have less-intensive investment relations. Moreover, the positive association of FDI and output co-movement is more apparent in the most recent years, as evidenced by the larger point estimate and t-statistic of the slope coefficient β for the sub-period 1995–2001 (5.36 for OLS; 6.30 for WLS), compared to that for the complete sample (2.83 for OLS; 4.01 for WLS). The estimate of β indicates that a difference in FDI exposure of one percentage point is associated with a 0.02 percentage point higher output correlation in recent years.

Table 6.3 (part (b)) shows that there is also a statistically significant positive association between the intensity of FDI relations and the correlation of output gaps for all sub-periods considered. This holds for both the OLS and the WLS estimates. However, the relationship does not appear to have gained in strength in recent years. Measuring output co-movement by business cycle coherence, we find a positive and significant β-estimate for the complete sample (1982–2001), but for the eighties there seems to be no connection between FDI relations and output co-movement (Table 6.3, part (c)). Finally, the results for correlations derived from annual data also point to a positive association of FDI exposures and business cycle linkages (Table 6.3 parts (d) and (e)). Lastly, parameter tests show that the pooled regression design is appropriate, as (with one exception) the hypothesis of equal slope coefficients across reporting countries cannot be rejected at conventional significance levels, while the hypothesis of equal intercepts is rejected in a number of cases.[10]

The evidence presented thus far only focuses on FDI links between countries. Economies are also linked by international trade ties, however, which is an alternative explanation of international business cycle co-movement. Moreover, it is likely that countries that invest a lot in each other will also tend to trade a lot with each other. The countries of the European Union, or the US and Canada, are a case in point. Investment ties and trade ties may also vastly differ, however. For example, the share of the US in the foreign trade of the Netherlands is only four per cent, whereas its share in Dutch FDI capital is more than twenty per cent. The fact that geographical distributions of FDI exposures and foreign trade relations are correlated, implies that the estimates in Table 6.3 may partly reflect the effects of trade relations (or economic relations in general).

---

[10] There is also some evidence that the FDI-output co-movement relationship may be non-linear. Regression equations that feature the square root of FDIP generally perform somewhat better than specifications in which FDIP enters linearly, especially for the more recent periods which are characterised by higher FDI exposures. Results are available upon request.

To shed light on this issue, we examine the role of bilateral trade in explaining output co-movement patterns. Estimation results indicate that for the years 1982–2001 bilateral trade ties are most important while bilateral FDI ties are not. However, correlations of real GDP growth rates are found to be more closely related to FDI relations than trade relations. Consequently, there is strong and robust evidence for a link between bilateral economic relationships and bilateral business cycle correlations. However, it is difficult to disentangle the effects of FDI relations and those of foreign trade relations.

The results for the various sub-periods suggest, however, that a remarkable change has occurred over the past twenty years. According to both estimation methods, bilateral FDI relations are far more closely linked to bilateral output co-movement patterns than trade relations in the most recent period 1995–2001. This holds in particular for correlations of real GDP growth rates, but the same pattern emerges for the output gap and the other co-movement measures. The finding that trade relations have become less important could partly be explained by the fact that horizontal FDI is a substitute for international trade. By contrast, the years 1990–1994 appear to have been characterised by a more-dominant influence of foreign trade relations. For the early years of the sample (1982–1989) the picture is mixed. In most cases the estimates of both β and γ are insignificant, implying that it is difficult to disentangle the roles of trade and FDI as transmission channels of disturbances. For the output gap correlations we find a significant effect of FDI relations, but not of trade relations when estimating by OLS. We get a similar pattern using WLS for correlations of real GDP growth rates.

6.5 Role of FDI from a labour market perspective

This section outlines how FDI may affect domestic labour market conditions. Given the low degree of international labour mobility, labour markets are typically thought of as being determined by national regulations and governmental policies, negotiations between national employer organisations and trade unions and domestic economic conditions and so on. Blanchflower, Oswald and Sanfey (1996) argue that, with increasing globalisation, this closed economy perspective may miss important aspects of wage setting.

Multinational companies are by their very nature internationally oriented. As foreign-owned firms' shares in employment and output are substantial in quite a number of countries (Table 6.1), their behaviour may be an important determinant of wage and employment outcomes in host countries. Multinational firms have a strong incentive to create an internal market across national borders. They may impose company strategies and labour practices on local production units. The option to reallocate activities to other countries or to withdraw from markets altogether gives multinational firms a strong bargaining position (Edwards, Rees and Coller 1999).[11] Unlike (direct investment) capital, labour throughout the world has been, so far, unable to organise itself across nation states (Ietto-Gillies 2000). Edwards, Rees and Coller (1999) examine the consequences of corporate restructuring, based on information provided by trade unions in European countries. They find that unions are at best involved in negotiating the consequences of mergers and acquisitions, but are rarely involved in the initial decision.

Rent sharing

Within an industry, profits are often shared with local firms and local workers belonging to that particular industry (Christofides and Oswald 1992; Oswald 1996). Apart from local factors, such as the profitability of the individual company, industry-wide profits exert a separate, independent influence on wages paid by the firms in the industry. In the literature, this phenomenon is known as *economic rent sharing*.

Within a multinational corporation, firm-specific assets – such as innovations and knowledge, management skills, brands, distribution networks and so on – are a joint input. Typically these firm-specific assets cannot be split and often require a large investment in research and development. Organising production within a multinational firm protects intangible assets, creating economies of scale and scope at the company level rather than the level of the local business unit. Cross-border profit (or loss) sharing is the natural consequence of the sharing of firm-specific assets with subsidiaries that is essential to a multinational operation. The recent global economic downturn has seen quite a few examples of multinational parent losses that had major consequences for wages, employment, investment projects and (internal and external) financing at the affiliate level in host countries. However, subsidiaries may also affect parents, as a number of recent accounting scandals have shown. Wages and employment at the affiliate level may therefore be determined by local factors as well as profitability at the multinational's top level.

Budd and Slaughter (2000) and Budd, Konings and Slaughter (2002) are the first empirical studies on cross-border profit sharing within

---

[11] An interesting example is the Volkswagen agreement in 2001, which led to more flexible work conditions and wage moderation. It was quite clear that the management explicitly used the argument that production could be relocated if the outcome was not satisfactory for the management (Andersen 2003).

multinational firms. Budd and Slaughter (2000) analyse 1,000 Canadian labour contracts in manufacturing from 1980 up to 2000. They find support for profit sharing across the borders of the US and Canada in both directions: US industry profits have a significantly-positive effect on wages of US-owned affiliates located in Canada. Canadian industry profits affect positively wages of Canadian-owned affiliates located in the US. However, US industry profits had a negative impact on wages in Canadian domestic companies. As high profits in the US also point to strength of the American businesses, domestically Canadian-owned companies feel competitive pressure and respond by restraining wages. Budd, Konings and Slaughter (2002) also find micro-evidence of cross-border profit sharing by multinationals within Europe. Their study is based on panel data analysis for almost 900 parent companies concentrated in Western Europe (France, Germany, Italy and Belgium) and about 2,000 affiliates operating in Europe from 1993–1998. With an elasticity of foreign affiliate wages to parent profits per worker of 0.03, about twenty per cent of observed variation in affiliate wages could be explained.

We are not aware of firm-level studies on cross-border profit sharing in terms of employment. However, there is ample anecdotal evidence to be found in newspaper reports on employment decisions in foreign affiliates that appear to be motivated by the financial needs of the multinational parent company rather than by purely local economic conditions. For this reason, we will also investigate whether international rent sharing might express itself in a sensitivity of domestic employment to profitability conditions abroad.

Empirical analysis

Inspired by the empirical evidence for profit sharing within industries as well as within multinational firms, this section investigates whether some sort of profit sharing can be detected at the level of national economies. In the spirit of the rent-sharing literature, we look at whether profits at a higher level of aggregation than the unit of observation (country) exert an independent influence on national real wages. In addition, we investigate whether employment is directly affected by this mechanism. Given the facilitating role of FDI and multinational firms, our empirical analysis focuses on the six largest recipients of direct investment capital: the US, the UK, Germany, France, the Netherlands and Belgium. Together, they host over seventy per cent of all FDI capital in the OECD area. The sample consists of annual observations in the period 1982–2000.

Our empirical work utilises standard equations for the real wage rate and aggregate employment to which we have added a variable that may capture international rent sharing. The standard analytical framework underlying the empirical modelling of the labour market assumes that unions and employers first bargain about the wage rate and that employers then choose employment. Wages are typically explained by domestic factors such as consumer prices, labour productivity and national wage pressure variables such as the unemployment rate. Employment mainly depends on the real wage rate and the level of output. We estimate the following equations for real wages and aggregate employment in the business sector:

$$\Delta w = \alpha_0 + \alpha_1 \Delta apl - \alpha_2 \Delta ur_{-1} + \alpha_3 fp_{-i} - \lambda(w - \delta_1 apl + \delta_2 ur_{-1})_{-1} \quad (2)$$

$$\Delta l = \gamma_0 + \gamma_1 \Delta w + \gamma_2 \Delta y + \gamma_3 fp_{-i} - \varphi(l - y - \phi_1 w - \phi_2 t)_{-1} \quad (3)$$

w	log of real wage per employee
apl	log of average productivity of labour
ur	unemployment rate
fp	foreign profitability variable
l	log of employment in business sector
y	log of production volume of business sector
t	linear trend

Since the time series involved are non-stationary, equations (2) and (3) are of the error-correction type, with the long-run relationship appearing in the last term. The parameters λ and ϕ measure the speed of adjustment towards the long-run equilibrium. The expected sign of all slope coefficients is positive. Real wages are determined by labour productivity and the bargaining power of labour, which is negatively related to the unemployment rate. The employment equation is derived from a CES-production function, in which employment depends on real wages, output and a (labour saving) autonomous rate of technology progress.

To investigate whether the micro-evidence on international rent sharing might have a counterpart at the aggregate level; we introduce into the regression equations a variable measuring foreign profitability (*fp*). Conceptually, the variable *fp* plays the same part as industry-wide profitability in studies on rent sharing within industries using firm-level data (Christofides and Oswald 1992). The variable *fp* for country *i* is calculated as the weighted average of the capital income shares in the business sector in the countries of origin of the direct investors in country *i*.[12]

---

[12] The weighting scheme aggregates across eight countries of origin, the six countries for which the analysis is done plus Italy and Japan. Data on the geographical composition of inward FDI capital are taken from UNCTAD (2002). It would also have been interesting to do the analysis with *fp* defined as the weighted average of profits at the parent company level of all foreign-owned firms operating in country *i*. Unfortunately, such data are unavailable.

The weighting scheme to calculate fp is inspired by the idea that foreign direct investment and multinational firms are the channel through which domestic labour markets are affected. The FDI channel may also explain why the economic developments in the US are more important for European countries than seems to be justified based on international trade patterns alone. For example, for the Netherlands exports to the US amount to five per cent of total exports, whereas over twenty per cent of imported FDI capital originates from the US.

As we focus here on the business-cycle effects of FDI through the cross-border transmission of economic shocks, the foreign-profitability measure is added to the dynamic part of the equation only.[13] Empirical work on rent sharing finds that changes in industry profits take time to pass through to firm-level wages, with the lag ranging from one to three years (Christofides and Oswald 1992; Blanchflower, Oswald and Sanfey 1996). Based on preliminary experiments, foreign profitability enters the wage equations with a two-year lag and the employment equations with a one-year lag. Later, we conduct a sensitivity analysis, varying the lag from one to three years.

Throughout the exercise, we use uniform specifications and lag structures across countries, as we are primarily interested in the influence of foreign profitability. Furthermore, with an eye on the limited number of observations in our sample from 1982–2000, we have imposed some cross-country equality restrictions on the parameters of conventional determinants. We have freely estimated the coefficients of foreign profitability and the speeds of adjustment towards long-run equilibrium, whose t-statistics are equivalent to a cointegration test (Kremers, Ericsson and Dolado 1992). The imposed parameter restrictions are easily accepted by the data. The marginal significance level of the Wald test regarding the restrictions on the wage equations is 0.79. Its counterpart for the employment equations is 0.85. Finally, for both labour market variables we jointly estimate the six country equations by the Seemingly Unrelated Regression (SUR) method in order to exploit the possibility of contemporaneously-correlated disturbances across the equations.

Empirical results

Tables 6.4 and 6.5 present our preferred regressions for the real wage rate and employment respectively. Turning to the results on the regular determinants first, the estimated coefficients generally have the expected sign and are significantly different from zero. This holds for both short-run

---

[13] This is also consistent with the time series properties of the foreign profitability variable, which is found to be stationary.

Table 6.4 *Parameter estimates of country wage equations with* fp *lagged two years (1982–2000)*

Country (a)	Belgium	Netherlands	Germany	France	UK	US
Δapl	0.12	0.12	0.49	0.40	0.89	0.63
	(1.5)	(1.5)	(2.6)	(3.7)	(8.0)	(3.8)
Δur_{-1}	0	−0.007	−0.016	−0.007	−0.007	−0.007
	–	(7.7)	(3.3)	(–)	(–)	(–)
fp_{-2}	0.005	0.001	0.013	0.003	0.004	−0.003
	(1.6)	(0.8)	(4.4)	(2.6)	(2.0)	(1.4)
$LT(\lambda)$	0.41	0.42	0.60	0.57	0.54	0.24
	(2.6)	(3.3)	(10.5)	(5.0)	(2.9)	(2.4)
apl_{-1}	0.88	0.40	0.88	0.61	0.88	0.88
	(21.6)	(7.9)	(–)	(12.8)	(–)	(–)
ur_{-2}	−0.012	−0.012	−0.030	−0.018	−0.012	−0.012
	(10.6)	(–)	(6.9)	(5.5)	(–)	(–)
$dumGE$ (b)	–	–	0.12	–	–	–
			(12.7)			
$\overline{R}^2$	0.38	0.60	0.90	0.61	0.63	0.32
SE	0.014	0.006	0.012	0.006	0.009	0.012
LM1 (c)	0.66	0.74	0.76	0.11	0.26	0.23
LM2 (c)	0.90	0.05	0.32	0.26	0.19	0.44

T-values between brackets.
(a) Wald-test on all combined parameter restrictions: associated p-value = 0.79.
(b) DumGE is a German re-unification dummy: 0 in the period 1981–1990 and 1 from 1991 onwards.
(c) Associated p-values.

dynamics and long-run equilibrium relations. Gains in labour productivity boost real wages, while an increase in unemployment depresses real wages. In the UK and the US, real wages display a much-stronger short-run response to changes in labour productivity than in continental Europe, in particular the small open economies in Belgium and the Netherlands. In the long run, real wages move almost one-for-one with labour productivity in four countries.[14] Regarding the sensitivity of wages to unemployment, differences between the European countries and the US are limited. German wages are the most sensitive to unemployment, in the short run as well as in the long run. In Belgium, wages do not react to unemployment in the short run. The error correction coefficient in the real wage equations is significant for all countries, consistent with

---

[14] The long-run effect of productivity is rather muted in the Netherlands in particular. This might be due to the long-sustained policy of wage moderation, which was the result of the 1982 Wassenaar agreement (Den Butter and Mosch 2003).

Table 6.5 *Parameter estimates of country employment equations with* fp *lagged one year (1982–2000)*

Country (a)	Belgium	Netherlands	Germany	France	UK	US
Δw	−0.14	0.05	−0.13	−0.17	−0.52	−0.33
	(3.2)	(0.5)	(4.1)	(1.2)	(4.3)	(5.7)
Δy	0.28	0.14	0.24	0.72	0.42	0.63
	(6.8)	(1.5)	(5.2)	(7.0)	(3.5)	(19.6)
fp_{-1}	0.004	0.006	−0.001	−0.001	0.000	−0.000
	(6.2)	(4.1)	(0.7)	(0.8)	(0.1)	(0.2)
$LT(\varphi)$	0.11	0.34	0.46	0.15	0.58	0.45
	(7.2)	(6.3)	(5.9)	(3.5)	(4.5)	(5.1)
$w-1$	−0.72	−0.72	−0.72	−0.72	−0.72	−0.72
	(9.8)	(−)	(−)	(−)	(−)	(−)
t	−0.002	−0.002	−0.002	−0.002	−0.002	−0.006
	(2.0)	(−)	(−)	(−)	(−)	(6.0)
dumGE (b)	–	–	0.012	–	–	–
			(2.6)			
$\bar{R}^2$	0.89	0.88	0.89	0.68	0.83	0.88
SE	0.003	0.006	0.004	0.008	0.009	0.004
LM1 (c)	0.23	0.25	0.67	0.51	0.10	0.58
LM2 (c)	0.33	0.48	0.13	0.27	0.03	0.71

T-values between brackets.
(a) Wald-test on combined parameter restrictions: associated p-value = 0.85.
(b) DumGE is a German re-unification dummy: 0 in the period 1981–1990 and 1 from 1991 onwards.
(c) Associated p-value.

cointegration. In three countries, more than half of the deviation of actual and long-run equilibrium values is corrected within the space of one year.

The estimates for the employment equations show that in the short run, employment reacts more strongly to changes in real wages and output in the Anglo-Saxon countries than in continental Europe. The estimates for the UK and the US tend to be two to three times larger than their continental European counterparts. The high short-run output elasticity of France is the exception to this pattern. For Belgium and France, we also find that employment very slowly adjusts to deviations from the long-run equilibrium, although the estimated coefficients are significantly different from zero. In the case of France, it takes about four years to cut the initial disequilibrium in half. The corresponding number for the fastest adjusting labour market (UK) is less than one year. Remarkably, Germany has the same adjustment speed as the US. However, one should keep in mind that, given the shock in wages or output, deviations from the long-run equilibrium will be much less sizeable to begin with in the US. Overall, our findings are consistent with the widely-held view that labour markets in continental Europe are characterised by poor flexibility compared to the UK and the US.

We next discuss the main results on the influence of foreign profitability on national labour markets conditions. For wages, we find a statistically-significant effect at the five per cent level for Germany, France and the UK, while for Belgium there is some tentative supportive evidence for an influence of foreign profitability. Regarding employment, we find strong evidence for a role of foreign profitability in Belgium and the Netherlands. Consequently, the US is the only country for which we fail to detect any effects of foreign profitability. This may be related to the fact that, due to the large size of the American economy compared to the other countries, foreign-owned firms still account for a relatively minor part of US GDP (see Table 6.1). The phenomenon of international rent sharing may therefore not be widespread enough to register at the aggregate level in the US. As a sensitivity analysis, we also estimate equations (2) and (3) for other lag structures. The results from this sensitivity analysis do not alter our insights fundamentally.

Painting with a broad brush, an increase in capital income share abroad by one percentage point stimulates employment by around 0.5 per cent after one to two years in Belgium and the Netherlands, and raises real wages by around 0.5 per cent after two to three years in the larger European countries. In all countries, total compensation is temporarily 0.5 percentage points higher, providing a spending impulse to the domestic economy. Between 1997 and 2000 foreign profitability declined by about 1.5 percentage points for all six countries. The unusually-synchronised nature of the downturn of in 2001 may be partly due to the rent-sharing phenomenon. Of course, these numbers are rough approximations. For example, the rise in real wages will also affect employment, competitiveness and so on. Therefore, it might be useful to further analyse the overall implications of international rent sharing in the context of a macroeconomic multi-country model.

Tables 6.4 and 6.5 suggest that in small countries (Belgium and the Netherlands) it is employment that benefits from an improvement in profitability abroad, while in large countries (France, Germany and the UK) it is wages. One could say that the 'foreign dividend' is mostly paid out in the form of more jobs in Belgium and the Netherlands and in the form of higher wages in France, Germany and the UK. This might reflect differences in preferences of trade unions with respect to the trade-off between wages and employment. Trade unions in small open economies might be more aware of the negative effects of high wages on competitiveness of domestic firms in home and foreign markets. They may therefore be more avid to protect jobs or expand employment than to extract high wages from firms. By contrast, unions in large countries may feel less constrained by such considerations and focus more on securing high wages.

6.6   Summary and policy implications

This chapter examines to what extent the rapid expansion of foreign direct investment (FDI) and the internationalisation of production can be related to the phenomenon of more-synchronised business cycles. Both larger inward and outward investment positions may make the domestic economy more susceptible to economic disturbances abroad.

From our investigation, we conclude that before 1995 there is no strong evidence in favour of an independent role of FDI in explaining cross-country business cycle patterns. Although the degree of output co-movement tends to be higher for economies that have relatively-intensive investment relations, we find the same to be true for international trade relations. We thus find strong and robust evidence for a link between bilateral economic relationships and bilateral business cycle correlations, but multi-collinearity problems prevent a precise assessment of the respective contributions of trade and FDI. Trade patterns tend to explain the pattern of output co-movement better than FDI linkages in the years immediately following German reunification and the collapse of the Japanese asset market bubble (1990–1994). The strong growth of FDI since 1995 appears to have changed this picture. FDI linkages are much better able to explain the pattern of international business cycle linkages than foreign trade relations in the years 1995–2001. Regarding the vulnerability to foreign output spillovers that occur with a lag, we find that FDI exposures are relevant, but international trade relations are not. In contrast to the case of contemporaneous linkages, this result is also obtained for the complete sample, not just the most recent period.

The empirical results are supportive evidence for the view that apart from the foreign trade channel, FDI now constitutes a separate channel through which economies may affect each other in an economically-significant fashion. Moreover, foreign disturbances may influence the domestic economy for a longer time-span when relayed through the FDI channel than through the trade channel, which mainly operates contemporaneously.

Our research has two policy implications. The first one is that the trend towards greater economic interdependence through FDI implies an underlying tendency for business cycles to display a more synchronised behaviour than in the past. However, this is not to say that we will actually observe greater output co-movement in the future. As the experience of the 1990s teaches, the effects of large asymmetric shocks may overshadow the upward influence on account of increasing interdependence.

The second lesson for policy makers is that FDI appears to have become an important channel for the international transmission of disturbances. This aspect of global linkages should be incorporated into the macroeconomic models that are used for making forecasts, evaluating scenarios and conducting policy analyses by national policy makers and international organisations, such as the IMF and the OECD. Up until now, international trade and financial asset prices have served as the main linkages among individual economies in these models. Finding out exactly how the FDI channel operates constitutes an interesting research agenda. In related research, we present evidence for several countries that domestic labour market conditions (wages and/or employment) are partly determined by the profitability of firms abroad (Jansen and Stokman 2003). International rent sharing may thus be an important aspect of global economic linkages at the macro-level. Adding a variable measuring foreign profitability to the specification of wage or employment equations could be a useful first step towards the incorporation of the FDI channel into (large-scale) econometric models.

REFERENCES

Andersen, T. N. (2003),' Wage formation and European integration', *EC Economic Papers* No. 188.

Artis, M. J. and W. Zhang (1999), 'Further evidence on the international business cycle and the ERM', *Oxford Economic Papers* 51, pp. 120–132.

Banque de France (2002), *La balance des paiements et la position extérieur de la France* 2001 (Annex).

Barnett, S. A. and P. Sakellaris (1998), 'Nonlinear response of firm investment to Q: Testing a model of convex and non-convex adjustment costs', *Journal of Monetary Economics* 42, pp. 261–288.

Barrell, R. and N. Pain (1997), 'Foreign direct investment, technological change, and economic growth within Europe', *Economic Journal* 107, pp. 1770–1786.

Berben, R. P. and W. J. Jansen (2005), 'Co-movement in international equity markets: A sectoral view', *Journal of International Money and Finance*, Vol 24, No. 5, pp. 832–857.

Bernanke, B. S., M. Gertler and S. Gilchrist (1999), 'The financial accelerator in a quantitative business cycle framework'. In J. B. Taylor and M. Woodford (eds.), *Handbook of macroeconomics*, North-Holland, Elsevier, pp. 1341–1393.

Blanchflower, D. G., A. J. Oswald, and P. Sanfey, (1996), 'Wages, profits and rent sharing', *Quarterly Journal of Economics* 111, pp. 227–251.

Blomström, M., S. Globerman and A. Kokko (2000), 'The determinants of host country spillovers from foreign direct investment', CEPR Discussion Paper 2350.

Boone, L., C. Giorno and P. Richardson (1998), 'Stock market fluctuations and consumption behavior: Some recent evidence', Economics Department Working Paper 208 (December), OECD.

Boone, L., N. Girouard and I. Wanner (2001), 'Financial market liberalization, wealth and consumption', Economics Department Working Paper 308 (September), OECD.

Borga, M. and R. J. Mataloni (2001), 'Direct investment positions for 2000: Country and industry detail', Survey of Current Business, July, pp. 16–29.

Borga, M. and D. R. Yorgason (2002), 'Direct investment positions for 2001: Country and industry detail', Survey of Current Business, July, pp. 25–35.

Braconier, H., P. J. Norbäck and D. Urban (2002), 'Vertical FDI revisited', Working Paper No. 537, Research Institute of Industrial Economics, Stockholm.

Brainard, S. L. (1997), 'An empirical assessment of the proximity-concentration trade-off between multanational sales and trade', American Economic Review 87, pp. 520–544.

Budd, J. W., J. Konings and M. J. Slaughter (2002), 'International rent sharing in multinational firms', NBER Working Paper 8809.

Budd, J. W. and M. J. Slaughter (2000), 'Are profits shared across borders? Evidence on international rent sharing', NBER Working Paper 8014.

Carr, D. L., J. R. Markusen and K. E. Maskus (2001), 'Estimating the Knowledge Capital Model of the multinational firm', American Economic Review 91, pp. 693–708.

Carvalho, V. M. and A. C. Harvey (2003), 'Convergence and cycles in the Eurozone', Paper presented at the First Workshop of the Euro Area Business Cycle Network, Madrid.

Christofides, L. N. and A. J. Oswald (1992), 'Real wages and rent sharing in collective bargaining agreements', Quarterly Journal of Economics 107, pp. 985–1002.

Cummins, J. G., K. A. Hassett and R. G. Hubbard (1996), Tax reforms and investment: a cross-country comparison, Journal of Public Economics 62, pp. 237–273.

De Haan, J., R. Inklaar and O. Sleijpen (2002), 'Have business cycles become more synchronized?', Journal of Common Markes Studies 40, pp. 23–42.

Den Butter, F. A. G. and R. H. J. Mosch (2003), 'The Dutch miracle: institutions, networks ands trust', Journal of Institutional and Theoretical Economics 159, pp. 361–392.

Deutsche Bundesbank (2003), 'Kapitalverflechtung mit dem Ausland, Statistische Sonderveröffentlichung' 10 (June).

Dunning, J. H. (1970), Studies in international investment, London, Allen & Unwin, p. 4.

Edwards, T. C. Rees and X. Coller (1999), 'Structure, politics and the diffusion of employment practices in multinationals', European Journal of Industrial Relations 5, pp. 286–306.

Ewe-Ghee Lim (2001), 'Determinants of, and the relation between, foreign direct investment and growth: A summary of recent literature', IMF Working Paper WP/01/175.

Frankel, J. A. and A. K. Rose (1998), 'The endogeneity of the optimum currency area criteria', *Economic Journal* 108, pp. 1009–1025.

Gilchrist, S., C. Himmelberg and G. Huberman (2002), 'Do stock price bubbles influence corporate investment?', Working Paper, Federal Reserve Bank of New York.

Goetzmann, W. N., L. Li and K. G. Rouwenhorst (2001), Long-term global stock market correlations, NBER Working Paper 8612.

Griever, W. L., G. A. Lee and F. E. Warnock (2001), 'The US system for measuring cross-border investment in securities: A primer with a discussion of recent developments', *Federal Reserve Bulletin*, October, pp. 633–650.

Hanson, H., J. Gordon, R. J. Mataloni Jr. and J. M. Slaughter (2001), 'Expansion strategies of US multinational firms'. In D. Rodrik and S. Collins (eds.), *Brookings Trade Forum 2001*, pp. 245–294.

Harris, R. and C. Robinson (2002), 'The effect of foreign acquisitions on total factor productivity: Plant-level evidence from UK manufacturing, 1987–1992', *Review of Economics and Statistics* 84, pp. 562–568.

Helbling, T. and T. Bayoumi (2003), 'Are they all in the same boat? The 2000–2001 growth slowdown and the G-7 business cycle linkages', IMF Working Paper 03/46 (March), International Monetary Fund.

Ietto-Gillies, G. (2000), 'What role for multinationals in the new theories of industrial trade and locations?', *International Review of Applied Economics* 14, pp. 413–426.

IMF (2002), 'Recessions and recoveries', chapter III in *World Economic Outlook* (Spring), 44–77, International Monetary Fund.

Jansen, W. J. and N. J. Nahuis (2003), 'The stock market and consumer confidence: European evidence', *Economics Letters* 79, pp. 89–98.

Jansen, W. J. and A. C. J. Stokman (2003), 'The importance of multinational companies for global economic linkages', *DNB Staff Report* 99/2003, De Nederlandsche Bank (www.dnb.nl).

Kremers, J. J. M., N. L. Ericsson and J. J. Dolado (1992), 'The power of cointegration tests', *Oxford Bulletin of Economics and Statistics* 54, pp. 325–348.

Luginbuhl, R. and S. J. Koopman (2003), 'Convergence in European GDP series: a multivariate common converging trend-cycle decomposition', Working Paper 2003–031/4, Tinbergen Institute.

Lumsdaine, R. L. and E. S. Prasad (2003), 'Identifying the common component of international economic fluctuations: A new approach', *Economic Journal*, 113, 101–127.

McGuckin, R. H. and S. V. Nguyen (1995), 'On productivity and plant ownership change: New evidence from the longitudinal research database', *RAND Journal of Economics* 26, 257–276.

Moran, T. (1998), *Foreign direct investment and development: the new policy agenda for developing countries and economies in transition.* Institute for International Economics, Washington, DC.

Obstfeld, M. and K. Rogoff (2000), 'The six major puzzles in international macroeconomics: is there a common cause?', *NBER Macroeconomics Annual 2000.*

OECD (2002a), *International Direct Investment Statistics Yearbook 2001*, Paris.

OECD (2002b), 'Measuring globalization: The role of multinationals in OECD economies, Vol I: Manufacturing Sector, 2001 edition, Paris.

Oswald, A. J. (1996), 'Rent sharing in the labour market', University of Warwick, Dept. of Economics Research Papers No 474.

Otoo, M. W. (1999), 'Consumer sentiment and the stock market', Discussion Paper 1999–60 (November), Federal Reserve Board.

Peersman, G. (2002), 'What caused the early millennium slowdown? Evidence based on vector autoregressions', unpublished manuscript (November), Bank of England.

Poterba, J. M. (2000), 'Stock market wealth and consumption', *Journal of Economic Perspectives* 14, 99–118.

Ravenscraft, D. J. and F. M. Scherer (1989), 'The profitability of mergers', *International Journal of Industrial Organization* 7(1), pp. 101–106.

Slaughter, M. J. (2003), 'Host country determinants of US foreign direct investment'. In H. Hermann and R. E. Lipsey (eds.), *Foreign direct investment in the real and financial sector of industrial countries*, Springer-Verlag Berlin, 7–32.

Sparling, R. P. (2002), 'Het externe vermogen van Nederland', Special issue of Statistisch Bulletin (February), De Nederlandsche Bank.

Starr-McCluer, M. (2002), 'Stock market wealth and consumer spending', *Economic Inquiry* 40, 69–79.

Statistics Canada (2002), *Canada's international investment position 2001.*

UK National Statistics (2002), Foreign direct investment in the UK analysed by area and main country.

UNCTAD (2002), 'World Investment Report 2002: *Transnational Corporations and Export Competitiveness*', United Nations.

Zeile, W. J. (2002), 'US affiliates of foreign companies: Operations in 2000, *Survey of Current Business*, August, 149–166.

7 Shocks and shock absorbers: the international propagation of equity market shocks and the design of appropriate policy responses

Ray Barrell and E. Philip Davis[1]

7.1 Introduction

Equity prices and equity markets are major sources of shocks to the world economy and major channels for the propagation of these shocks. In this chapter we seek to calibrate their effects, and assess what policy responses can best absorb them. We first briefly discuss the evidence for the effects of equity prices on real economic activity and look at some evidence on the relationship between equity prices and output using Vector Error Correction (VECM) Models. We compare these results for the US and the major euro area countries to those produced using the National Institute Global Econometric Model (NiGEM). We assess the implications of equity price falls comparable to those seen in 2000–2002 in the context of NiGEM, presenting a range of simulations on the model. These give a view of the macroeconomic impact of equity market falls, viewed in the context of the high degree of correlation between equity price changes in the recent past, and also give an indication of the effect of differing policy responses.

7.2 The macroeconomic importance of equity markets

There is a significant literature investigating the impact of wealth – itself driven partly by share prices – on consumption. Davis and Palumbo's (2001) study of the US consumption function attempts to determine whether changes in wealth affect the growth rate of consumer spending. They examined quarterly aggregate US data from 1960–2000 and modelled long-run relationships to investigate whether (logged) consumption, income and wealth share a common trend. They found that there

---

[1] Ray Barrell is a Senior Research Fellow, NIESR and Visiting Professor, Imperial College. E.Philip Davis is a Professor of Economics and Finance, Brunel University and Visiting Fellow, NIESR.

is a statistically-significant long-run wealth effect on consumer spending. Ludvigsen and Steindel (1999) also examined wealth effects in a loglinear long-run consumption relationship and found a statistically-significant wealth and income effect. They also showed that these variables share a common trend, using quarterly US data, as do Lettau and Ludvigsen (2001).

Barrell and Davis (2004a) look at a similar standard model of consumption for the G5 economies. Income and wealth effects are significant, and there is a clear role for both the level and the change in financial wealth. However, they also find that wealth effects differ between countries, with no impact from changes in equity-based wealth in Germany but a relatively-strong effect in the US. Complementing this, Byrne and Davis (2003a) investigated the impact of disaggregated financial wealth on consumption for G7 countries, and found that, contrary to earlier empirical work, illiquid financial wealth, (equities, bonds, life insurance and pension assets less mortgage debt) scaled by personal disposable income (PDI), tends to be a more-significant long-run determinant of consumption than liquid financial wealth (deposits and money market instruments less other debt) across the G7. Again, the effect varied across countries. They suggested that the overall pattern reflects a shift from liquidity constrained to life-cycle behaviour following financial liberalisation, and also a more disaggregated pattern of wealth holding. Barrell and Davis (2006) indeed found that financial liberalisation is accompanied by a rise in wealth effects and fall in income effects consistent with elimination of liquidity constraints.

The differences in response of consumption to wealth found in these papers reflect the relative importance of both direct and indirect holding of equities in household portfolios. Table 7.1 shows the ratio of wealth to personal disposable income (PDI) in the major economies. As regards changes in wealth which could impact on consumption, the table shows that falls in the UK and US over 1999–2001 were 100 per cent of PDI can be seen to be much greater by end-2002. Falls in France and Italy were around half those in the UK and US, while the data showed relatively-small declines in Germany, Canada and Japan. The penultimate line shows direct equity holdings,[2] while the bottom line, from Byrne and Davis (2003b), makes a correction for institutional holdings on behalf of households. It shows that portfolio

---

[2] Note from the memo line that the direct holdings of equity are largest in France, Canada and the US and lowest in Germany and Japan. The large difference between this figure and illiquid financial wealth is largely a consequence of the importance of institutional investors, albeit also in some countries reflecting bond holdings.

Table 7.1 *Household wealth-income ratios*

	UK	US	Germany	Japan	Canada	France	Italy
			Net financial wealth/personal disposable income ratio				
1998	3.45	3.79	1.48	3.02	2.29	2.66	2.72
1999	3.96	4.18	1.57	3.35	2.35	2.92	3.02
2000	3.63	3.65	1.56	3.50	2.34	3.03	3.05
2001	3.05	3.23	1.56	3.56	2.33	2.63	2.75
2002	2.48	2.67	1.50	3.54	2.28	2.52	2.80
2003	2.51	2.95	1.64	3.65	2.22	2.63	2.79
		Memo: Personal sector direct equity holdings/personal disposable income ratio					
2001	0.59	0.85	0.36	0.34	0.99	1.08	0.62
		Memo: Total direct plus indirect equity holdings/total financial wealth %					
2000	53.4	48.5	27.1	13.1	39.8	47.8	30.5

Source: National flow-of-funds balance sheet data, Datastream.

shares of equity allowing for indirect holdings are quite comparable across the G7, with the outliers being Japan and to a lesser extent Germany and Italy. The ratio of direct to total equity holdings is an indicator of the immediate visibility of equity price changes to consumers, and might be expected to affect the speed of response to a change in equity prices.

Turning to investment, as shown in IMF (2003), declines in investment often have a substantial impact on GDP growth after equity price falls, and falls in investment were sizeable in the recent bear market, partly linked to the high level of corporate debt and reliance on external finance generally in the bull period. The potential channels of transmission[3] include Tobin's Q (the valuation of firms relative to the replacement cost of the capital stock) and the financial accelerator, (whereby the level of corporate net worth eases concerns of lenders over moral hazard, and hence external finance constraints). Evidence for the US suggests that the stock market bubble of the late 1990s influenced corporate investment, raising it significantly (Gilchrist, Himmelberg and Huberman, 2004). More generally there is a significant body of evidence for the US that stock prices affect the level of investment and hence have an impact on the level and rate of change in GDP, although other factors such as the existence of external finance constraints over and above those shown by the financial accelerator, appear to explain investment behaviour as well (Hubbard 1998).

[3] See Ashworth and Davis (2001).

Firms in the US are generally more dependent on equity markets for their finance than are firms in the euro area, where the strength of links with banks should reduce the importance of financial constraints and equity prices on investment. Bank finance has historically been important in Italy, France and Germany. In general, we would expect more market-based economies to have more impact from equity prices and from external finance constraints and this does appear to be the case. For instance Bond *et al.* (2003) construct a set of company panel data for Belgium, France, Germany and the UK over the period 1978–1989 and find that financial constraints and the associated variations in market-based equity risk premia were perhaps more important in the UK, which is more similar to the US in terms of the structure on investment finance than are the members of the euro area.

The differences in financial structure that we discuss above impact on the reactions of economies to equity market shocks and influence the differences between countries that we observe in the Monetary Transmission Mechanism (MTM). The traditional money-based view of this mechanism is that interest rates affect consumption and investment in perfect capital markets and induce substitution over time. Imperfect capital markets and the existence of liquidity constraints are at the core of the credit view of the transmission mechanism, in the spirit of the pattern of wealth effects and the financial accelerator and these can at least partly be picked up by investigating the role of equity prices in the overall economy. Allen, Chui and Maddeloni (2004) discuss the impacts of financial systems in Europe and the US on the transmission mechanism, stressing the role of bank- versus market-based systems as well as the importance of equity markets.

The impacts of equity prices on GDP can be evaluated either with Vector Autoregressive (VAR)-based models or with more structural approaches. Pesaran *et al.* (2004) build a compact Vector Error Correction (VECM)-based global model of twenty-five linked countries in which they focus on domestic equity price effects on GDP, showing that they are both significant and vary across countries. Pesaran *et al.* (2005) build on this model to evaluate credit risk using this large dynamic global macroeconomic VAR model attached to descriptions of portfolios. They apply generalised impulse response functions[4] for equity price shocks, calculating the correlations between past shocks and applying sets of shocks to all equity prices. Barrell and Davis (2005) use a set of VECM models to evaluate the impacts of changes in equity prices on the economy in the

---

[4] This requires calculating the correlation between innovations across countries, and applying a shock with its appropriate partner shocks in other countries.

EU and US and draw a distinction between effects in bank-based and market-based economies. The strength of impact of equity price shocks in the US is emphasised in all these results.

7.3   Estimation of cointegrating relationships

As a counterpart to work with the Institute macromodel NiGEM in this chapter, we first follow Barrell and Davis (2005) and seek to extend the work of Pesaran and others by further assessing links of equity prices to the real economy via estimating VECMs for the large EMU countries and the US. These have the advantage of a reduced-form approach, not imposing restrictions on the data, while also allowing both short- and long-run (cointegrating) effects to be discerned. In each case we estimate a four-variable VAR system, and we look for factors that would cause output to cycle around its equilibrium value. As we are investigating real output we would like to use other real variables unless there is a strong case for not doing so. We presume that we should look for policy variables and for an exogenous shock variable such as equity prices. Hence besides real equity prices (LREQP) we utilise real GDP (LY), the government surplus to GDP ratio (GBR) as an indicator of the stance of fiscal policy, and the three-month real short rate (RR) as an indicator of the stance of monetary policy. In order to be sure that we may find a cointegrating vector, we use the data period 1971–2003, covering the era since the end of Bretton Woods, including several cycles.

As at least two of our variables, (LY and LREQP) are integrated of order one we should work in error correction form to avoid spurious regressions. We may write this as:

$$\Delta y = \Sigma_i \, \beta_i \, \Delta y(-i) + \gamma \, y(-1) + \varepsilon \tag{1}$$

Where β_i is a matrix of dynamic response coefficients, γ is the matrix of coefficients on the long-run levels terms and y is the vector of the four explanatory variables in each country. Using standard tests we find that the length of lag in the VAR we should use does not exceed two quarters, and the trace and eigenvalue tests show us that there is one cointegrating vector in each country. Following Johansen (1995), we then estimate these and place them in the VAR. We normalise on one variable in order to aid interpretation of this vector and then analyse variance decompositions. (Key to cointegration specifications: specification 2 is intercept in cointegrated equation CE and no intercept in VAR, and specification 3 is intercept in CE and VAR).

The normalised cointegrating vectors above show a much closer relationship between equity prices and GDP in the market-based US than in

Table 7.2 *Estimation results – co-integrating vector 1971:1–2003:4*

Normalised on log real equity prices	France	Germany	Netherlands	Italy	US
LREQP(−1)	1.0	1.0	1.0	1.0	1.0
LY(−1)	−3.5	−2.1	−1.9	−4.0	−1.5
	(2.1)	(10.1)	(5.7)	(2.5)	(6.3)
GBR(−1)	0.8	−0.31	−0.06	−0.08	−0.13
	(3.6)	(8.6)	(1.2)	(0.9)	(2.5)
RR(−1)	0.6	0.11	0.04	−0.12	0.02
	(5.7)	(3.6)	(1.4)	(1.4)	(0.7)
C	19.3	11.9	21.7	22.3	13.7
Co-integration specification	3	3	2	2	2
period	1971–2003	1971–2003	1971–2003	1971–2003	1971–2003

the five mainly bank-based euro area economies reported in the table. Real interest rates have the expected negative relationship with both equity prices and output in all countries except Italy, whilst the sign of the impact of improvements in the fiscal position (the level of public borrowing as a per cent of GDP) is negative in four countries, but only significant in two, and positive in one, suggesting that the direction of causation between borrowing and output is not at all clear.[5]

Examination of estimation results gives some information, but for our purposes the main outputs of interest from a VECM are variance decompositions. As a first step we use the decomposition of the variances of twenty step ahead forecasts by components of the error correction equation to evaluate the structure of the economies we are studying. As shown in Table 7.3, we may note in particular the 'autonomy' of share prices in variance decompositions, compared with a marked (albeit variable) impact of share price variance on real GDP. In the variance decomposition for equity prices the extremes are France and the Netherlands, with the forecast variance for most share prices being explained solely by the past history of equity prices themselves. Most economies in our sample have virtually autonomous equity markets reflecting their forward-looking rate.

The variance decompositions for output are much more varied, with past history for output contributing between 22 and 87 per cent, with

---

[5] Barrell and Davis (2005) suggest that in most countries there is evidence of an association between large deficits and low GDP, indicating expansionary fiscal contractions are possible.

Table 7.3 *Selected variance decompositions of LREQP and LY after twenty quarters*

Decomp of/by	France	Germany	Netherlands	Italy	US
LREQP	96	94	72	95	93
LY	3	1	1	2	5
GBR	0	5	26	2	1
RR	1	0	0	0	1
LY	87	87	76	49	22
LREQP	12	4	22	32	51
GBR	2	6	1	1	26
RR	0	2	0	18	0

equity prices contributing between 4 and 51 per cent. The largest role for equity prices in the decomposition of output variance is in the US, with a share above 50 per cent. The large share for the US does fit with our priors and there is clearly a strong case to be made for there being a difference between this large equity-based economy and the others.

We argue that changes in US equity prices impact directly on the European economies through direct holdings of US equities in European portfolios and as US share price movements lead other markets. As a variant, we included real US share prices in the VECM for the larger EU countries. We reran the tests for these EU countries with the log of real US share prices coming first in the Choleski ordering. As can be seen from the variance decomposition, there is a major impact of including the US on share price variance – indicating a considerable influence of the US on EU markets – but no change to the overall autonomy of share prices. US equity prices seem to be relatively important in the very-open equity market in the Netherlands. As regards the determination of domestic output, there is now a large contribution by US share prices, with it being more important in the decomposition than domestic equity prices in all economies except for Germany. The overall impact of share prices is comparable to the basic results.

7.4   Modelling the impact of equity prices

Over the last eighteen years, NIESR has developed the global macro model NiGEM for use in policy analysis.[6] NiGEM is an estimated model, which uses a 'New-Keynesian' framework in that agents are presumed to

---

[6] See Barrell *et al.* (2004) for a brief description.

Table 7.4 *Selected variance decompositions of LREQP and LY after twenty quarters including US share prices (per cent)*

Decomp of/by	France	Germany	Netherlands	Italy
LREQP	60	57	29	54
USLREQP	37	39	48	43
LY	1	0	1	1
GBR	0	3	22	1
RR	1	0	0	0
LY	82	61	76	68
USLREQP	13	1	18	14
LREQP	3	8	3	9
GBR	2	12	2	5
RR	0	19	0	5

be forward-looking, but nominal rigidities slow the process of adjustment to external events. All countries in the OECD are modelled separately. All economies are linked through the effects of trade and competitiveness. There are also links between countries in their financial markets via the structure and composition of wealth, emphasising the role and origin of foreign assets and liabilities. There are forward-looking wages and exchange rates, while long-term interest rates are the forward convolution of short-term interest rates. The model has complete demand and supply sides and there is an extensive monetary and financial sector. NiGEM contains expectations and uses the Extended Path Method to obtain values for the future and current expectations and iterate along solution paths.

International propagation of shocks to US equity prices in the model relies on two main sets of channels. Those due to model structure, notably trade and the effects of financial asset valuations on consumption, propagate the shock through US demand for foreign output or through the impact on the demand of foreign residents for all output. We detail aspects of the underlying equations below. In addition, policy responses can be part of the propagation of the shock. If both demand and inflation in the US fall then the Federal Reserve can be expected to cut short-term interest rates. This will help to absorb the shock, but it will also cause the dollar to fall. The depreciation of the dollar improves US competitiveness and also helps to absorb the shock in the US. It will raise US exports and reduce imports compared to where they would otherwise have been without the improvement in competitiveness. The improvement in competitiveness must be matched elsewhere by deterioration in other countries' competitiveness and this also propagates the shock to other countries.

Shocks are not only absorbed by the operation of policy rules, but also by the market mechanism. If policy reduces short-term interest rates and is expected to continue to do so, then this causes the long-term interest rate to fall, inducing a rise in bond prices that should partly offset the impact on wealth of the fall in equity prices.[7] A decline in US consumption driven by a fall in equity prices and hence wealth raises US saving. The long-term real interest rate in our model, which drives the user cost of capital, will fall in the US and elsewhere as a result of changes in the saving and investment balance. This gives a potential boost to investment both in the US and elsewhere, and reduces the impact of a rise in the risk premium.

7.4.1   The structure of NiGEM

Trade in goods and services

These equations depend upon demand and relative-competitiveness effects, and the latter are defined in similar ways across countries. It is assumed that exporters compete against others who export (X) to the same market via relative prices (RPX) and demand is given by the imports in the markets to which the country has previously exported (S)

$$\Delta \ln X = \lambda [\ln X(-1) - \ln S(-1) + b^* \ln \text{RPX}]$$
$$+ c1^* \Delta \ln X(-1) + c2^* \Delta \ln S + \text{error} \qquad (2)$$

while imports (M) depend upon import prices relative to domestic prices (RPM) and on demand (TFE)

$$\Delta \ln M = \lambda [\ln M(-1) - b1^* \ln \text{TFE}(-1)] + b2^* \ln \text{RPM}$$
$$+ c1^* \Delta \ln M(-1) + c2^* \Delta \ln \text{TFE} + \text{error} \qquad (3)$$

As exports depend on imports, they will rise together in the model. Of particular relevance for this chapter, we can be certain that if US imports fall that will be reflected in declines in exports elsewhere in the world.

---

[7] Bond prices depend on the long rate on bonds, and revaluations change with the level of the rate. Japanese long rates have been much lower than elsewhere for some time, hence revaluations differ in that country.

Financial markets

Forward-looking nominal long rates LR and long real rates have to look T periods forward using expected short-term nominal and real interest rates respectively using:

$$(1 + LR_t) = \Pi_{j=1,T}(1 + SR_{t+j})^{1/T} \tag{4}$$

Forward-looking exchange rates RX have to look one period forward along the arbitrage relation involving domestic and foreign short-term interest rates (SRH and SRF)

$$RX_t = RX_{t+1}(1 + SRH_t)/(1 + SRF_t) \tag{5}$$

Forward-looking equity prices are solved out from the discounted sum of expected future profits (Π), divided by the real stock of capital (K). The discount factor is made up of the nominal interest rate, r, and the risk premium on equity holding decisions, *rpe*.

$$EQP_t = \sum_{i=1}^{\infty}((\Pi_{t+i}/K_{t+i})/((1 + r_i)(1 + rpe_i))) \tag{6}$$

This can be written as an infinite forward recursion that depends only on current profits and the expected equity price next period, which embeds information on future profits:

$$EQP_t = \Pi_t + EQP_{t+1}/(1 + r_t)(1 + rpe_t) \tag{7}$$

The equity price will jump when any of its future determinants changes, and the risk premium is set at its recent value unless reset in the experiment, as it is here.

Wealth and asset accumulation

The wealth and accumulation system allows for flows of saving onto wealth and for revaluations of existing stocks of assets in line with their prices determined as above. In the medium term, personal sector liabilities are assumed to rise in line with nominal personal incomes and if there are no revaluations, gross financial wealth will increase by the nominal value of net private sector saving plus the net increase in nominal liabilities. Revaluations come from three sources, as follows:

(1) *Domestic equity prices* These revalue the proportion of the domestic share of the portfolio that is held in equities, both quoted and unquoted. We assume that unquoted shares rise in line with quoted shares. Balance of payments data include an estimate of the equity stock of the domestic production sector held abroad.

(2) *Domestic bond prices*   The scope of revaluations to bonds is calculated using information on the maturity structure of government debt. When long rates jump down, bond prices jump up. Data are available on the proportion of debt held abroad and this is used in revaluations.

(3) *Foreign assets and liabilities*   There is information on the structure of liabilities to foreigners, hence when equity and bond prices change, the value of gross liabilities also changes. Countries receive revaluations in proportion to their stock of gross assets as a share of the world total after factoring out banking sector deposit assets. Hence a change in US (and other) equity prices affects gross assets and hence wealth in other countries 'correctly', as do changes in the value of bonds held abroad.

Cross-country differences in the importance of assets as a per cent of income, and in the structure of assets, as well as the responsiveness of consumption to them are important factors driving the following results.

Consumption and personal income

The consumption (C) relations are based on Barrell and Davis (2004a), with a role for real net financial wealth (RNW) and real personal disposable income (RPDI), as well as for housing wealth and house prices where appropriate. Dynamic terms in real wealth and real income are included as appropriate. Although in the long run real wealth effects are similar everywhere, as Barrell and Davis (2004a) stress, they are absent in the dynamics in for instance, Germany, and important in the dynamics of adjustment in the US. The resulting equation with all variables in logs is:

$$\Delta \ln C = \lambda [\ln C(-1) - a^* \ln RPD1(-1) - (1 - a)^* \ln RNW(-1)]$$
$$+ b_1 \Delta \ln C(-1) + b_2 \Delta \ln RPDI + b_3 \Delta \ln RNW \quad (8)$$

As outlined above, it is assumed that besides being cumulated saving, wealth is affected by financial market activity through equity and bond prices and if these markets 'expect' something in the future then it will be reflected in prices. News that changes expectations will cause wealth to be revalued and hence will affect behaviour now. Published data on Net Financial Wealth[8] are used, and the ratios of wealth to income and of wealth to consumption will influence the properties of the model.

---

[8] Data for the G-7 are discussed in Byrne and Davis (2003b), and are generally available, for instance in OECD sources. For some small countries we have constructed data in consultation with the Central Bank.

Production

For each country there is an underlying CES production function which constitutes the theoretical background for the specification of the factor demand equations for employment and the capital stock, and which form the basis for unit total costs and the measure of capacity utilisation which then feed into the price system. A CES production function that embodies labour augmenting technological progress (denoted λ) with constant returns to scale can be written as:

$$Q = \gamma \left[s\,(K)^{-\rho} + (1-s)(Le^{\lambda t})^{-\rho} \right]^{-1/\rho} \qquad (9)$$

γ and s are production function scale parameters, and the elasticity of substitution, σ, is given by $1/(1+\rho)$. Variables K and L denote the net capital stock and labour input measured in terms of employee hours. In general we find that the elasticity of substitution is around one half. The parameters of the production function vary across countries and w, c and p denote respectively labour costs per head, nominal user costs of capital and the price of value added (at factor cost) and β denotes the mark-up. With long-run constant returns to scale, we obtain log-linear factor demand equations of the form:

$$Ln(L) = [\sigma \ln \{\beta(1-s)\} - (1-\sigma)\ln(\gamma)]$$
$$+ \ln(Q) - (1-\sigma)\lambda t - \sigma \ln(w/p) \qquad (10)$$

$$Ln(K) = [\sigma \ln(\beta s) - (1-\sigma)\ln(\gamma)]$$
$$+ \ln(Q) - \sigma \ln(c/p^*(1+rp)) \qquad (11)$$

These long-run factor demands are embedded in error correction models, with adjustment to equilibrium after a shock taking place more quickly in the US than in the euro area countries. The speed of adjustment can also depend upon Tobin's Q, here measured as the ratio of the value of the equity market to the current value of the private business sector capital stock. The influence of Q on the speed of adjustment in the US is statistically important, as we would expect, but we have not found a role for it in the euro area countries. The long-term parameters are used in the construction of an indicator of capacity utilisation, which affects the mark-up of prices over unit total costs. The capital stock adjustment equation depends upon the long-term equilibrium capital stock, and the user cost of capital is influenced by the forward-looking real long-term rate, as well as by taxes and depreciation. The speed of adjustment to equilibrium in the investment/capital stock adjustment equations also depends upon the short-term real interest rate, with this effect being similar across countries.

Labour markets and prices

It is assumed that employers have the power to manage, hence the bargain in the labour market is over the real wage. In the long term, wages rise in line with productivity, all else being equal. Given the determinants of the trajectory for real wages, if unemployment rises, then real wages fall relative to trend, and conversely. The equations were estimated in an equilibrium-correction format with dynamics estimated around the long run. Both the determinants of equilibrium and the dynamics of adjustment can change over time and adjustment, especially in Europe, is slow. We assume that labour markets embody rational expectations over the inflation rate and we assume that wage bargainers use model-consistent expectations, either for the immediate period ahead or over a longer-term horizon. These compensation equations are discussed at some length in Barrell and Dury (2003) and all these equations are dynamically homogenous. Price equations are a profit-related mark-up over total costs, with speeds of adjustment reflecting data and these are much lower in the euro area than in the US. In general these equations are dynamically homogenous and if target inflation rises, it will have no significant effect on the level of output.

7.4.2   Policy rules

Fiscal and monetary policy rules are important in 'closing the model' and the rules are discussed at greater length in Barrell and Dury (2000). We use simple rules that are designed to reflect policy frameworks rather than optimal rules.

Fiscal policy rules

Budget deficits are kept within bounds in the longer term, and taxes rise to do this. This simple feedback rule is important in ensuring the long-term stability of the model. Without a solvency rule (or a no-Ponzi games assumption) there is no necessary solution to a forward-looking model. The simple fiscal rule can be described as:

$$\text{Tax}_t = \text{Tax}_{t-1} + \phi[\text{GBRT} - \text{GBR}] \tag{12}$$

Where Tax is the direct tax rate, GBR and GBRT are the government surplus target and actual surplus, ϕ is the feedback parameter, which is designed to remove an excess deficit in less that five years. We relax GBRT for five years in one of our experiments, allowing government debt as a per cent of GDP to increase to a new, higher equilibrium level.

Monetary policy rules

It is assumed that the monetary authorities adopt simple targeting rules that stabilise the price level (P_t) or the inflation rate ($\Delta \ln P_t$) in the long term. If we use different rules in different countries then some of the difference we observe would depend on that policy choice. In this chapter, we initially use the same rule for all countries. The European Central Bank (ECB) has been set the objective of maintaining price stability in the medium term. It has set itself a target for inflation within the constraints of a nominal target for the stock of money, and it describes this as the two-pillar strategy.[9] A combined policy of nominal aggregate and inflation rate targeting – with targets denoted with * – would give:

$$r_t = \gamma_1(\ln(P_t Y_t) - \ln(P_t^* Y_t^*)) + \gamma_2(\Delta \ln P_{t+j} - \Delta \ln P_{t+j}^*) \tag{13}$$

The combined rule is chosen as the default monetary policy rule because it may provide a reasonable rule to proxy the framework that is used in Europe by the ECB. We choose to use it elsewhere as the proportional controller on inflation dominates responses. Note that a fiscal expansion in the model leads to inflation via changes in the saving/investment balance – given the monetary policy rule, this will drive up short rates and hence long rates. We also report experiment where we utilise the 'industry standard' Taylor Rule where interest rates respond to the difference between actual and target inflation as well as to the output gap, which is the difference between actual (Y_t) and trend output (*YTREND*).

$$r_t = \gamma_0 + \gamma_1(\ln Y_t - \ln YTREND_t^*) + \gamma_2(\Delta \ln P_{t+j} - \Delta \ln P_{t+j}^*) \tag{14}$$

The coefficients are set at industry standard levels, with $\gamma_1 = 0.5$ and $\gamma_2 = 1.5$, whilst the intercept is endogenous, taking the value of the steady rate long-term interest rate.

7.4.3 Model residuals for equity prices, consumption and income

In assessing the behaviour of the global economy during the bear market using the model, it is important to evaluate the cross-country correlation of unexplained components of key variables, which indicate structural shocks. There are many sources of structural shocks and we can address their changing nature by looking at a selected set of structural equation shocks from NiGEM, and we choose consumption, compensation (the main component of personal income) equity price and business

---

[9] Barrell and Dury (2000) discuss these issues. We do not target money, as this is a poor indicator of the underlying target, which we take to be nominal GDP, $P_t Y_t$.

Table 7.5 *Correlation of structural shocks between US and others*

	Consumption	Compensation	Business investment	Equity prices
	0.12	0.45	0.22	0.51
Germany	0.05	−0.19	0.01	0.33
Italy	−0.04	−0.16	−0.13	0.35
UK	−0.50	0.24	0.12	0.65
Japan	−0.07	−0.31	−0.23	−0.10
Canada	0.12	0.11	0.28	0.55

investment residuals to see if there are noticeable correlations across countries. Specifications of these equations are as described above.[10]

Table 7.5 looks at the correlation of these structural shocks across countries between 1991(q1) and 1999(q4). We present correlations with the US, which is our main interest in the present context of the transmission from the US to the rest of the G7. It is evident that the correlations between countries for consumption, business investment and for the compensation variable residuals are low. On the other hand the correlation of the unexplained component of the equity price equation is high over this period except for Japan. It is especially high for France, the UK and Canada *vis à vis* the US equity market. This suggests that transmission of shocks affecting consumption and to a lesser extent investment tends to occur indirectly via asset prices and does not impact on expenditures or incomes directly.

7.5   The 2000–2002 bear market

The interest in equity price simulations is of course heightened by share price trends in recent years. Equity markets fell around 50 per cent over 2000–2002, and it is clear that we witnessed a bear market comparable to that of the early 1970s, as is discussed in Davis (2003). Table 7.6 derived from Davis (2003) shows that unconditional volatility exhibited a steady rise over 1972–1975 with conditional volatility (measured using GARCH(1, 1) estimation) starting higher and rising less. Unconditional and conditional volatility saw a peak in 1998 after which unconditional volatility declined sharply before rising again, while conditional volatility was also on a gradual uptrend albeit never recovering the level of

---

[10] See also Barrell, Becker, Byrne, Gottschalk, Hurst and van Welsum (2004) for a discussion of these equations and of model properties.

Table 7.6 *Average volatility of share price in the G7 (per cent)*

	Standard deviation	Conditional volatility	Difference		Standard deviation	Conditional volatility	Difference
1972	3.68	5.23	−1.55	1998	7.23	6.16	1.08
1973	5.57	5.47	0.10	1999	4.81	5.65	−0.85
1974	6.85	6.50	0.34	2000	5.08	5.79	−0.71
1975	7.13	6.98	0.16	2001	5.97	5.82	0.15
				2002	6.85	6.22	0.63

Source: MSCI.

1998. The differences between the two types of volatility are potentially instructive given conditional volatility is a closer proxy for expectations and uncertainty. Furthermore, uncertainty proxied by conditional volatility may have an additional effect on consumption over and above wealth effects per se.

In 1972, unconditional volatility was below conditional, suggesting uncertainty in markets at the sustainability of the bull market. Thereafter conditional volatility fell somewhat short of unconditional, especially for the US in 1974 and the UK in 1975 when markets were hit by unpredictable and uncorrelated shocks such as the oil shock as well as expected volatility. Similarly, in 1998 the markets may not have anticipated the level of volatility seen in the Russia/LTCM crisis and hence unconditional was highest, but thereafter as the bear market took hold it was conditional volatility that tended to be higher until 2002 when unconditional was again higher.

The correlation of domestic share prices with world indices tends to increase in bear markets, reducing the seeming diversification benefits of international investment, and increasing the scope of international spillover effects illustrated in Table 7.4. Typically, this pattern is thought to reflect common behaviour of institutional investors as well as common fundamentals across the world. Global financial integration has ensured a much higher level of average correlations than in 1975 at the trough of the earlier bear market as Table 7.7 below from Davis (2003) shows.

Trends in risk premia are one of the key elements in the background to the bear market. There are generally substantially higher returns to saving in equities than other forms of asset holdings, but risk aversion and the need for liquid assets for precautionary and transactions purposes ensures that these holdings never dominate entirely. Theoretical portfolio models often predict a level of risk aversion which is much lower than that necessary to explain the level of share holdings (for recent evidence

Table 7.7 *Correlation of share price with world indices*

	UK	US	Germany	Japan	Canada	France	Italy	Country averages
1972	0.74	0.83	0.47	0.63	0.66	0.17	0.22	0.53
1973	0.64	0.96	0.51	0.65	0.88	0.45	0.03	0.59
1974	0.59	0.95	0.39	0.09	0.78	0.80	0.50	0.59
1975	0.72	0.96	0.51	0.72	0.72	0.50	0.69	0.69
1998	0.92	0.94	0.87	0.75	0.93	0.81	0.72	0.85
1999	0.71	0.97	0.88	0.61	0.85	0.86	0.54	0.77
2000	0.78	0.96	0.44	0.54	0.81	0.66	0.22	0.63
2001	0.96	0.98	0.95	0.72	0.89	0.95	0.90	0.91
2002	0.98	0.99	0.95	0.40	0.88	0.97	0.95	0.88

Source: MSCI.

see Haliassos and Michaelides, 2000). In particular, the equity premium puzzle suggests that over the past century or so, stocks were not sufficiently riskier than bonds to explain the spread in their returns (Mehra and Prescott, 1985).

Evidence from the 1990s suggested that the risk premium had declined or disappeared, possibly due to the institutionalisation of portfolios (Blanchard 1993), although there may also have been a cyclical element in the recent equity bull market, whereby risk premia fell everywhere for reasons that may not have been fully justified. Madsen and Davis (2003), for example, suggest that the response of share prices to productivity shocks was inappropriate, since the impact of the latter on profitability is temporary. The bear market may in this context be viewed partly as a correction of unsustainably low risk premia.

As shown by Jagannathan *et al.* (2000) the risk premium can be proxied by the dividend yield plus expected dividend growth less the real bond yield. IMF (2001) argues that the growth in potential output can be used to proxy expected earnings and dividend growth. Accordingly, Table 7.8 below shows a measure of the risk premium using a Hodrick Prescott filter on GDP growth to proxy dividend growth.[11] The stylised fact that premia declined in the 1980s and virtually disappeared in the 1990s is confirmed. The sizeable estimated risk premium in the low-inflation 1960s shows that the decline was not merely a consequence of the impact of disinflation on real bond yields. The peaks of the bull markets in 1972 and 1999 show

---

[11] We use the National Institute forecast of output in each of the G7 in the filter to avoid end point problems.

Table 7.8 *Estimated risk premia*

	Germany	US	UK	France	Canada
1960–69	7.6	4.4	4.5	6.6	5.1
1970–79	5.8	7.5	9.4	11.4	7.6
1980–89	2.3	1.8	3.2	4.1	1.1
1990–94	0.8	1.7	1.9	−0.3	−1.2
1995–99	0.4	0.4	1.6	−0.1	−0.6
Memo: 1972	5.9	3.5	4.3	8.9	5.3
Memo: 1999	0.0	−0.4	1.0	−0.4	−0.1

vast differences in estimated risk premia, albeit in each case generally below the decade-average, underpinning the suggesting of a bubble in 1999, while 1972–1975 is better explicable in terms of fundamentals.

7.6   Analysing the impact of equity prices

Using the NiGEM model, we undertook a number of simulations to assess the impact of an equity price decline and the appropriate policy responses. Our major concern was to assess the impact of a US stock market decline on the US and on other economies, with a particular focus on international propagation. This can take place through trade, through the impact of US equity prices on wealth in other countries and through contagion of the equity price fall to other countries' equity markets.

We first undertook a simulation using the NiGEM model of a re-evaluation of future profits in the US equity markets, engineering a fall of 34 per cent in the equity price in the US. We induce a temporary increase in the perceived equity risk premium, with it slowly declining back to historical levels after fourteen years.[12] This large equity price shock in the US spreads to the rest of the world through trade and asset holdings, and is denoted *US Premium* (USPREM) in the tables in section 5.1. Some of the potential impact of the fall on the US is absorbed by diversified portfolios and spreads to wealth elsewhere.[13]

Contagion to other countries takes place through equity markets as well as through trade and the impact on the value of foreign holdings of US assets. We can define such contagion in several ways. We note that the experience of 2000–2002, discussed above, is outside the range of

[12] See Barrell (2002) for a discussion of the assumptions.
[13] We undertook a simulation where wealth contagion was cut off and its effects are noted below. Available as USPREM-default2.txt on NiGEM model v205.

Table 7.9 *GDP effects of equity premia and equity price shocks* (percentage point difference from baseline level)

		Year 1	Year 2	Year 3	Year 4	Year 5	Year 6
US	ALLPREM	−2.54	−2.72	−2.58	−2.21	−1.71	−1.14
	USPREM	−2.55	−2.71	−2.53	−2.12	−1.59	−1.02
Euro Area	ALLPREM	−0.57	−0.73	−0.72	−0.64	−0.55	−0.44
	USPREM	−0.52	−0.57	−0.52	−0.45	−0.37	−0.29
Germany	ALLPREM	−0.53	−0.74	−0.82	−0.86	−0.83	−0.77
	USPREM	−0.49	−0.63	−0.68	−0.71	−0.69	−0.64
France	ALLPREM	−0.63	−0.71	−0.67	−0.62	−0.60	−0.58
	USPREM	−0.53	−0.46	−0.42	−0.42	−0.45	−0.48
Italy	ALLPREM	−0.56	−0.81	−0.79	−0.68	−0.55	−0.44
	USPREM	−0.50	−0.62	−0.48	−0.28	−0.09	0.05
Neths	ALLPREM	−0.98	−0.97	−0.81	−0.64	−0.50	−0.35
	USPREM	−0.89	−0.78	−0.66	−0.56	−0.47	−0.36

correlations observed in the 1990s, hence using historical correlations of structural residuals to calibrate the expected change in the equity premium elsewhere, is not an adequate description of recent events. Accordingly, we simulated a fall in the risk premium of the same magnitude everywhere, except in Japan and this is noted as *All Premia* (ALLPREM) in the tables in section 5.1. The Japanese premium fall is 40 per cent of that in the US, which is consistent with the correlations in the previous section. Equity price falls are lower in other countries than in the US, reflecting in part the greater impact of equity prices on the US economy and hence greater second round effects on equity prices. In particular the greater the impact of the shock on output, the proportionately greater the impact is on future profits, and hence their discounted future value changes more. Similar declines in equity premia generate falls of equity prices of 23 per cent in France and the Netherlands and 15–18 per cent in Germany and Italy as compared to 33 per cent in the US.

7.6.1   *Equity shocks*

The results of our two equity simulations are reported in Table 7.9. We report on the US, the euro area, Germany, France and Italy and we include the Netherlands because of the scale of its equity markets. It is clear that in all cases the fall in output is largest in the US, reflecting larger wealth effects as well as the impact through the role of q in determining investment. In the case of the rise in the *US premium* alone, the results for other countries are driven by lower US demand as well as effects on wealth

Table 7.10 *US effective exchange rate and long rates*
(percentage points difference from baseline in first year)

	Long rate	Long real rate	dollar euro rate	dollar effective rate
ALLPREM	−2.04	−1.60	−7.64	−4.48
USPREM	−1.92	−1.52	−7.81	−4.51

of US shares in foreign portfolios. It is partly offset by lower bond yields, as discussed below. The simulation[14] gives an initial 2.5 per cent fall in US GDP, with much smaller effects elsewhere, as we might expect given the VECM results above. The decline in US equity prices reduces long-term interest rates everywhere, albeit by more in the US, (see changes in Table 7.10). This raises bond prices everywhere, offsetting the direct impact of US equities on wealth elsewhere.

Compare these results with Table 7.3 that takes account of both domestic and US equity price effects in euro area country VECMs. The VECM results suggest that the impact of US and European equity prices on the European economies accounts for only 10 to 20 per cent of the variance of output, whilst US equities account for 50 per cent of the variance of US output. Hence it is not at all surprising that our concerted equity price shock has around three times the effect on the US as it has on the euro area countries.

If we restrict contagion via wealth effects (implicitly assuming all US assets are held domestically), the impact on US output is greater, with US output being 0.1 and 0.3 percentage points further below baseline in the second and years of the analysis. Wealth in Canada would be two per cent higher, in the UK it would be 2.5 per cent higher after three years if there were no wealth stock contagion and in both countries the output effects would be 0.1 to 0.2 per cent of GDP smaller. In the euro area wealth would be two per cent higher in France and three per cent higher in Germany, reflecting the relative size of their foreign investment stocks, but in both countries the output effects would be smaller by 0.1 per cent than in the US premium shock.

Contagion to other equity markets marginally increases the scale of the shock in the US, whilst it increases the impact of the shock by 30–40 per cent in the euro area countries in the second and third years of the simulation, much in line with the variance decomposition reported above. The increased effects in the US reflect both the trade effects of

[14] Available as USPREM-default1.txt and ALLPREM-default1.txt on NiGEM model v205.

lower output elsewhere and the impact of lower wealth in the US because of a decline in the value of foreign assets. There are marked disinflationary effects of the shocks, especially in the US where inflation is on average 0.4 per cent below base for the first five years of the scenario, although the sharp depreciation of the dollar that we discuss below offsets the effects of lower demand on prices in the first year of the simulation. This is because demand is lower so inflation and output fall below baseline. Disinflationary effects are greater when there is contagion of share price falls. In response, the monetary authority is expected to cut nominal rates now and in the future. Reflecting these patterns, Table 7.10 shows that US nominal and real long rates also fall in each simulation, as does the effective exchange rate. All these changes help absorb the shock in the US, although the fall in the US effective exchange rate propagates the shock. Table 7.10 also gives the changes in exchange rates under the set of shocks. In general, currencies other than the US dollar appreciate, and propagation takes place through competitiveness effects in addition to the demand and wealth effects. However, the appreciation is marginally less when the equity price shock propagates to other countries, and this helps absorb some the extra shock suffered outside of the US.

It is useful to trace the monetary reaction in the model and in the world in more detail. We have undertaken a simulation with equity-based wealth permanently lower as a ratio of GDP and hence in the simulation saving has to rise to achieve the equilibrium wealth-income ratio embedded in the equation for consumption. This changes the saving and investment balance and *ceteris paribus*, investment will be less than saving. If this happens, nominal rates would be cut in every period that inflation and output would be below target. Nominal rates will be cut until demand reaches capacity and inflation settles on target, and this requires that the real interest rate is lower period by period than it is on our baseline. Hence the long real rate is also lower. Long real rates fall elsewhere, but not by as much. Euro area rates fall by 40 per cent of the US fall, for instance. Euro area inflation rates fall by 0.3 percentage points in the first year and 0.2 percentage points over the next four years of the all equity price simulation. The effects are marginally less in the US-only equity price fall simulation, moderated by the smaller appreciations associated with equity price contagion.

7.6.2   Policy responses to the shock

The impact of the shock is not given solely by the behavioural relationships of the private sector, asset price dynamics and the pattern of international trade and asset holdings, but also depends on the policy response

Table 7.11 *Impacts on output of a larger monetary reaction in the US*
(Percentage difference in GDP from US equity premium results)

	Year 1	Year 2	Year 3
Euro area – US Taylor Rule	0.16	0.14	0.04
(% of shock)	−31.27	−25.21	−8.36
Euro area – US double output feedback	0.16	0.14	0.06
(% of shock)	−31.16	−25.51	−11.12
US – US Taylor Rule	0.15	0.19	0.14
(% of shock)	−6.05	−7.18	−5.65
US – US double output feedback	0.36	0.42	0.30
(% of shock)	−14.03	−15.49	−12.00

of the authorities. The VECM results above represent the average policy response we have seen over the last thirty years, hence neither take account of improvements we may have seen in macroeconomic management, nor do they allow us to look at the effects of short-term policy innovations. As noted, NiGEM has inbuilt rules which target inflation in the case of monetary policy and seek budget balance over five years in the case of fiscal policy. The monetary policy rules use the short-term interest rate as an instrument and long-term interest rates are determined by the market in the light of their expectations of future short-term rates given their knowledge of the feedback rule and the structure of the economy.

Changing the monetary feedback in the US
It is useful to analyse the impact of easier monetary policy via raising the response to inflation of the monetary authorities in the monetary rules. We can change the monetary response in the US, either by doubling the feedback on inflation by implementing a Taylor Rule[15] in that country, or by increasing the feedback coefficient on the output gap within a Taylor Rule, and the results are presented in Table 7.11.

The Taylor Rule has twice the feedback on inflation as compared to our default, and hence the deflationary shock in the US leads to a larger fall in interest rates and hence to a smaller fall in output. Short rates fall by 1.2 percentage points in our base simulation, by 1.5 in our greater inflation response simulation, and by 2.0 in our additional greater output

[15] Available as USPREM-USTR-default.txt and USPREM-USTR-BIGIG2.txt on NiGEM model v205.

Table 7.12 *Impacts on output of a larger monetary reaction outside the US* (Percentage difference in GDP from US equity premium results)

	Year 1	Year 2	Year 3	Year 4
US	0.00	0.00	0.00	0.00
(% of shock)	0.02	−0.04	−0.05	0.14
Euro Area	0.03	0.07	0.08	0.08
(% of shock)	−6.32	−12.26	−16.21	−18.09
Germany	0.03	0.07	0.09	0.08
(% of shock)	−6.96	−11.58	−12.87	−11.61
France	0.04	0.07	0.08	0.07
(% of shock)	−6.79	−14.66	−18.81	−17.88
Italy	0.03	0.06	0.08	0.08
(% of shock)	−5.41	−10.30	−16.82	−27.14
Neths	0.05	0.09	0.10	0.09
(% of shock)	−5.40	−11.20	−14.66	−15.28

response simulation. The associated fall in long rates is the same in the last two simulations, and is twice the size of the base case fall. This action in the US removes about seven per cent of the shock, with the same absolute impact on the euro area (where the shock is smaller). Doubling the feedback coefficient on output in the US Taylor Rule is especially beneficial for the US, where a further eight per cent of the initial shock is removed, but there is no additional gain to the euro area from this change as it has no impact on world long-term interest rates.

Monetary responses outside the US
We can also focus on the monetary response in the rest of the world and we assume in the external extra monetary response scenario that the coefficient on inflation in the feedback rule used by all central banks outside the US is doubled.[16] Given the disinflationary impact of the equity price shock, interest rates are cut further. Table 7.12 shows that the impact on GDP of the US equity price shock in the euro area can be attenuated by a monetary response. Doubling the feedback coefficient removes about 20 per cent of the impact on the euro area of an equity price shock in the US. The stronger feedback in response to lower inflation reduces interest

[16] We used $r = 0.75(\text{inflation} - \text{target}) + .5(\text{Nominal output} - \text{target})$ and then we raised 0.75 to 1.5. Available as USPREM-DEFAULT1 + FEED.txt on NiGEM model v205.

Table 7.13 *Impact on output of turning solvency off in the US*
(Percentage difference in GDP from US equity premium results)

	Year 1	Year 2	Year 3	Year 4
Euro Area	0.00	0.02	0.04	0.06
(% of shock)	0.25	−3.27	−8.50	−12.75
US	−0.05	0.06	0.24	0.31
(% of shock)	2.06	−2.24	−9.37	−14.59

rates by 0.8 percentage points in the first year, rather than 0.6 percentage points as in our base case. However, there is little impact on long-term interest rates, and hence the effects are smaller in the bank-based German economy than in the slightly more market-based economies of Italy and particularly France and the Netherlands.

Fiscal feedbacks in the US
The US does have the possibility of loosening its fiscal stance. Our standard mode of operation has a fiscal feedback rule in place from the start of the run and this will induce a rise in direct taxes in response to the reductions in revenues and increases in spending that come from the reduction in demand and output that follow from the equity shock. There are various ways to change the fiscal response in the US, but the simplest is to assume that the fiscal feedback rule does not operate for the first five years of the scenario[17] (denoted 'turning solvency off'). This will induce an increase in the budget deficit, and after four years the US debt stock would be more than one per cent of GDP higher than it would otherwise have been. The real long-term interest rate (and the nominal long rate) is 0.12 higher than it would otherwise have been in response to an increase in the US deficit of 0.33 per cent of GDP on average over four years. It would also be possible to simulate a direct fiscal response to the decline in equity prices, and indeed we may have seen that in the US, where the budget moved from a surplus of around 1.5 per cent of GDP in 2000 to a deficit of $3^1/_4$ per cent of GDP in 2002.

The impact of the fiscal loosening on GDP is given in Table 7.13. Clearly, the US is the main beneficiary, and output would be 0.25 percentage points higher after three years than in the base US premium shock

---

[17] Available as USPREM-default1-NOSP.txt on NiGEM model v205.

by the third year of our simulations. However, the direct effects of this passive fiscal response are slow to come through, as they operate through a lower tax take. Some of the potential expansionary effects will be offset by higher real interest rates in the US, and as financial markets are presumed to be forward looking, long real rates jump up, and hence output effects are slightly larger in the first year than in our base case. This contractionary fiscal expansion only lasts for one year, however. Elsewhere the rise in long term real rates partly offsets the demand effects, and output is only marginally above that in the base case simulation in the euro area.

7.7   Conclusions

Equity price falls over 2000–2002 were comparable to the bear market of the mid-1970s, although evidence of a bubble is much stronger in recent years (given the low level of the risk premium) and correlations between equity markets have been much stronger. Based on estimated relationships, falls in equity prices of the scale observed can have significant recessionary effects on the world economy. In our VECM results we show that the contribution of equity prices to a variance decomposition of output is around three times greater in the US, at 50 per cent, than in the larger euro area economies. Composition of wealth, openness and trade patterns are among the key factors which influence the scope of output responses internationally. For the US in particular, the reliance of firms on market-based finance helps explain why equity prices have a much more sizeable impact on output than they do in Europe. Variance decompositions in VECM studies can only evaluate the 'average' policy response in the sample period, however, and we need to use structural models to explain how policy may mitigate the effects of shocks.

We undertake simulations on our model NiGEM and show that falls in equity prices have around three times greater an impact in the US than they do in the euro area, much as we would expect from the VECMs. However, the scale of impacts is not immutable. Monetary easing can help absorb such a shock. Fiscal-policy loosening can also help offset the effects of a collapse in equity prices, but it will mean higher long-term real interest rates and hence it moderates one of the automatic shock absorbers provided by the market mechanism. In our experiments we show that a monetary easing either in the US or the euro area associated with a change in feedback parameters can remove up to one-fifth of the impact of the initial shock in the area where the easing takes place. A loosening of the solvency constraint also allows ten per cent of the shock to be absorbed in the country where loosening takes place by increasing the debt stock. Clearly in both cases monetary and fiscal actions could be stronger, but if the US were to respond to an equity market shock by reducing the emphasis on inflation in its policy setting and loosening fiscal constraints, it could remove up to a third of the impact of the shock on the economy. We would conclude both that active policy in response to equity price falls is wise and that structural models are a useful part of the policy analysis toolkit.

REFERENCES

Allen, F., M. Chui, and A. Maddeloni (2004), 'Financial systems in Europe, the US and Asia', *Oxford Review of Economic Policy* Vol 20, pp. 490–508.
Ashworth, P. and P. E. Davis (2001), 'Some evidence on financial factors in the determination of aggregate business investment for the G7 countries' Discussion Paper No 187, NIESR, London.
Barrell, R. (2002), 'Equity markets, block realignments and the UK exchange rate', *National Institute Economic Review*, 181 (July), pp. 38–43.
Barrell, R., B. Becker, J. Byrne, S. Gottschalk, I. Hurst, and D. van Welsum (2004), 'Macroeconomic policy in Europe: Experiments with monetary responses and fiscal impulses' *Economic Modelling*, 21, pp. 977–1031.
Barrell, R., J. Byrne and K. Dury (2003), 'The implications of diversity in consumption behaviour for the choice of monetary policy rules in Europe' *Economic Modelling*, 20, pp. 275–299.
Barrell R. and E. P. Davis (2004a), 'Consumption, financial and real wealth effects in the G5', *Discussion Paper No. 232*, NIESR, London.
Barrell R. and E. P. Davis (2006), 'Financial liberalisation, consumption and wealth effects in seven OECD countries', *Scottish Journal of Political Economy* (forthcoming).
Barrell R. and E. P. Davis (2005), 'Equity prices and the real economy – a Vector Error Correction approach'. Paper presented at the FINPROP conference, *DIW*, Berlin, July 2005.
Barrell, R. and K. Dury (2000), 'An evaluation of monetary targeting regimes', *National Institute Economic Review No. 174*, October 2000.
Barrell, R. and K. Dury (2003), 'Asymmetric labour markets in a converging Europe: Do differences matter?' *National Institute Economic Review*, 183, January, pp. 56–65.
Blanchard, O. J. (1993), 'The vanishing equity premium', in R O'Brien (ed.), *Finance and the international economy 7*, Oxford University Press.
Bond, S., J. A. Elston, J. Mairesse and B. Mulkay (2003), 'Financial factors and investment in Belgium, France, Germany and the United Kingdom: a comparison using company panel data'. *Review of Economics and Statistics* Vol 85, pp. 153–165.
Byrne J. and E. P. Davis (2003a), Disaggregate wealth and aggregate consumption: an investigation of empirical relationships for the G7', *Oxford Bulletin of Economics and Statistics*, 65, pp. 1–23
Byrne J. and E. P. Davis (2003b), *Financial structure*, Cambridge University Press.

Davis, E. P. (2003), 'Comparing bear markets – 1973 and 2000', *National Institute Economic Review*, 183, pp. 70–81.

Davis, M. A. and M. G. Palumbo (2001), 'A primer on the economics and time series econometrics of wealth effects, finance and economics' Discussion Paper, Federal Reserve Board, Washington.

Gilchrist, S., C. Himmelberg, and G. Huberman (2004), 'Do stock price bubbles influence corporate investment?' *NBER Working Paper* 10537.

Haliassos, M. and A. Michaelides (2000), 'Calibration and computation of household portfolio models. In Guiso, L. Haliassos, M. and Jappelli, T. (eds.) *Household portfolio*. Cambridge, MA, The MIT Press.

Hubbard, R. (1998), 'Capital market imperfections and investment' *Journal of Economic Literature* Vol 36, pp. 193–225.

International Monetary Fund (IMF), (2001), 'Asset prices and the business cycle,' in *World Economic Outlook*, April, pp. 101–149.

International Monetary Fund (IMF), (2003), 'When bubbles burst', in *World Economic Outlook*, April, pp. 61–94.

Jagannathan, R., E. McGrattan, and A. Scherbina (2000), 'The declining US risk premium', *Federal Reserve Bank of Minneapolis Quarterly Review*, 24/4, pp. 3–19.

Johansen, S. (1995), *Likelihood-based inference in cointegrated vector autoregressive models* Oxford University Press.

Lettau, M. and S. Ludvigsen (2001), 'Consumption, aggregate wealth and expected stock returns'. *Journal of Finance*, Vol. 56(3), pp. 815–849.

Ludvigsen, S. and C. Steindel, C. (1999), 'How important is the stock market effect on consumption?' *Economic Policy Review*, Federal Reserve Bank of New York, July, Vol. 5(2)5 pp. 29–51.

Madsen, J. and E. P. Davis (2003), 'Equity prices, productivity growth and the "New Economy", *Economic Journal*, Vol. 116, pp. 791–811.

Mehra, R. and E. C. Prescott (1985), 'The equity premium: A puzzle', *Journal of Monetary Economics* 15, pp. 145–161.

Pesaran, M. H., T. Scheurmann, and S. Weiner (2004), 'Modelling regional interdependencies using a global error-correcting macroeconometric model' *Journal of Business and Economic Statistics* Vol. 22, pp. 129–162.

Pesaran, M. H., T. Scheurmann, B. J. Treutler, and S. Weiner (2005), 'Macroeconomic dynamics and credit risk, a global perspective' *Journal of Money, Credit and Banking* (forthcoming).

8 The euro area in the global economy: its sensitivity to the international environment and its influence on global economic developments

Alessandro Calza and Stephane Dees[1]

Introduction

External developments affect the euro area through a variety of transmission channels. While trade remains the predominant source of linkages between the euro area and the rest of the world, several studies show that other channels, notably financial markets, play an increasingly important role in the transmission of shocks and spillover effects to the euro area.[2]

The degree of exposure of a country to the international environment is traditionally measured by its trade-openness ratio. It is generally assumed that relatively-closed countries are rather immune from developments abroad, since in their case the trade channel is expected to play a limited role in the transmission of external shocks to domestic variables. Besides, it is often assumed that a country's sensitivity to external developments varies depending on its geographical trade structure. However, such measures of external exposure may be misleading as they can only capture the effect via direct trade of a shock. Beyond this direct effect, there are additional channels – third-market, second-round and spillover effects – through which economies are indirectly affected by the original shocks. Moreover, given increasing financial development and integration, financial markets have gained influence in the transmission of shocks across countries.

The purpose of this chapter is to assess the strength of international linkages using the extension by Dees *et al.* (2005, hereafter DdPS) of the Global Vector Auto-Regressive (GVAR) approach proposed by Pesaran *et al.* (2004). The GVAR approach consists of a comprehensive modelling

---

[1] Respectively Senior Economist, and Principal Economist, External Development Division, European Central Bank. All views expressed in this chapter are the authors' and do not necessarily reflect those held by the European Central Bank.

[2] See, for example, Anderton *et al.*(2004) for an overview.

framework that allows us to consider the responses to various types of global and country shocks through a number of transmission channels. These channels include both trade flows and financial linkages – notably, through capital, equity and currency markets – which have proved particularly relevant in the recent past. The GVAR model by DdPS includes twenty-six economic areas, linked through area-specific vector error-correcting models allowing for simultaneous inter-relations between domestic and foreign variables.[3] In order to deal with the modelling issues arising from European Monetary Union (notably, common nominal exchange and short-term interest rates since 1999), the GVAR model is estimated with the countries forming the euro area being treated as a single economy.

Using the DdPS' GVAR model, we assess the importance of changes in global economic conditions for developments in the euro area and, more generally, evaluate the dependence of the euro area economy on external factors. In addition, we analyse in detail the impact of changes in economic conditions in the US, the world's largest economy and a key euro-area economic partner. The effect of changes in the international environment of the euro area is simulated on the basis of generalised impulse response functions (GIRFs), which summarise the information derived from the correlations between the endogenous variables and their foreign counterparts as well as from the model estimates.

As a complement to the simulations of the effects of global and US shocks on the euro area, we assess the impact of changes in the economic conditions of the euro area on its main trading partners, with a view to evaluating the importance of the euro area in the global economy.

The chapter reviews the most recent contributions to the literature on international linkages and discusses the relative merits of the different approaches, gives an overview of the version of the GVAR used in this chapter, and presents a generalised impulse-response analysis of the impact of global and (selected) area-specific shocks.

How to account for international linkages?

It is often argued that the globalisation arising from increased cross-country trade and financial integration over the past few decades has strengthened international business-cycle linkages. In recent years a substantial empirical literature aiming to test this hypothesis has accumulated. Most recent studies focus on quantifying the importance of

---

[3] See Appendix 1 for details about the geographical coverage of the model.

common factors in determining national macroeconomic developments. A strand of the literature also investigates whether co-movements in economic activity reflect the increased role of common shocks or the enhanced transmission of shocks across countries and regions. More recently, the simultaneous economic slowdown in the United States and Europe observed in 2000 and 2001 has prompted a renewed flow of contributions.

It is fair to say that so far the results of this literature remain relatively mixed. For instance, using a variety of country samples and econometric techniques, several authors (e.g. Gregory *et al.*, 1997; Kose *et al.*, 2003; and Lumsdaine and Prasad, 2003) provide empirical evidence of a common component of international business cycles. Kose *et al.*(2003) specifically refer to this component as a 'world business cycle'. These studies usually find that the fraction of output fluctuations explained by the common component varies significantly by country, but is typically higher for developed industrialised economies than for emerging countries.

Monfort *et al.* (2003) also find that the output developments in G7 countries are driven to a substantial extent by common dynamics, which they relate to oil prices (an important and easily-identifiable common shock). These authors also find evidence of asymmetric spillovers between America and Europe (with spillovers running from the former to the latter but not vice versa) and argue that such spillovers have become stronger in recent years, reflecting the process of globalisation.

By contrast, Kose *et al.* (2003) find that the fraction of output fluctuations explained by the common factor has not significantly increased in recent decades and has in fact decreased over the 1990s. This finding leads them to the conclusion that there is little evidence that increased integration has resulted in stronger business-cycle synchronisation. In addition, Doyle and Faust (2005) argue that recent increases in the cross-section correlation across the G7 economies are not statistically significant, once one allows for breaks in the means and variances of the variables.

An influential work by Stock and Watson (2003) shows that over the last four decades there has been a decrease in output-growth volatility owing to weaker international shocks as well as key structural changes (such as new stock management methods and more credible monetary policy). However, this has not translated into closer international business-cycle synchronisation over time: depending on the methodology used, the G7 average cross-country correlation is either unchanged across the two sub-samples considered (1960–1983 and 1983–2002) or slightly drops over time.

More specifically on the US, Doyle and Faust (2002) find that there is little evidence of a structural rise in the correlation between GDP growth in the US and in the G7 in recent decades, while Heathcote and Perri (2003) argue that over the last forty years US output has become less synchronised with that of the rest of the world. As regards evidence for the euro area, Anderton *et al.* (2004) show that the correlation between euro-area GDP growth and a common factor derived from GDP data for the US, Canada, the UK and the euro area has pronouncedly increased in recent years, yet it has followed a declining trend over the last three decades.

One shortcoming of most recent empirical studies is that they are usually based on purely-statistical methods (e.g. factor analysis) and, as a result, remain silent about the channels through which shocks are transmitted across countries. By contrast, earlier work has been typically based on more-traditional structural approaches and aimed to explicitly model the various channels and to quantify their role in the transmission process. Global macroeconometric models – such as those developed by international organisations (e.g. IMF's Multimod, OECD's Interlink) or by research institutes (e.g. NIESR's NIGEM) – consist of estimated and/or calibrated large-scale structural models providing interesting insights into the linkages that exist among the main economies. However, as argued in Pesaran *et al.*(2004), these models do not typically account for the financial linkages among the world's major economies and may be rather cumbersome to use in practice. In addition, the different economic relationships implying linkages among the individual country models are sometimes hard to interpret or may be difficult to uncover because of lack of transparency regarding the country-specific models.

More recently, in the context of the New International Macroeconomics, several authors have developed multi-country Dynamic Stochastic General Equilibrium (DSGE) models featuring nominal rigidities and imperfect competition to analyse the transmission of shocks across countries (e.g. Corsetti and Pesenti, 2001). Yet, even using this category of models, the modelling of international linkages is not always straightforward, with the estimated spillover effects remaining in some cases limited (e.g. Adjemian *et al.*, 2004). In addition, the reliability of these models has been in the past undermined by their difficulty to fit the data (Kim and Pagan, 1995), though this is an area in which substantial progress is being currently made.

To sum up, two main approaches have been typically used to assess the impact of the international environment on domestic economies: purely statistical methods (such as factor models) or structural models (e.g. traditional large-scale macroeconometric models or, more recently, micro-founded open economy models). As explained in the next section, the application of the GVAR approach to the study of the international transmission of shocks may bridge the gap between these alternative approaches and overcome some of the limitations usually faced with the modelling of international business cycle linkages.

GVAR approach: an overview

As mentioned earlier, the GVAR approach consists of specifying and estimating a set of country-specific vector error-correcting models that are consistently combined to generate a global model that can be simultaneously solved for all the variables in the world economy. This approach addresses the problem of consistently modelling interdependencies among many economies through the construction of 'foreign' variables, which are included in each individual country model. Thus, each country model includes domestic variables plus variables obtained from the aggregation of data on the foreign economies using weights derived from trade statistics. Because the set of weights for each country reflects its specific geographical trade composition, foreign variables vary across countries. Subject to appropriate testing, the country-specific foreign variables are treated as weakly exogenous during the estimation of the individual country models.

DdPS show that, through the inclusion of such country-specific foreign variables, the GVAR approach provides an approximate solution to a global unobserved common factor model, such as those surveyed in the previous section. In addition, Pesaran and Smith (2005) argue that each country-specific model can be derived from a DSGE model of a small open economy, such as Gali and Monacelli (2005). Based on these observations, it can be argued that the GVAR approach bridges the gap between the alternative approaches – factor analysis and structural modelling – previously used to model international business cycle linkages. The rest of this section presents a short overview of the GVAR approach, while referring the reader to DdPS for a more detailed discussion.

Suppose that there are $N+1$ countries indexed by $i = 0, 1, \ldots, N$, with $i = 0$ for the US, the numeraire country. The GVAR can be written as the collection of individual country VAR(p_i, q_i) models:

$$\Phi_i(L, p_i)\mathbf{x}_{it} = \mathbf{a}_{i0} + \mathbf{a}_{i1}t + \Upsilon_i(L, q_i)\mathbf{d}_t + \Lambda_i(L, q_i)\mathbf{x}_{it}^* + \mathbf{u}_{it}, \quad (1)$$

where $\mathbf{x}_{it}$ is the $k_i \times 1$ (with k_i usually five or six) vector of modelled variables, $\mathbf{d}_t$ is the vector of observed international variables common to all countries, and $\mathbf{x}_{it}^*$ is the $k_i^* \times 1$ vector of foreign variables specific to country i. $\Phi_i(L, p_i)$ and $\Lambda_i(L, q_i)$ are the $k_i \times k_i$ and $k_i \times k_i^*$ matrix polynomials in the lag operator L of the coefficients of the domestic and country-specific foreign variables, respectively. $\mathbf{a}_{i0}$ and $\mathbf{a}_{i1}$ are the $k_i \times 1$ vectors of coefficients of the deterministic variables, here intercepts and linear trends. $\Upsilon_i(L, p_i)$ is the $k_i \times k^d$ matrix polynomial of coefficients of the international variables $\mathbf{d}_t$. $\mathbf{u}_{it}$ is a $k_i \times 1$ vector of idiosyncratic country-specific shocks.

The country-specific models can be consistently estimated separately, treating $\mathbf{x}_{it}^*$ as weakly exogenous, which is compatible with a certain degree of weak dependence across $\mathbf{u}_{it}$.[4] The country-specific foreign variables $\mathbf{x}_{it}^*$ are constructed as country-specific trade-weighted averages over the values of the other countries:

$$\mathbf{x}_{it}^* = \sum_{j=0}^{N} w_{ij}\mathbf{x}_{jt}, \text{ with } w_{ii} = 0, \tag{2}$$

where w_{ij} is the share of country j in the trade (exports plus imports) of country i.[5]

After selecting the lag length-order p_i and q_i for each country by means of the Akaike Information Criterion (allowing for a maximum lag-order of 2), the VAR(p_i, q_i) models are estimated separately for each country, allowing for the possibility of cointegration among $\mathbf{x}_{it}$, $\mathbf{x}_{it}^*$ and $\mathbf{d}_t$.

Once the individual country models are estimated, all the $k = \sum_{i=0}^{N} k_i$ endogenous variables of the global economy, collected in the $k \times 1$ vector $\mathbf{x}_t = (\mathbf{x}_{0t}', \mathbf{x}_{1t}', \ldots, \mathbf{x}_{Nt}')'$, are solved simultaneously. To do this (1) can be written as:

$$\mathbf{A}_i(L, p_i, q_i)\mathbf{z}_{it} = \varphi_{it}, \text{ for } i = 0, 1, 2, \ldots, N \tag{3}$$

where

$$\mathbf{A}_i(L, p_i, q_i) = [\Phi_i(L, p_i), -\Lambda_i(L, q_i)], \mathbf{z}_{it} = \begin{pmatrix} \mathbf{x}_{it} \\ \mathbf{x}_{it}^* \end{pmatrix},$$

$$\varphi_{it} = \mathbf{a}_{i0} + \mathbf{a}_{i1}t + \Upsilon_i(L, q_i)\mathbf{d}_t + \mathbf{u}_{it}.$$

Let $p = \max(p_0, p_1, \ldots, p_N, q_0, q_1, \ldots, q_N)$ and construct $\mathbf{A}_i(L, p)$ from $\mathbf{A}_i(L, p_i, q_i)$ by augmenting the $p - p_i$ or $p - q_i$ additional terms in powers of L by zeros. Also note that:

$$\mathbf{z}_{it} = \mathbf{W}_i\mathbf{x}_t, \; i = 0, 1, 2, \ldots, N, \tag{4}$$

where $\mathbf{W}_i$ is a $(k_i + k_i^*) \times k$ matrix, defined by the country-specific weights, w_{ji}.

---

[4] For further details see DdPS.
[5] See Appendix 1 for more details on the computation of the trade-based weights.

With the above notations (3) can be written equivalently as:

$$\mathbf{A}_i(L, p)\mathbf{W}_i\mathbf{x}_t = \varphi_{it}, \ i = 0, 1, \ldots, N,$$

and then stack to yield the VAR(p) model in $\mathbf{x}_t$:

$$\mathbf{G}(L, p)\mathbf{x}_t = \varphi_t, \tag{5}$$

where:

$$\mathbf{G}(L, p) = \begin{pmatrix} \mathbf{A}_0(L, p)\mathbf{W}_0 \\ \mathbf{A}_1(L, p)\mathbf{W}_1 \\ \vdots \\ \mathbf{A}_N(L, p)\mathbf{W}_N \end{pmatrix}, \varphi_t = \begin{pmatrix} \varphi_{0t} \\ \varphi_{1t} \\ \vdots \\ \varphi_{Nt} \end{pmatrix}. \tag{6}$$

The GVAR(p) model (5) can now be solved recursively and used for forecasting or generalised impulse response analysis in the usual manner.

The GVAR model developed in DdPS covers thirty-three countries, where eight of the eleven countries that originally joined Stage Three of European Monetary Union on 1 January 1999 are grouped together, while the remaining twenty-five countries are modeled individually.[6] The present GVAR model, therefore, contains twenty-six countries/regions estimated over the sample period 1979(2)–2003(4).

The endogenous variables included in the GVAR, when available, are the logarithm of real output (y_{it}); the rate of quarterly inflation ($\pi_{it} = p_{it} - p_{it-1}$), with p_{it} the logarithm of a domestic price index; the real exchange rate ($e_{it} - p_{it}$), with e_{it} the logarithm of the nominal exchange rate against the dollar; the logarithm of real equity prices (q_{it}); a short-term interest rate $\left(\rho_{it}^S = 0.25 * \ln(1 + R_{it}^S/100)\right)$, where R_{it}^S is a short-term annualised rate of interest measured in per cent; and a long-term interest rate $\left(\rho_{it}^L = 0.25 * \ln(1 + R_{it}^L/100)\right)$, where R_{it}^L is a long-term annualised rate of interest (typically a long-term government bond yield) measured in per cent. The time series data for the euro area were constructed as cross-section weighted averages of $y_{it}, \pi_{it}, q_{it}, \rho_{it}^S, \rho_{it}^L$ over Germany, France, Italy, Spain, Netherlands, Belgium, Austria and Finland, using average Purchasing Power Parity GDP weights over the 1999–2001 period.

The vector of common international variables $\mathbf{d}_t$ includes only the logarithm of oil prices. With the exception of the US model, all individual models include the country-specific foreign variables, $y_{it}^*, \pi_{it}^*, q_{it}^*, \rho_{it}^{*S}, \rho_{it}^{*L}$ and oil prices (p_t^o). Based on the results of appropriate tests, these variables are included as weakly exogenous. The specification of the US

[6] See Table 8.2 for the list of modelled countries. Although not all the euro-area countries are modelled, the eight countries included provide a fairly extensive coverage of the euro-area economy. For instance, in 2000 these countries jointly accounted for around 93% of the euro area's GDP (at PPP exchange rates) and for about 92% of its labour force.

model differs from that of the other countries in that oil prices are included as an endogenous (rather than exogenous) variable, while only $e^*_{U.S.,t} - p^*_{U.S.,t}$, $y^*_{U.S.,t}$, and $\pi^*_{U.S.,t}$ are included as weakly exogenous foreign variables. The endogeneity of oil prices reflects the large size of the US economy. The omission of $q^*_{U.S.,t}$, $R^{*S}_{U.S.,t}$ and $R^{*L}_{U.S.,t}$ from the vector of US-specific foreign financial variables reflects the results of tests showing that these variables are not weakly exogenous with respect to the US domestic financial variables, in turn reflecting the importance of the US financial markets within the global financial system.

Applications

In the GVAR, international linkages are taken into account through three distinct, but interrelated channels: (1) direct dependence of $\mathbf{x}_{it}$ on the vector of foreign variables $\mathbf{x}^*_{it}$; (2) dependence of $\mathbf{x}_{it}$ on common global exogenous variables $\mathbf{d}_t$ (in our case, only oil prices); and (3) non-zero contemporaneous dependence of shocks in country i on the shock in country j, as measured by the cross-country covariances, Ω_{ij}.

In order to better understand the mechanics of the first channel, the next subsection will study the links between the domestic endogenous and foreign country-specific variables, using simple correlation analyses. In addition, selected results of the estimation of the GVAR model will be reported to assess the statistical significance and magnitude of the direct impact of foreign influences (both country-specific and common factors) on the euro-area domestic variables, thereby also shedding light on the second channel. Thereafter, simulations based on GIRFs will be shown in order to illustrate more comprehensively the dynamics of the linkages between the euro area and its international environment through the three different channels underlying the GVAR model.

How strong are the linkages between the euro area and its international environment?

Correlations between euro-area variables and their foreign counterparts

As mentioned earlier, it is often argued that global integration (e.g. via trade and financial markets) has, in recent decades, led to a larger degree of business-cycle synchronisation across the main economies. The analysis of the contemporaneous correlations between euro-area variables and the corresponding foreign variables included in the GVAR model may potentially shed light on the degree of synchronisation between the euro-area economy and its international environment. Figure 8.1

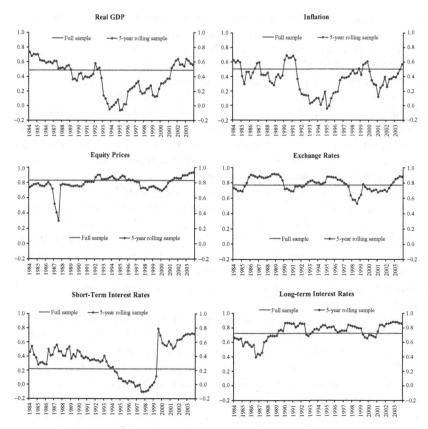

Figure 8.1. Correlation between quarterly changes in euro area and foreign variables (*Correlation coefficients*)

shows the developments in the indices of correlation between quarterly changes in euro-area GDP, inflation and selected asset prices (equity prices, exchange rate and interest rates) and those in the respective foreign variables over the period 1979(1)–2003(4). In addition, in order to assess whether such correlations have changed over time, we compute the indices over five-year rolling sample periods, starting from the period 1979(1)–1983(4) and shifting the sample ahead by one quarter at a time.

The full-sample period correlation between domestic and foreign variables is fairly high for both output (0.49) and inflation (0.5). In particular, the correlation index for GDP is slightly higher than that obtained by Doyle and Faust (2002) for the US (0.44) on the basis of a similar exercise. This confirms evidence of a somewhat larger sensitivity to changes in conditions in the international environment of economic activity in the euro area relative to the US.

The relatively-high correlation between euro area and foreign inflation is likely to reflect at least to some extent the impact of common inflationary shocks, notably related to oil price developments.[7] The correlation between euro area and foreign variables is generally higher for the asset prices considered (with the exception of short-term interest rates) than for output and inflation. This is not entirely surprising given the well-known evidence of stronger cross-country integration in capital markets than in markets for goods and services.

The correlation indices over five-year rolling samples reveal, though, significant fluctuations over the sample period. The correlation index between euro area and foreign GDP is very high in the first half of the 1980s, but declines gradually throughout the rest of the decade, dropping sharply at the beginning of the 1990s, in correspondence with the European recession in the wake of German reunification. Hereafter, the correlation index recovers, returning to fairly high levels towards the end of the sample period.

Similar fluctuations can be observed for the correlation between euro-area and foreign inflation. Also in this case the correlation index markedly falls in the 1990s, possibly reflecting idiosyncratic factors such as the above-mentioned recession in the wake of German reunification as well as the sharp disinflation in the run-up to the start of Stage Three of European Monetary Union. The fluctuations are significantly less pronounced for asset prices, with the correlations remaining relatively steady at fairly high rates. The main exception is the large fluctuation observed for the short-term interest rates in the second half of the 1990s, largely reflecting sharp movements in interest rates in some emerging countries after the Asian crisis.

Significance and magnitude of the contemporaneous impact of foreign variables on euro-area variables

The direct effect of developments in the international economic environment on the euro area can be formally assessed from the estimated coefficients of the contemporaneous foreign variables in the equations for the corresponding domestic variables. These coefficients can be interpreted as impact elasticities between domestic and foreign variables

---

[7] Ciccarelli and Mojon (2004) have recently argued that a common factor derived from national inflation data accounts for around 70% of the variance of inflation in OECD countries, which leads them to the conclusion that inflation is predominantly a global phenomenon.

Table 8.1 *Contemporaneous effects of foreign variables on their euro area counterparts*

	Domestic variables				
	y	Δp	q	ρ^S	ρ^L
Country-specific foreign variables					
y^*	0.50*	0.02	−0.08	0.01	−0.03
	(0.10)	(0.09)	(1.11)	(0.03)	(0.02)
Δp^*	−0.29*	0.12	1.81	−0.03	0.00
	(0.10)	(0.08)	(1.04)	(0.02)	(0.02)
q^*	−0.01	0.01	1.16*	0.00	0.00
	(0.01)	(0.01)	(0.08)	(0.00)	(0.00)
ρ^{*S}	0.32*	−0.02	0.38	0.09*	0.01
	(0.09)	(0.08)	(0.99)	(0.02)	(0.01)
ρ^{*L}	0.49	0.87*	7.40	0.05	0.62*
	(0.49)	(0.41)	(5.22)	(0.12)	(0.08)
Common foreign variables					
p^o	0.00	0.01*	−0.12*	0.00	0.00
	(0.00)	(0.00)	(0.03)	(0.00)	(0.00)

Source: Dees *et al.* (2005).
Note: * denotes statistical significance at the 5% level or less. Standard errors are in parentheses.

(see Table 8.1). The elasticities are statistically significant at the conventional levels for all variables, except inflation, and have the expected positive sign. This confirms that developments in international economic conditions spill over directly into the euro area.

More precisely, a one percentage point rise in foreign output leads to a contemporaneous 0.5 percentage point increase in domestic output in the euro area. As noted by DdPS, this value of the point elasticity is close to the estimates for other large economies, such as Japan (0.48) and the UK (0.44), but somewhat larger than that obtained for the US (0.34). The higher-impact elasticity of foreign output for the euro area relative to the US is consistent with the euro area's relatively-larger degree of trade openness.

Foreign inflation and short-term interest rates have statistically-significant contemporaneous effects on euro-area output of comparable magnitude but of opposite sign, implying a positive impact of (ex-post) real interest rates. The statistical significance of foreign output and real interest rates in the euro-area output equation implies that the model adequately controls for changes in global demand conditions.

Foreign prices have no statistically-significant contemporaneous effect on euro-area prices, while the effect of oil prices is limited. This suggests that in the short-run, euro-area prices are not very sensitive to external influences. By contrast, real equity prices and long-term interest rates are highly sensitive to contemporaneous foreign developments, as can be evinced from their large and statistically-significant impact elasticities. In particular, the estimated impact elasticity for real equity prices is above unity (1.16), suggesting that in the short-term, euro-area equity markets tend to amplify movements in foreign equity prices.

There is also distinct evidence of a negative impact of higher oil prices on euro-area equity prices. This negative impact may reflect the expected effects of oil price rises on production costs and corporate profitability as well as their impact through consumer and investor confidence and other channels.

The impact elasticity between foreign and domestic short-term interest rates is statistically significant but rather small, especially compared with that estimated for long-term interest rates. This difference reflects the predominance – at least for the large economies – of domestic factors in determining the behaviour of short-term interest rates (which are closely linked to policy rates). By contrast, long-term interest rates are generally linked to a larger extent to foreign rates through integration in international capital markets.

The sensitivity of the euro-area economy to its international environment

This section examines the sensitivity of the euro-area economy to (selected) real and financial shocks to the international environment on the basis of an impulse response function analysis. We first analyse the impact of global (negative) shocks to aggregate demand and to real equity prices. We subsequently replicate the simulations for shocks originating from the US in order to assess the role of this country within the international environment of the euro area. For the sake of comparison, we present the effects of these shocks for both the euro area and other main countries.

While 'global shocks' can be intuitively defined as unexpected events simultaneously hitting all economic areas in the world, the analysis in this section requires a precise technical definition. More precisely, we consider shocks common to all countries but specific to individual variables. Such shocks are computed as cross-country weighted averages of variable-specific shocks, with the weights reflecting the relative importance of each country in the world economy.[8]

---

[8] For technical details on the definition of global shocks see Appendix 2.

Impact of external 'aggregate demand shocks' on the euro area

Figure 8.2 shows the impact on the main economic areas of a negative one-standard error shock to global real GDP. The direct impact of the shock on output in the various countries and regions ranges between −0.15 and −0.35 per cent. In most cases the peak of the response is reached after two to four quarters, though in the case of the euro area the response is more sluggish. The US and the euro area are the two regions where the peak effect is the largest (around −0.4%), though with significant differences in terms of persistence. While the effect on US output returns to baseline after few quarters, it is more persistent for the euro area.

The initial reaction of inflation is negative in most areas, which lends support to the interpretation of the shock as a global 'aggregate demand shock'. The impact of the shock tends to be relatively large in the short-term, especially for the UK and fairly persistent in most regions.

As regards asset prices, the sign of the equity price responses varies across regions: in Japan, the euro area and the rest of Western Europe equity prices are negatively affected by the global output shock; by contrast, the response is positive in the remaining regions. However, the magnitude of the responses is relatively small in all areas. Currencies tend to depreciate permanently *vis-à-vis* the US dollar in all countries, with the exception of Japan, where the yen appreciates to some extent. Nevertheless, like in the case of equity prices, the currency movements following the unexpected decline in global aggregate demand remain overall rather limited.

The responses of interest rates are relatively synchronous and qualitatively homogeneous across regions for both policy-related short-term rates and long-term bond yields. The US is the country with the largest reaction of interest rates to the world aggregate demand shock. By contrast, in Japan the interest rate responses are fairly small and even slightly positive in the case of the short-term interest rate. The significant decline in the US short-term rate may implicitly reflect a policy response, given the relatively large weight of the US in global output and the important role of domestic economic growth in the reaction function of the US monetary authorities.

More specifically on the evidence for the euro area, the responses to an aggregate demand shock worldwide are qualitatively similar to those of the other main economic areas, though the impact on output seems to be more persistent in the euro area. Admittedly, a global aggregate demand shock may be a somewhat artificial concept. Even shocks with worldwide implications are likely to originate from a specific region. More specifically, given the relatively-large importance of the US in the global

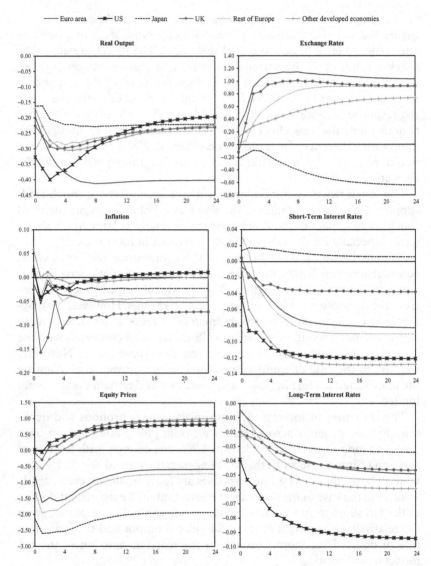

Figure 8.2. Impulse responses of a negative standard error (−1σ) shock
to global real GDP on various variables across regions
(Units on horizontal axis: quarters; vertical axis: percentage change)

economy, developments in this country are likely to have global implications. For instance, the slowdown in worldwide economic growth observed between 2000 and 2001 followed to a large extent developments in the US. In order to explore this issue, it may be useful to replicate the previous impulse response analysis for a US aggregate demand shock. This analysis may shed light on the relevance for the euro-area economy of changes in US domestic economic conditions.

From a static perspective, the US economy should have a relatively limited weight in the international environment of the euro area. This is because the US directly accounts for 'only' around 15 per cent of euro-area foreign demand, compared to over 40 per cent accounted for by its neighbouring countries (the UK plus the rest of Europe). However, this assumption would be misleading, since it is based only on the geographical composition of euro area direct trade and ignores the broader role of the US in the world economy. In fact, the impact of changes in US economic conditions on the euro area may be amplified through additional trade-related channels effects (namely, second-round and third-country effects) and/or other channels, such as financial linkages. As these multiple indirect effects remain difficult to identify and gauge, the GVAR approach may prove helpful in providing a quantification of the total impact on the euro area of a shock originating from the US economy.

The results of this simulation are reported in Figure 8.3. As in the previous case, the fall in US output can be interpreted as a negative aggregate demand shock, since it is followed by a decline in US inflation. The negative one-standard error shock to US real GDP leads to a 0.5 per cent reduction in domestic real GDP on impact (-0.35% after four years) and also has a relatively-large dampening impact on world output. While euro-area output is not affected on impact, thereafter the external shock gradually propagates and leads after one year to a persistent decline in area-wide real GDP of around 0.10 per cent.

A rapid back-of-the-envelope calculation based on the weight of the US in euro-area foreign demand and the openness ratio of the latter would suggest a long-run elasticity of euro-area output to a change in US GDP of just below 0.10.[9] The GVAR results show a significantly-larger sensitivity of euro area output to a shock on US economic activity (around three times the elasticity based on the back-of-the-envelope calculation).

[9] Using an import elasticity of US imports to GDP of 2 and a share of the US in the euro area foreign demand of 17%, a 1% increase in US GDP would translate into a 2% increase in US imports, increasing in turn euro-area exports by 0.35%. Given the share of exports in euro-area GDP (17%), this increase in export would translate into an initial increase of 0.06% in euro area GDP. Assuming the Keynesian demand multiplier equal to 1.5, this initial increase in GDP would lead to a total long-run impact on GDP equal to 0.09%.

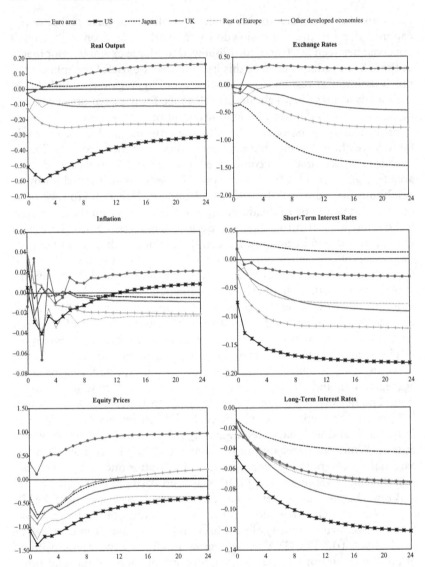

Figure 8.3. Impulse responses of a negative standard error (-1σ) shock to US real GDP on various variables across regions
(Units on horizontal axis; quarters; vertical axis: percentage change)

Figure 8.3 also shows that the group labelled 'other developed countries' is one of the most affected – in terms of output losses – by the US aggregate demand shock. As Canada belongs to this group, this result is not entirely surprising, given the trade exposure of this country to the US.

As regards the other variables, inflation in the US becomes negative in the short-term and takes over two years to return to baseline. The reaction of inflation in the other regions is similar but remains limited. The reaction of real exchange rates is also very small, with only the Japanese yen somewhat appreciating. The other variables react in a relatively synchronous manner, especially long-term interest rates and equity prices (with the exception of the UK).

Overall, this analysis reveals that, once indirect effects are factored in, the long-run impact of domestic US shocks on the euro area is likely to be larger than could be expected only on the basis of direct trade flows. More generally, this result can be interpreted as effectively illustrating the role of indirect channels in determining the ultimate impact of global economic developments on the euro area.

Impact of external 'equity shocks' on the euro area

The previous analysis has focused on how (specific) real shocks are transmitted through international linkages. As the impacts of such shocks seem to be larger than could be expected from a trade perspective, additional channels are likely to play a major role in the amplification and propagation of the original impulses. In order to investigate the role of financial channels in the transmission mechanism, the following simulations analyse the impact of shocks to real equity prices. As in the previous case, we distinguish between shocks to global and US equity prices.

Figure 8.4 shows the responses of the endogenous variables to a negative one standard error shock to real equity prices worldwide. On impact, the shock hits the various equity markets similarly, leading to immediate decreases in real equity prices ranging between 3 and 6 per cent. Over the next few quarters, the magnitude of the responses tends to increase, especially in the euro area and the rest of Western Europe, where after two years the reduction in equity prices becomes larger than 10 per cent. In the other regions, the long-run response of equity prices to the shock is more moderate and varies between −4 and −6 per cent.

The impact of the global equity shock on real GDP in the various countries is negative, with persistent output losses ranging between 0.1 and 0.7 per cent. Inflation decreases, with no marked differences across countries. By contrast, the responses of real exchange rates diverge across countries, with no clear pattern emerging at the global level. Interest rates

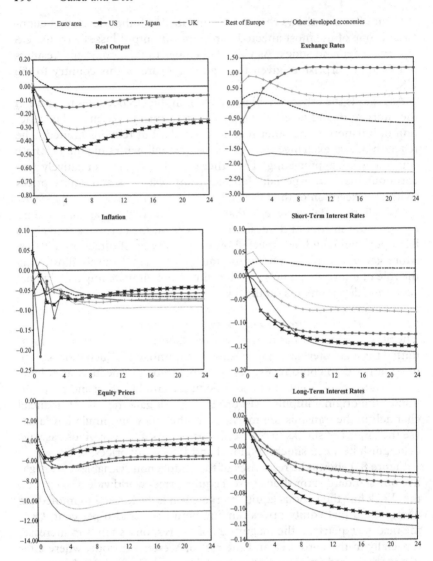

Figure 8.4. Impulse responses of a negative standard error (-1σ) shock to global real equity prices on various variables across regions
(Units on horizontal axis; quarters; vertical axis: percentage change)

decline, probably reflecting both the deterioration in economic activity and the disinflationary impact of the shock.

Figure 8.5 shows the results of a shock of the same nature, but initially located in the US. The impulse responses to a US equity price shock look strikingly similar to those following a world equity shock for all countries other than the US (particularly the euro area). Not surprisingly, the responses from US variables look now more pronounced, but this mainly reflects the larger scale of the domestic shock. Perhaps, the main difference between the responses to a global and a domestic equity shock regards the exchange rate, since in the latter case there is clearer evidence of a depreciation of the dollar *vis-à-vis* the currencies of the other main regions (with the notable exception of the UK).

Overall, the results of this analysis illustrate, first, the large role of the US in the global financial system and, second, the significant synchronisation in equity markets across countries.

The weight of the euro area in economic developments worldwide

An interesting feature of the previous simulations is the similarity in the responses to external shocks between the euro area and the rest of Western Europe. In order to further analyse the nature and strength of the inter-relationships between the euro area and its neighbours, we also perform an impulse response analysis for both an 'aggregate demand shock' and an 'equity shock' originating from the euro area. These simulations allow us to assess the role of the euro area in the world economy and also complement the evidence presented in the previous section for shocks to US variables.

Impact of 'aggregate demand shock' to the euro area and *transmission to its partners*

Figure 8.6 shows the responses to a negative one-standard error shock to euro area real GDP. Real GDP decreases on impact by 0.3 per cent in the euro area before converging to a persistent decline of almost 0.5 per cent after two years. The shock also has a relatively large impact on the neighbouring economies. Real output in the rest of Western Europe is reduced by 0.2 per cent on impact and by about 0.3 per cent in the long-run. The decline in UK output is slightly more muted: 0.1 per cent on impact and around 0.2 per cent after two years.

Inflation declines by a very small amount in the euro area and the rest of Western Europe, consistent with evidence of nominal rigidities in these areas. The response of equity prices is very similar between the euro

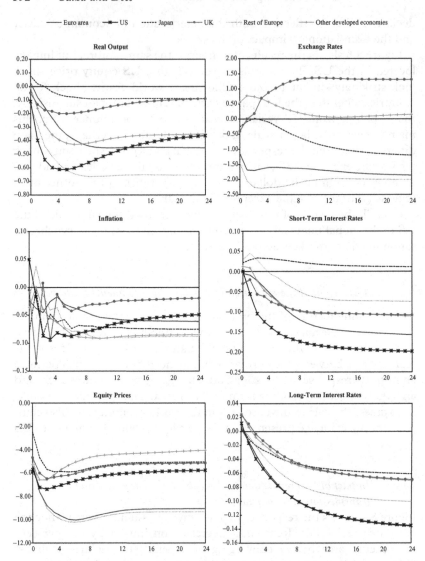

Figure 8.5. Impulse responses of a negative standard error (-1σ) shock to US real equity prices on various variables across regions
(Units on horizontal axis: quarters; vertical axis: percentage change)

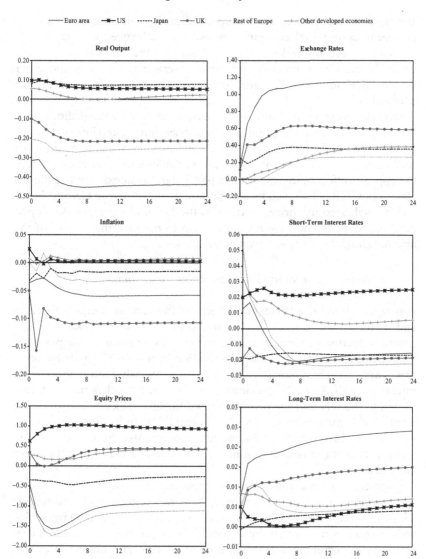

Figure 8.6. Impulse responses of a negative standard error (-1σ) shock to euro area real GDP on various variables across regions
(Units on horizontal axis: quarters; vertical axis: percentage change)

area and the rest of Western Europe, indicating that integration among European continental economies is also fairly advanced as regards capital and financial markets. By contrast, the reaction of real equity prices in the UK is more akin to that observed for the US and other developed economies. The euro tends to depreciate *vis-a-vis* the other currencies.

Overall, this analysis shows that an euro aggregate-demand shock has a significant effect on its neighbouring countries, but limited impact beyond Europe. The responses of the other countries and regions to a euro-area shock remain relatively limited for most variables and in some cases, have the opposite effect than expected. In particular, the unexpected decline in euro area GDP is followed by a slight rise in output in the US and Japan and by higher equity prices in the US, the UK and the other developed economies. These positive responses help to mitigate the impact of the original shock for the European economies.

Impact of an 'equity shock' on the euro area and transmission to its partners

Figure 8.7 shows the effects of a shock on the euro-area equity markets and its transmission to the rest of the world. The shock leads to a persistent reduction in euro-area real equity prices by around nine per cent. Domestically, this shock leads to a decline in real GDP (by 0.1% after two years), a slight decrease in inflation and somewhat lower short-term interest rates. Like in the previous simulation, the shock is mainly transmitted to the UK and the rest of Western Europe, which also experience a fall in real equity prices, a decrease in real GDP and a marginal decline in inflation. In terms of exchange rate movements, the European currencies (except the British pound) tend to appreciate *vis-à-vis* the other currencies.

Long-term interest rates increase, though to a limited extent. Even in the euro area, the long-term rates follows the pattern displayed worldwide. This might indicate that bond markets are more affected by worldwide responses rather than by domestic developments (as indicated also by the large correlations between domestic long-term interest rates and their foreign counterparts).

Beyond Europe, the responses of most variables to a euro-area equity shock remain relatively limited, that is close to zero or even slightly positive in the case of real GDP and the short-term interest rate. These positive effects on the rest of the world might be explained by the appreciation of the euro, which allows the other economies to gain some competitiveness *vis-à-vis* the euro area.

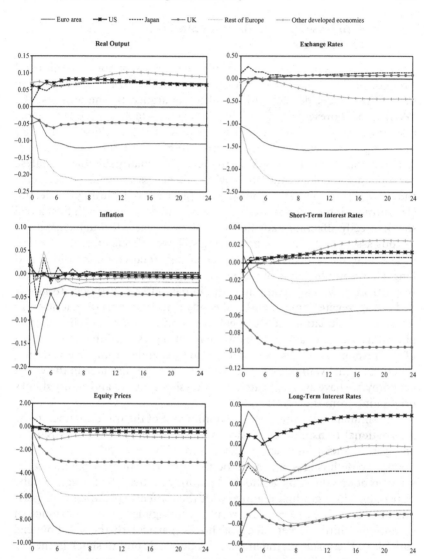

Figure 8.7. Impulse responses of a negative standard error (-1σ) shock
to euro area real equity prices on various variables across regions
(Units on horizontal axis: quarters; vertical axis: percentage change)

Main lessons from the simulations and concluding remarks

This chapter has provided some empirical evidence on the dynamics and strength of the international transmission mechanism of shocks, using the GVAR model developed by DdPS. As argued by the authors, the GVAR model presents a comprehensive, yet tractable approach to apply a spatio-temporal structure to the analysis of the world economy. By providing a framework capable of accounting for both trade and financial transmission channels, the GVAR model is particularly suitable to analyse the transmission of real and financial shocks across countries and regions. Indeed, the transmission of shocks takes place not only through trade, but also through interest rates, exchange rates and equity prices. Thus, a real shock directly affecting trade flows is also propagated through changes in various asset prices, in turn generating spillover effects on real variables.

The analysis in this chapter has specifically focused on the direct and longer-term implications of (selected) external shocks for the euro area. In particular, we have computed the impact effects of shocks to global and US aggregate demand and real equity prices on short- and long-term interest rates, inflation, output, real equity prices and real exchange rates in various countries and regions. We have also presented the time profiles of the responses of these variables, using generalised impulse response functions. Finally, in order to assess the role of the euro area in the world economy, we have also replicated the analysis for output and equity shocks originating from the euro area.

The simulations confirm the predominance of the trade channel in the international transmission of shocks, despite the more recent strengthening in financial integration (consistent with e.g., Forbes and Chinn, 2004). Trade linkages appear to be the first transmission channel to be set in motion following a shock. This implies that shocks are initially transmitted in a gradual manner with their effects spreading over periods of two to three years. The results also highlight the importance of second-and third-market effects of shocks (particularly those to financial variables). For instance, the impact of a domestic output shock in the US is likely to be amplified over time through second-round effects, since the US will eventually be affected by the return impacts of the shock on the rest of the world. In addition, other regions such as the euro area will be indirectly affected by the shock through the impact of the US shock on their trade partners, implying third-country effects.

The simulations show that financial shocks (specifically, to equity prices) tend to be transmitted much faster than shocks to output and are often amplified as they travel from the originating country to the rest of the world. This is consistent with the results of the analysis of cor-relations between domestic and foreign variables showing that financial variables are significantly more-correlated with their foreign counterparts than real output or inflation. Nevertheless, there are some differences in behaviour across financial markets, with the responses of equity and bond markets to shocks generally more-synchronous than those of foreign exchange markets.

Interestingly, the further increase in correlation between domestic and foreign variables observed in recent years for equity prices and long-term interest rates has not been accompanied by a similar rise in the correlation of output. After some increase in the correlation between euro-area and foreign GDP in the 1990s, this seems to have plateaued over the last few years. This might confirm the results by Heathcote and Perri (2004), who show that increased financial integration results in lower synchronisation in business cycles, as agents use international financial markets to reduce deviations from the optimal mix between home and foreign goods. The simulations also show that the financial variables move more synchronously than inflation and output.

Finally, one interesting feature of the simulations is that the responses to external shocks by the euro area and the rest of Europe tend to exhibit strong similarities. These similarities are confirmed also in the case of shocks to euro-area variables. The synchronisation in the responses of the euro area and the neighbouring economies certainly reflects their high degree of integration through trade (euro-area countries account for more than half the trade of the rest of Western Europe). In addi-tion, the highly-synchronised responses from financial variables indicates that the integration between these areas also operates through financial markets.

Appendix 1: Countries included in the GVAR model and composition of regional groups

Table 8.2 presents the countries included in the GVAR, while Table 8.3 reports the trade weights of the main countries and regions. The version of the GVAR model developed by DdPS and used in this chapter covers thirty-three countries: eight of the eleven countries that originally joined the euro area on 1 January 1999 are grouped together, while the remain-ing twenty-five are modelled individually. Therefore, the present GVAR model contains twenty-six economic areas.

The trade shares used to construct the country-specific foreign vari-ables (the 'starred' variables) are given in the 26 × 26 trade-share matrix provided in a Supplement to DdPS (available on request). Table 8.3

Table 8.2 *Countries and regions in the GVAR model*

United States	Euro area	Latin America
China	Germany	Brazil
Japan	France	Mexico
United Kingdom	Italy	Argentina
	Spain	Chile
Other developed economies	Netherlands	Peru
Canada	Belgium	
Australia	Austria	
New Zealand	Finland	
Rest of Asia	Rest of W. Europe	Rest of the world
Korea	Sweden	India
Indonesia	Switzerland	South Africa
Thailand	Norway	Turkey
Philippines		Saudi Arabia
Malaysia		
Singapore		

Table 8.3 *Trade weights based on direction of trade statistics*

Country/ region					Rest of W. Europe			
	US	E.A.	Japan	U.K.	Sweden	Switz.	Norway	Rest*
US	0.000	0.155	0.124	0.052	0.008	0.012	0.004	0.644
E.A.	0.227	0.000	0.072	0.238	0.057	0.090	0.028	0.288
China	0.236	0.164	0.248	0.029	0.010	0.007	0.003	0.304
Japan	0.319	0.132	0.000	0.032	0.007	0.009	0.003	0.499
U.K.	0.180	0.537	0.042	0.000	0.027	0.028	0.023	0.163
Sweden	0.104	0.517	0.035	0.115	0.000	0.017	0.099	0.113
Switz.	0.113	0.670	0.039	0.066	0.015	0.000	0.004	0.094
Norway	0.090	0.449	0.030	0.181	0.132	0.008	0.000	0.109

Note: Trade weights are computed as shares of exports and imports displayed in rows by region such that a row, but not a column, sums to one.
*'Rest' gathers the remaining countries. The complete trade matrix used in the GVAR model is given in a supplement that can be obtained from the authors on request. Source: *Direction of Trade Statistics*, 1999–2001, IMF.

presents the trade shares for the eight largest economies (seven countries plus the euro area), with the 'Rest' category showing the trade shares for the remaining countries. As regards the euro area's trading partners, we can see that the US, the UK and the rest of Western Europe have a similar share in euro-area trade (around 1/5) and that jointly accounts for almost two-thirds of total euro-area trade. Another important piece of information that emerges from the trade matrix includes the very-high share of the euro area in the trade of the UK and the rest of Western Europe (more than half of the trade of these countries is with euro-area countries). Hence, these countries play a key role in the transmission of shocks to the euro area via third market, or through second-round effects.

Appendix 2: Definition of global shocks

In the empirical section, we have considered the effects of 'global' shocks, that is innovations that might not necessarily originate from a particular country, but are common to the world economy as a whole. Examples of such shocks include major developments in technology, or global innovations to commodity or equity markets. In particular, it is possible to consider the effects of a global shock to a specific variable, defined as a weighted average of variable-specific shocks across all the countries in the model. To see how this can be done, consider the GVAR model (5), and abstracting from deterministic terms and higher order lags write it as

$$\mathbf{G}\mathbf{x}_t = \mathbf{H}\mathbf{x}_{t-1} + \ldots + \mathbf{u}_t, \ \mathbf{u}_t \sim IID(0, \Sigma_u) \tag{7}$$

with a total of $k = \sum_{i=0}^{N} k_i$ domestic variables for the $N + 1$ countries.

A global shock at time t to a specific variable can now be defined as a shock to say the ℓth variable in all $N + 1$ countries simultaneously aggregated to a single shock using a set of weights reflecting the relative importance of the individual countries in the world economy. For example, using PPP GDP weights a global shock to the ℓth variable can be defined as $u_{\ell t}^g = \mathbf{a}_\ell' \mathbf{u}_t$, where a_ℓ is a $(k \times 1)$ selection vector, $a_\ell = (a_{0\ell}', a_{1\ell}', \ldots, a_{N\ell}')'$ and $a_{i\ell}$ is the $k_i \times 1$ vector with zero elements except for its element that corresponds to the ℓth variable which is set equal to w_i, the weight of the ith country in the world economy. By construction $\sum_{i=0}^{N} w_i = 1$.

The generalised impulse response function in the case of a one standard error global shock is given by:

$$\psi(h, \mathbf{x} : u_\ell^g) = E(\mathbf{x}_{t+h}|\Omega_{t-1}, u_{\ell t}^g = \sqrt{\mathbf{a}_\ell' \Sigma_u \mathbf{a}_\ell}) - E(\mathbf{x}_{t+h}|\Omega_{t-1}),$$

and in the case of the above GVAR model is easily seen to be:

$$\psi(0, \mathbf{x} : u_\ell^g) = \frac{\mathbf{G}^{-1} \Sigma_u \mathbf{a}_\ell}{\sqrt{\mathbf{a}_\ell' \Sigma_u \mathbf{a}_\ell}}. \tag{8}$$

The effect of a one standard error global shock on expected values of x at time $t + h$, for $h = 1, 2, \ldots$ can then be obtained recursively by using (8) and solving forward in the light of the difference equation (7).

REFERENCES

Adjemian, S., M. Darracq-Paries and F. Smets (2004), 'Structural analysis of US and euro area business cycles'. Mimeo presented at the ECB-IMF Workshop on 'Global financial integration, stability and business cycles: Exploring the links', Frankfurt am Main, 16–17 November 2004 (http://www.ecb.int/events/conferences/html/ecbimf.en.html).

Anderton, R., F. di Mauro and F. Moneta (2004), 'Understanding the impact of the external dimension on the euro area: Trade, capital flows and other international macroeconomic linkages', European Central Bank Occasional Paper No. 12.

Ciccarelli, M. and B. Mojon (2004), 'Global inflation', European Central Bank Working Paper No. 537.

Corsetti, G. and P. Pesenti (2001), 'Welfare and macroeconomic interdependence', *Quarterly Journal of Economics*, 116 (2), pp. 421–445.

Dees, S., F. di Mauro, M. H. Pesaran and L.V. Smith (2005), 'Exploring the international linkages of the euro area: A Global VAR analysis', European Central Bank Working Paper No. 568, (forthcoming), *Journal of Applied Econometrics*.

Doyle, B. and J. Faust (2002), 'An investigation of the co-movements among the growth rates of the G-7 countries', *Federal Reserve Bulletin*, 88 (10), pp. 427–437.

Doyle, B. and J. Faust (2005), 'Breaks in the variability and co-movement of G-7 economic growth', *The Review of Economics and Statistics*, 87(4), pp. 721–740.

Forbes, K. J. and M. D. Chinn (2004), 'A decomposition of global linkages in financial markets over time', *The Review of Economics and Statistics*, 86(3), pp. 705–722.

Gali, J. and T. Monacelli (2005), 'Monetary policy and exchange rate volatility in a small open economy', *Review of Economic Studies*, 72 (3), pp. 707–734.

Gregory, A. W., A. C. Head and J. Raynauld (1997), 'Measuring world business cycles', *International Economic Review*, 38 (3), pp. 677–701.

Heathcote, J. and F. Perri (2003), 'Why has the US economy become less correlated with the rest of the world?', *American Economic Review*, 93 (2), pp. 63–69.

Heathcote, J. and F. Perri (2004), 'Financial globalization and real regionalization', *Journal of Economic Theory*, 119 (1), pp. 207–243.

Kim, K. and A. Pagan (1995), 'The econometrics of calibrated models'. In M. H. Pesaran and M. R. Wickers (eds.), *Handbook of applied econometrics*, Oxford: Blackwell, pp. 356–390.

Kose, M. A., C. Otrok and C. H. Whiteman (2003), 'International business cycles: World, region and country-specific factors', *American Economic Review*, 93(4), pp. 1216–1239.

Kose, M. A., E. S. Prasad and M. E. Terrones (2003), 'How does globalization affect the synchronization of business cycles?', *American Economic Review*, 93(2), pp. 57–62.

Lumsdaine, R. L. and E. S. Prasad (2003), 'Identifying the common component of international economic fluctuations: A new approach', *Economic Journal*, 113 (484), pp. 101–127.

Monfort, A., J. P. Renne, R. Rüffer and G. Vitale (2003), 'Is economic activity in the G7 synchronized? Common shocks versus spillover effects', CEPR Discussion Paper No. 4119.

Pesaran, M. H., T. Schuermann and S. M. Weiner (2004), 'Modelling regional interdependencies using a global error-correcting macroeconometric model', *Journal of Business & Economic Statistics*, 22 (2), pp. 129–162.

Pesaran, M. H. and R. Smith (2005), 'Macroeconometric modelling with a global perspective', *The Manchester School*, 74, Supplement 1, pp. 24–49.

Stock, J. H. and M. W. Watson (2003), 'Understanding changes in international business cycle dynamics', NBER Working Paper No. 9859.

Index

Printed in the United States
By Bookmasters